The Fourth Gospel
and the Quest for Jesus

The Fourth Gospel and the Quest for Jesus

Modern Foundations Reconsidered

Paul N. Anderson

t&t clark

Published by T&T Clark
A Continuum imprint
The Tower Building, 11 York Road, London SE1 7NX
80 Maiden Lane, Suite 704, New York, NY 10038

www.continuumbooks.com

First published 2006
This edition 2007

Paul N. Anderson has asserted his right under the Copyright, Designs and Patents Act, 1988, to be identified as Author of this work.

British Library Cataloguing-in-Publication Data
A catalogue record for this book is available from the British Library.

Typeset by Free Range Book Design & Production Ltd
Printed and bound in the USA

ISBN-10: 0-567-04394-0 (hardback)
ISBN-13: 978-0-567-04394-8 (hardback)

ISBN-10: 0-567-03330-9 (paperback)
ISBN-13: 978-0-567-03330-7 (paperback)

CONTENTS

TABLES

ACKNOWLEDGEMENTS

No accomplishment is achieved in isolation, and much indebtedness to many is deeply felt. To begin with, a great deal is owed to conversations and inter- actions within the John, Jesus and History seminar, a new Group at the national SBL meetings. In addition to the 250 scholars around the world that are on our listserve and the two dozen scholars that have presented papers since our opening sessions in 2002, I owe a great deal to my colleagues on the steering committee – Tom Thatcher, Alan Culpepper, Mary Coloe, Felix Just, Jamie Clark-Soles, and D. Moody Smith. I also appreciate the opportunity to include in this book a revision of the paper presented at the Atlanta 2003 national SBL meetings under the title, 'John, Jesus and History – Why This Study is Needed, and Why It is Needed Now', as Part II below. It is hoped that the present work will also contribute to possible ways forward within this venue of inquiry and beyond.

A further word of gratitude is expressed to Peter Hofrichter and the other scholars who gathered at the Salzburg Symposium, 'Für und wider die Priorität des Johannesevangeliums', held on the Monchstein in March 2000. A shorter version of Part III below was presented at that Symposium, and appreciation is also expressed to Georg Olms Verlag for the permission to publish again the essay, 'Interfluential, Formative, and Dialectical – A Theory of John's Relation to the Synoptics', first published in Peter Hofrichter (ed.), *Für und wider die Priorität des Johannesevangeliums* (TTS, 9; Hildesheim, Zürich, and New York: Georg Olms Verlag): 19–58. Within the present work, that essay is recrafted into Part I ('Modern Foundations for the Critical Investigation of John, Jesus and History') and Part III, 'Interfluential, Formative and Dialectical – A Theory of John's Relation to the Synoptics'. Table 3.3, 'A Charting of Johannine-Synoptic Interfluential Relations', was first presented at the 'Gospel of John and Christian Theology Conference' at St Andrews, Scotland (July 2003), and it has also been distributed at the John, Jesus and History Consultation in Atlanta, Georgia (November 2003), the New Testament and Hellenistic Religions Section of the Pacific Northwest SBL meetings in Seattle, Washington (May 2005), the 'Death of Jesus in the Fourth Gospel Conference' at the University of Leuven, Belgium (July 2005), and at the 'Imagery in the gospel of John Conference' in Eisenach, Germany (July 2005). Responses from scholars at those sessions and otherwise have been very helpful indeed.

I also want to thank David Landry and Shawn Kelley, and Francisco Lozada and Adele Reinhartz, for the opportunity to present the paper, 'Mark,

John and Answerability: Aspects of Interfluentiality Between the Second and Fourth Gospels', at a joint session of the Synoptic Gospels and Johannine Literature Sections of the Toronto 2001 SBL meetings (see http://catholic-resources.org/John/SBL2001-Anderson.html), and I thank Mary Ann Tolbert and Adeline Fehribach for their helpful responses.

Appreciation is also expressed to James Charlesworth and the 'Millennial Conference on Jesus and Archeology' held at the Notre Dame Pontifical Center in Jerusalem (August 2000) for the opportunity to develop many of the ideas central to various sections of this book. Some elements of Part II (especially parts of Section B:3) is similar to parts of the essay, 'Aspects of Historicity in John – Implications for the Investigations of Jesus and Archaeology', in James Charlesworth (ed.), *Jesus and Archaeology* (Grand Rapids: Eerdmans, 2006: pp. 587–618). Further aspects of the larger argument are also developed in that essay, including implications for other studies.

Likewise, appreciation is expressed to the organizers and participants of several other seminars in which components of the present work were presented. Regarding the history of the Johannine situation, John's composition, and Cognitive-Critical analyses of gospel-tradition developments, the Psychology and Biblical Studies Section of SBL, the Johannine Literature Section of SBL, and the New Testament and Hellenistic Religions Section of the Pacific Northwest SBL are thanked. In particular, a fuller paper developing the material outlined in Table 2.2, 'Similar *Egō Eimi* Sayings of Jesus in Mark and John', was presented at the 2005 Philadelphia meetings under the title, 'The Origin and Development of the Johannine *Egō Eimi* Sayings in Cognitive-Critical Perspective', and Wayne Rollins is thanked for his engaging response.

Gratitude is also felt for the many responses to *The Christology of the Fourth Gospel*, upon which the present work builds. Appreciation is also expressed to its publishers: to Martin Hengel and Georg Siebeck for including it in the WUNT II series (Mohr/Siebeck) a decade ago, to Hal Rast for making it available to an American audience (Trinity Press International), and to David Root and K.C. Hanson for its third printing (Wipf & Stock) scheduled for this year. References to it and other publications by the author are intended to point the interested reader to places where particular points are developed in further detail, aspiring to serve the stewardship of time. The present work is also part of a larger set of projects including more extensive treatments of 'Matters Johannine', including: John's composition and particular relations to Synoptic traditions, the history of the Johannine situation, Jesus studies in Johannine perspective, analyses of the origin and meanings of John's Christological tensions, and literary readings of John. For some of those studies the present work also lays something of a foundation for a more nuanced approach to relevant issues.

Regarding this book in particular, appreciation is expressed to Robert Webb for including this book in the new 'Library of Historical Jesus Studies', and to Rebecca Vaughan-Williams, Joanna Taylor and Haaris Naqvi of T&T

Clark, as well as editor Jane Boughton, for their excellent editorial help. I especially thank Robert Kysar for his helpful and gracious Foreword. I consider Professor Kysar to be the leading authority over the last three decades on Johannine scholarly literature, and it is a privilege to include his astute situating of the contributions of *The Christology of the Fourth Gospel* and *The Fourth Gospel and the Quest for Jesus* within the larger trajectories of international Johannine studies. I also appreciate the supportive words contributed by Martin Hengel, Craig Keener and James M. Robinson, suggesting the value of the present work for Johannine and Jesus Studies alike.

Finally, I want to thank my students at George Fox University (especially Patrick Willis and Annie Weare) and Yale Divinity School (during the year 1998–99) for their help and encouragement along the way. I also thank Princeton Theological Seminary for granting Visiting Scholar status during the fall semester of 2004, and likewise the libraries at the Universities of Chicago, Cambridge, Glasgow, Harvard, Yale and Princeton, as well as those at George Fox University, Princeton Theological Seminary, the Berkeley Graduate Theological Union and Mount Angel Seminary, for their helpfulness. To those who have assisted with reading and responding to my work at various stages of its development (in addition to those mentioned above), I express my gratitude, including: John Painter, Frank Moloney, Craig Koester, Folker Siegert, Jörg Frey, Thomas Söding, Michael Labahn, Christina Hoegen-Rohls, François Bovon, Brian Blount, George Parsenios, Elaine Pagels, Charles Hill, Harry Attridge, Jeremy Hultin, Hans-Josef Klauck, Jeff Staley, Richard Bauckham, Gilbert Van Belle, Jutta Lonhardt-Balzer, Mark Matson, Sidney Sowers, James Fowler, James Loder, Hal Ellens, Andreas Köstenberger and Mark Goodacre; and to my George Fox University and Newberg colleagues, Chuck Conniry, Kent Yinger, Howard Macy, Tom Johnson, Corey Beals, Shannon Hinkle, Robin Baker, Cella Jaffee, Arthur Roberts, William Green, Ed Liebman, Vince Corbin and Bill Jolliff, a personal word of thanks is due.

I am especially indebted to my wife Carla and our three daughters, Sarah, Della and Olivia. This book is dedicated to our parents, Alvin and Lucy Anderson, and Dealous and Lois Cox, whose help and encouragement along the way have been immeasurable.

Paul Anderson
1 January 2006

of dialectic is of great importance and deserves more attention than it has been given in understanding the fourth evangelist's thought.[7] In this volume, you will find Anderson furthering his concept of dialectic in Section C of Part I.

With his assertion that Johannine thought is dialectical rather than monological, Anderson challenges a significant weakness in modern source criticism. Bultmann provides us a good example. He contends that 6.51c-58 is the addition of an 'ecclesiastical redactor' who sought to make the Gospel speak more 'correctly' in terms of the convictions of the church. He writes, for instance, that in the light of the bread discourse preceding 6.51c Jesus is himself the bread God gives and 'there is no need for a sacramental act, by means of which the believer must make the life his own.'[8] He also contends that 6.22-4 breaks 'the continuity between v. 21 and v. 25' and must, therefore once again be the work of the redactor.[9]

The method by which scholars have come to distinguish between an author's own work and the inclusion of source material has included the use of 'content criticism'. The basis for much of the distinction between source and redaction is what seem to be contradictions in the Gospel, much of which for Anderson is the essence of Johannine dialectical thought. Stylistic differences and other matters also figure into a case for distinguishing, say, Fortna's 'signs gospel' and the work of the evangelist. However, the detection of what scholars perceive as contradictions in ideas has even more importance.[10] Consequently, the possibility of dialectical thought is entirely dismissed.

Anderson brings a dialectical mode of thought to the question of the relationship between John and the Synoptics as well as source criticism. For one who has followed Anderson's scholarly work, especially in the last ten years, it is clear that he has introduced another entirely different facet into the question of the relationship among the Gospels. The standard mode of operation is for the scholar to find points at which the Fourth Gospel seems to reflect the influence of one or more of the Synoptics.[11] Or, the claim of the

7. See Robert Kysar, 'Pursuing the Paradoxes of Johannine Thought: Conceptual Tensions in John 6,' *Voyages with John* (Waco: Baylor University Press, 2006). First published in *The Living Test: Essays in Honor of Ernest W. Saunders* (Dennis E. Groh and Robert Jewett, eds.; Landham, MD: University Press of America, 1985), pp. 189–206.

8. Rudolf Bultmann, *The Gospel of John: A Commentary* (G.R. Beasley-Murray, R.W.N. Hoare and J.K. Riches, trans. and ed.; Oxford: Basil Blackwell, 1971), p. 219.

9. *Ibid*, p. 84. See Dwight Moody Smith's excellent deciphering of Bultmann's work: *The Composition and Order of the Fourth Gospel: Bultmann's Literary Theory* (New Haven and London: Yale University Press, 1965).

10. See for instance W. Nicol, *The Sēmeia in the Fourth Gospel: Tradition and Redaction* (Supplements to *Novum Testamentum*, vol. XXXII; Leiden: E.J. Brill, 1972), pp. 30–40 and Urban C. von Wahlde, *The Earliest Version of John's Gospel: Recovering the Gospel of Signs* (Wilmington, DE.: Michael Glazier, 1989), pp. 57–60.

11. See C. K. Barrett who argues for evidence of the influence of Mark on John. *The Gospel According to St. John: An Introduction with Commentary and Notes on the Greek Text* (2nd edition; Philadelphia: Westminster, 1978).

fourth evangelist's independence from the Synoptics must be supported by the absence of parallel material.[12] Anderson, on the other hand, refuses to think of the relationship as a one-way path. His diagram found in Table 3.3 illustrates what he calls the 'interfluential relations' not only between the Synoptics and John but among all four of the Gospels.

I find Anderson's suggestion of a two-way influence very valuable with numerous implications, such as his theory of a 'bio-optic perspective on Jesus'. He argues that one can identify the interfluentiality of each of the Synoptics and John, with each bringing its own peculiar perspective (Part III). With such a perspective how then does each of the four Gospels contribute to our understanding of the Jesus of history?

This volume challenges biblical scholars to rethink the foundations of much of our study. It will, I believe, make readers assess their own methods and stimulate new discussions of John and the quest for Jesus.

Robert Kysar
Bandy Professor Emeritus of Preaching and New Testament
Candler School of Theology, Emory University

---

12. For a more nuanced case for John's independence from the Synoptics, see Craig S. Keener, *The Gospel of John: A Commentary* (two volumes; Peabody, Mass.: Hendrickson, 2003), volume 1, pp. 42–7.

INTRODUCTION

John *versus* Jesus –
Modern Foundations of Biblical Scholarship

While the greatest theological controversies in the Patristic era revolved around the unitive and disunitive presentations of Jesus as the Christ within the Gospel of John, the greatest religious controversies in the Modern era have involved the quest for the Jesus of history, and in particular, the place of the Gospel of John within that investigation.[1] Whereas the epistemological origins of John's Christological tensions involve at least four dialectical factors,[2] the relation of the Johannine evangel to canons of historicity – and therefore, to Jesus of Nazareth – remains an enigma. In the late second century, Clement of Alexandria referred to the Synoptics as *somatic* and John as *pneumatic*, but does this mean the Synoptics are 'factual' and John is not?[3] Conversely, does the fact of John's theological character mean that it *cannot* be historical? Many would claim that these are critically established bases for divorcing John from historicity within modern scholarship,[4] yet the critical question is

---

1. Albert Schweitzer opens his epoch-making analysis (1906, 1964 trans., p. 1) with the striking claim that:

> When, at some future day, our period of civilization shall lie, closed and completed, before the eyes of later generations, German theology will stand out as a great, a unique phenomenon in the mental and spiritual life of our time. For nowhere save in the German temperament can there be found in the same perfection the living complex of conditions and factors – of philosophic thought, critical acumen, historical insight, and religious feeling – without which no deep theology is possible.
> And the greatest achievement of German theology is the critical investigation of the life of Jesus.

He was not incorrect in making such a claim.

2. The four epistemological origins of John's Christological tensions are John's agency Christology (rooted in the Prophet-like-Moses agency motif connected with Deuteronomy 18.15-22), the dialectical thinking of the evangelist, the dialectical situation of Johannine Christianity, and literary devices employed by the narrator (Anderson, 1996, pp. 260–5).

3. The words of Clement, *ta somatika* and *evangelion pneumatikon* (Eusebius, *Hist. Eccles.* 6.14), are *wrongly* translated 'bodily facts' versus 'spiritual gospel' if this implies a facticity-versus-spiritualization dichotomy. More accurately, *somatika* and *pneumatikon* refer to a 'body-and-spirit' complementarity of gospel presentations; any programme of interpretation making too much of a fact-versus-theology dichotomy – critical *or* traditionalistic – rests on a critical mistake.

4. Robert Funk builds from Reimarus to Strauss in describing the first two of 'the seven pillars

whether these inferences and their implications are solid foundations upon which to build one's critical approaches to these subjects. Assessing the degree to which such is the case is the central interest of the present work.

Until the nineteenth century, the historicity of John was largely unquestioned by biblical scholars and those searching for the Jesus of history. With the rise of historical-critical scholarship, however, especially in Europe, John came to be relegated to the canons of Christology and theology – casting light upon the Christ of faith, but having little or no value for investigating the Jesus of history. Therefore, the two prevalent modern opinions on the subject have come to involve the 'de-historicization of John' and its direct implication: the 'de-Johannification of Jesus'.[5] As these views go against the traditional acceptance of John's claims to eyewitness testimony, they have played ubiquitous roles in forcing a divide between critical and traditional biblical scholarship. Characteristic of the Modern era, religious arguments have pervasively lost out to scientific ones.

Scholars aspiring to identify themselves as scientific and critical (versus traditional and uncritical) understandably came to adopt these platforms, and indeed they do have their merits. Synoptic investigations of the Jesus of history can therefore be carried out unencumbered by the idiosyncrasies of John, the 'maverick gospel',[6] and the history of John's material may be ascribed to parallel religious typologies or the theological imagination of the Fourth Evangelist, rather than a dissonant witness. These platforms would all

---

of scholarly wisdom', which formed the foundations of the work of the Jesus Seminar (Funk *et. al.*, 1993), as follows:

> The choice Strauss posed in his assessment of the gospels was between the supernatural Jesus – the Christ of faith – and the historical Jesus. Other scholars in the German tradition developed a safer, but no less crucial, contrast between the Jesus of the synoptic gospels – Matthew, Mark, Luke – and the Jesus of the Gospel of John. Two pillars of modern biblical criticism were now in place. The first was the distinction between the historical Jesus, to be uncovered by historical excavation, and the Christ of faith encapsulated in the first creeds. The second pillar consisted of recognizing the synoptic gospels as much closer than the Fourth Gospel, which presented a "spiritual gospel" (p. 3).

The seventh 'pillar' claims that now the burden of proof has shifted so that supposedly 'historical elements in these [gospel] narratives must therefore be demonstrated to be so' (p. 5). Even a scholar as otherwise judicious as James Dunn (2003) recently sided with Baur and Strauss against the bulk of Johannine scholars in claiming: 'On the whole, then, the position is unchanged: John's Gospel cannot be regarded as a source for the life and teaching of Jesus of the same order as the Synoptics' (p. 166). John is 'a secondary source to supplement or corroborate the testimony of the Synoptic tradition' (p. 167). In essence, Dunn is claiming that Baur and Strauss are correct; for critical scholars, John must be confined to canons of myth and faith, rather than independent historical knowledge.

5. These terms became coined within the 'John, Jesus, and History Group' at the national SBL meetings as papers were commissioned for the 2001 meetings in order to investigate effectively the critical bases of these tendencies.

6. Robert Kysar's excellent book by that title (1993) helpfully covers many distinctive Johannine issues and themes.

be fine and good among critical scholars if the evidence were monolithic and univocal. Unfortunately, however, it is not, and this is what evokes – and even requires – a critical assessment of the prevalent modern opinions on these matters.

Indeed, the highly theological character of John with its radical departures from the Synoptic Gospels has bolstered such moves, but they come with new sets of critical problems. As well as being historical, Mark and the other Synoptic traditions are pervasively theological. Therefore, they cannot be relegated to the canons of factuality and bald historiography any more than John can. And, despite John's pervasive theological tone, John has more archaeological and topographical references, and more direct claims to first-hand familiarity, than all the other gospels put together.[7] In some ways the Synoptic presentation of Jesus is preferable in terms of historicity, but in others the Johannine demonstrates a greater sense of historical realism. These are factors of which nearly all critical scholars are aware, and yet discerning how they relate to the above foundations remains elusive. At the very least, a more rigorous exploration of the issues calls for a more *nuanced* demarcation of particular contributions made by each of these traditions. If even this small advance is achieved, a genuine contribution to the larger debates will have been made.

At the outset, some critical scholars will be put off by the challenging of purported critical consensus views, and this is understandable. The critical investigation of biblical subjects must be carried out on the basis of empirical evidence and rational argumentation, rather than appealing to traditionalistic sentimentality. Traditionalism, however, is not the same as tradition, nor is criticalism the same as criticism. This study is conducted as a critical investigation, welcoming and attempting to weigh all evidence on the basis of its merits. If critical scholars are threatened by critical theories being examined critically, one wonders if the theories or the scholars deserve the appellation, 'critical'. Dogmatic criticalism poses no practical or theoretical improvement over dogmatic traditionalism. Because scientific inquiry welcomes critical scrutiny from all sides, examining long-standing issues in the light of new evidence and approaches is the sort of thing authentic critical scholarship welcomes. Whether or not it is compelling, of course, is another matter.

Nor should the traditionalist or the postmodernist be encouraged to think that this project is intended to be a challenge to modernism in defence of an alternative set of views. It is not. It is a critical investigation intended to

---

7. Distinctive aspects of historicity in John include: rhetorical claims to first-hand knowledge, connections between Palestine and geographically removed settings, archaeological and topographical content, spatiality and topographical incidentals, aspects of personal familiarity, chronological references, and the fact of empirical detail (Anderson 2006a). It could be that *some*, or even *many*, of these details are disconnected from aspects of historicity, but arguing that *all* of them, or even *most* of them, are divorced from historical knowledge requires critical substantiation if such a claim is to be accorded critical merit.

hammer hard on traditional and critical views alike, aspiring to build upon the most compelling evidence, even if it goes against particular traditional views. On this matter, it may go without saying that the best of traditional scholarship has historically endeavoured to build upon the most plausible of critical inferences, and likewise, the best of critical investigations often find resonance with the best of exegetical scholarship. In both ventures, the quest for truth is central, and therefore compelling evidence should be welcome, whichever direction it may point.

By now an operative assumption is clear. Rather than maintaining a 'conflict' model of scientific investigation, whereby support is raised and allegiances are garnered along the lines of the triumphalistic winning of one side over another, this approach is intentionally 'synthetic' and integrative.[8] The goal is truth-seeking, and whether one's investments are confirmed or challenged by the inquiry, the quest for truth on these matters is the overarching concern. Whether such was the original intention of the Johannine dictum, that 'you shall know the truth, and the truth shall set you free' (Jn 8.12), it certainly *is* the case within the realm of critical inquiry. In drawing the best information in from various disciplines, perspectives, and approaches it is hoped that empirical veracity and theoretical validity will contribute to the soundness of any judgement made.

A comment also deserves to be made here regarding the place of paradigms within biblical and historical interpretation. As Thomas Kuhn (1996) points out in his important book on revolutions within the history of scientific inquiry, normal science involves puzzle-solving, puzzle-solving involves the posing and testing of hypotheses and paradigms. Paradigms that function well tend to be maintained and embraced as heuristic lenses through which to understand and approach scientific inquiry – maintained within communities of inquiry, but change and revolution happen by necessity when a critical mass of exceptions and problems force the reconsideration of the bases or components of a given paradigm. Finally, progress is made through the improving of one or more aspects of a paradigm, which then leads to the refining of an existing paradigm or the establishing of another. Parallel to the history of science, the history of biblical criticism shows similar developments.

The problem with the de-historicization of John and the de-Johannification of Jesus as corollary platforms is that several important issues cannot be resolved given these two foundational approaches to the critical investigations of John and Jesus. First, John claims explicitly to be based upon eyewitness memory. Are these claims totally false, or simply misguided? And, how would one know? The Johannine Gospel contains more assertions of first-hand

---

8. As with other science-religion debates in the Modern era, the four ways of relating these subjects as outlined by Ian Barbour include *conflict, independence, dialogue,* and *integration* (1997, pp. 77–105). Exchange 'history' for 'science', and 'tradition' for 'religion', and many of the issues regarding the critical investigation of the historicity of John are indeed parallel.

information than any other gospel tradition (including Thomas)! The evidence may be against such claims, but it must be robust to maintain its challenge. Second, John has more archaeological, topographical, sensory-empirical, personal knowledge and first-hand information than all of the other gospels combined. How is its presence explicable if John is truncated from history? Third, alternative theories of composition based on alien (non-Johannine) traditions fall flat when tested even by their own measures. If an alternative theory of composition is compelling, that is one thing; a failed alternative poses no improvement at all. Fourth, differences with the Synoptics are many, but so are John's similarities. The forcing of a dichotomous choice between John or the Synoptics itself is a factor of failed efforts to pose a plausible model of inter-traditional dialogue. If a workable model were advanced, would discussions of historicity also be different? Finally, many errors in logic and claim are committed by all sides of the debate. Traditionalists yoke theological convictions to historicity claims, while criticalists mount equal challenges to match. If modest approaches based on degrees of compelling evidence were to be advanced, including an acknowledgment of a view's limitations, a critical consensus might yet be possible. These considerable inadequacies with the present state-of-the-art opinion on the matter call for some advance to be made – or at least attempted.

A corollary in the quest for truth is also the humbling reality that the investigator's tools and approaches are always finite, and they always have weaknesses as well as strengths. Therefore, degrees of certainty also deserve to be declared. Truth claims among scholars always fall somewhere within the continuum of certainty, and a major flaw of critical and traditional scholars alike is the failure to describe the degrees of certainty between assertions forwarded and considered. Consider, for instance, the following gradations: 1) 'Certain' and 'necessarily true' require uncontrovertable and compelling logic and evidence. 2) 'Probable' and 'likely' require compelling evidence, although some questions will remain. 3) 'Plausible' and 'arguable' involve impressive evidence, though falling short of probability because of several unknowns. 4) 'Possible' simply holds open the fact of an assertion's potential actuality, although evidence against it may be as strong as evidence for it. 5) 'Implausible' and 'unarguable' acknowledge that the weight of evidence is against the assertion, but it is not beyond the realm of possibility. 6) 'Improbable' and 'unlikely' imply not only the lack of compelling evidence in favour of an assertion, but they acknowledge probable evidence against it. 7) 'Negative certainty' and 'necessarily untrue' imply that overwhelming evidence and compelling logic are both against an assertion so as to negate any possibility of veracity or validity.

Indeed, there may be other ways of describing degrees of certainty regarding one's truth claims as a biblical scholar, but this demarcation needs to be done. Serious disagreement between scholars may sometimes be a factor of the absence of nuance rather than disagreement over substance. For instance, because a particular claim is not necessarily true (level 1), this does *not* imply that it is *necessarily untrue* (level 7). It may fall within levels 5 or 6, and still be arguable, and yet the great logical flaw within positivistic reductionism is to equate 'not *positively* true' with 'positively *not* true'. Rather, a more nuanced approach to the critical investigation of the gospels and Jesus is to not only make an assertion, but to describe *why* it might and might not be true, seeking to locate the claim within the spectrum of certainty, functioning to narrow some options while leaving others open. Therefore, the assets of perspectives one ultimately rejects must be acknowledged as well as the limitations of the views one maintains. Such approaches make advances in the quest for truth possible, and even plausible.

Before proceeding, it must also be acknowledged that the descriptions of the modern foundations as 'the de-historicization of John' and 'the de-Johannification of Jesus' tend to overstate things a bit. Few scholars hold to an absolute embracing of such views, and even their advocates will have particular exceptions to the larger position. It is also not the case that 'all' critical scholars embrace both of these views, and this is especially the case among the leading Johannine scholars around the world. It might even be questioned whether the majority, or even the plurality, of Johannine scholars would hold strictly to either of these positions. The impression is that it is largely some Jesus scholars and generalists who constitute the highest numbers of these modernistic-platform adherents. This is what makes the present study all the more important as an evaluation of the foundations for effective investigations of the historical Jesus. The implications may extend to more than one field of inquiry.

As an approach to this inquiry in Part I, a brief survey of the scholarly literature over the last two centuries and more will be conducted, followed by an analysis of paradigms for interpreting John and the laying out of one's findings on the history and development of the Johannine tradition. Part II will explore the strengths and weaknesses of six planks in each of the platforms of the de-historicization of John and the de-Johannification of Jesus, seeking a more measured assessment of the issues. Part III will outline a larger theory of John's 'interfluential' relations to each of the Synoptic traditions, making inferences as to what similarities and differences are more and less historically problematic. Part IV will consider the Jesus of history through 'bi-optic' lenses, attempting to lay out eight features of bi-optic attestation, eight features of Synoptic historical plausibility and eight features of Johannine historical plausibility as a more nuanced approach to the issue. Part V will then consider the theological and interpretive implications of this attempted synthesis on the issue, concluding with suggestions for further study and inquiry. In all of this, it is hoped that a critical assessment of traditional and critical perspectives on the issues at hand will lead to a more nuanced view of the Fourth Gospel and the Quest for Jesus.

PART I
MODERN FOUNDATIONS
FOR THE CRITICAL INVESTIGATION OF JOHN, JESUS AND HISTORY

'But, last of all, John, perceiving that the *somatic material* had been made plain in the Gospel [of Mark?], being urged by his friends and inspired by the Spirit, composed a *pneumatic gospel*. This is the account of Clement'.

Eusebius, *Hist. Eccles.* 6.14

The rise of the Modern era produced many intellectual advances, especially in the Western world. With the emergence of the scientific era in the seventeenth century, technological advances paved the way for empirical methods of hypothesis verification. Following the Thirty Years War in Europe and the Civil War in England, rationalism replaced religious authority as the primary coin of intellectual exchange. With the rise of philosophic naturalism in the eighteenth century and the emergence of historical-critical methodology in the nineteenth, much of biblical content and perspective was expelled from canons of historicity – evoking defences of traditionalism on one hand, and requiring alternative critical approaches on the other. As a result, scientific and modernistic authorities came to be pitted against religious and traditionalistic authorities, and nowhere has this adversarial embattlement been more intense than within discussions of John, Jesus and history.

Within these discussions, particular sources of authority have been yoked to one agenda or another, bringing to bear the weightiest of authority claims of the times. 'Scientific investigation' was often pitted against 'authoritative tradition', and vice versa, at times obscuring the issues and deflecting the discussion away from a focused weighing of the evidence. Likewise, bolstering one theological view or another on the basis of John's historicity or apostolic authority has understandably evoked critical reactions. On the traditionalistic side, misappropriating the perspective of the Johannine Prologue, for instance, imposing it upon the more mundane Johannine narrative, has claimed too much out of too little. On the critical side, arguments constructed upon silence or upon Johannine-Synoptic differences have also overreached the evidence. As new theories have been posed as a means of addressing the Johannine riddles, each new set of theories comes with its own set of new problems. Any approach taken by scholars thus needs to be mindful of its particular strengths and weaknesses, seeking always to improve one's tools and approaches to these important issues. Therefore, the developing story of the investigations of John, Jesus and history deserves consideration at the outset.

A. *The Story of John's Historical Marginalization and its Implications*

The story of John's historical marginalization begins with questions of authorship and the distinctive origin and character of the Johannine tradition. As the purported source of an eyewitness tradition, John's historicity received few serious challenges for 17 centuries. Things changed in the Modern era with analysis shifting to comparisons and contrasts between John and the Synoptics, leading to inferences as to which tradition bore greater historical veracity. During the nineteenth and twentieth centuries, John became largely marginalized as a historical document, and critical scholars were forced to explain the origin of John's content otherwise. Historical investigations thus shifted to the history of comparative religions, tradition development and source analysis. Studies arguing in favour of John's historical origin abounded, but rather than being engaged and improved upon by critical scholarship, they were largely sidestepped. The same might also be said of some traditionalist approaches to historical-critical methods. A final development has been the circumventing of the modernist historical-critical project altogether, and the posing of fresh literary-critical theory to the Johannine riddles, as a means of contributing to meaningful interpretation. While these approaches overlap, their progression and relatedness deserve consideration.

1) *The Traditional View and its Development – From Papias (or Luke?) to Schleiermacher*
For the first 17 centuries of the Christian movement, neither the authorship nor the historicity of John was questioned seriously by interpreters. Some exceptions were taken to particular aspects of earlier theories, but by and large, John's composition by 'the eyewitness' and 'the theologian' carried the day within most analyses. They simply assumed that John's differences were either a factor of theological interest or particular traditional material. Some interpreters actually preferred John's historical presentation to the other gospels, although most interpreters sought to work out some sort of harmonization between them.[1] Discussions of historicity tended to hinge upon questions of John's authorship and apostolic character. As a review of the literature suggests, little improvement was made over the basic treatments of second-century witnesses and the impressions of Eusebius.[2]

The early second-century associations of the Apostle John with the Johannine writings were indirect. Echoes from the Gospel of John are apparent in the writings of 1 Clement, Ignatius of Antioch, Polycarp of Smyrna, Justin Martyr, the Gospel of Philip and certainly Tatian's 'Diatessaron'.[3] The sorts of contacts between John and these writings include their use of Johannine concepts and language, but most of the references are not direct ones. Due to this fact, critical scholars have tended to argue that the lack of explicit mention of the Apostle John suggests a lack of awareness that the Johannine tradition had anything to do with him. Their silence is taken as an argument against

1. See, for instance, Augustine's *Harmony of the Evangelists* and Johannes Albrecht Bengel's *Gnomon Novi Testamenti* (Tübingen, 1745) as examples of classic attempts to harmonize the gospels.
2. In reviewing Sean Kealy's analysis (2002, pp. 1–366) of 19 centuries of Johannine interpretation, it is clear that it is really not until the turn of the eighteenth century that the traditional view of Johannine authorship became questioned by serious scholars.
3. See Charles Hill's analysis of the near-unanimous second-century opinion regarding the apostolic origin of John (2004, pp. 294–446, 75–171). In this exhaustive treatment of the primary literature, Hill concludes that John was *not* the exclusively favourite gospel of heretics, and that John was *not* pervasively ignored by second-century Christian leadership. Rather, Hill shows that John was known and used by *no fewer than 43 different second-century sources* (p. 450), with some of these even involving multiple references (see, for example, the letters of Ignatius). Hill also demonstrates that orthodox writings referenced the Johannine writings far more than the Gnostic and heterodox writings did, thus challenging inferences of orthodox 'Johannophobia' in the early church.

the apostolicity, and thus veracity, of the Johannine tradition, but this assumption is hyperextended critically. Familiarity could just as easily have been a factor in leaving out particular statements of attribution. What is impressive is the fact that the Johannine writings are actually extensively discussed and referenced in the second century, and that there are more papyri and manuscript fragments from John than there are from any other ancient Christian text.[12]

A more striking discovery, however, pushing the connection even earlier into the late first century, is the fact that Luke attributes a Johannine phrase to the Apostle John in Acts 4.19-20. The reason this connection has been overlooked by all sides of the debate is likely the fact that it is 'Peter and John' who are credited with speaking, rather than John alone. Whereas scholars might have overlooked this passage as a joint statement, it is actually two separate statements, and a closer analysis of the first statement illuminates the second. In verse 19, the statement is very similar to ones made by Peter in Acts 5.29 and 11.17. In all three of these statements Peter is credited with saying something like, 'We must *obey God rather than man*'. This being the case, the association of the second statement, 'We cannot help but speak about *what we have seen and heard*', bears an unmistakably Johannine ring. Its closest parallel is 1 Jn 1.3, and in Jn 3.32 Jesus is the one who declares what he has 'seen and heard' from the Father. Add to this connection the facts that Luke departs from Mark no fewer than three dozen times in which he sides with John, that he includes Johannine theological content in his Gospel and Acts, and that he expresses appreciation in his first prologue to 'eyewitnesses and servants of the *Logos*', and this first-century connecting of the Apostle John with the Johannine tradition approximates a fact.[13]

Beyond Luke's unwitting connecting of John the apostle with the Johannine tradition, other references are more direct. The testimony of Papias, Bishop of Hieropolis, certainly makes a contribution here, although scholars are divided as to his diction, meaning and value. This may be because some of his connections appear to be incidental rather than emphatic, but the converse is also true. Papias identifies at least three Johannine leaders: John the disciple of the Lord, John the presbyter and Aristion. He connects all three of these with being actual followers of Jesus, even if not members of the Twelve, and

---

12. According to Victor Salmon (1976), there are over 300 biblical papyri in the Chester Beatty manuscript collection, and many of these are from John. Likewise, the earliness of the Bodmer Papyrus (Birdsall 1960; Roberts 1935) and other second-century fragments from the Gospel of John push the dating of the Fourth Gospel toward the turn of the first Christian century rather than the middle second century.

13. This discovery is laid out in the last appendix at the end of *The Christology of the Fourth Gospel* (Anderson, 1996, pp. 274–7), and it will be developed briefly in Part III. Even if Luke was misguided or wrong, or even if he was imitating reality mimetically, this first-century clue to Johannine authorship deserves critical consideration. It connects the Johannine Gospel with John the apostle a *full century before* Irenaeus.

this is another reason for some of the confusion. In particular, his emphasis is upon John the presbyter, of whom he claimed to be a hearer, and his preference for the living voice of the oral tradition over the written text suggests the primitivity of his opinion. A further problem with the Papias tradition is that we do not have access to any of his five books containing expositions on the Lord's sayings (arguably the first full history of the early church after the Acts of the Apostles), so we are left with interpreting a dozen or more fragments of his writings and references by later historians.[14]

Beyond the puzzling details of the presentation of Papias' fragments, scholars tend to make several sorts of mistakes regarding what Papias does and does not say. Errors by traditional scholars tend to include the following: a) inferring his references to 'John', 'the elder', or 'disciples of the Lord' imply a reference to John the apostle (this error appears to have been made by Irenaeus, who mistakes his being a follower of John the elder with John the apostle); b) inferring that he connected John the apostle with the authorship of the Fourth Gospel explicitly (again, Irenaeus makes this connection, although direct evidence from Papias is lacking); and c) assuming that he was a follower and disciple of John the apostle rather than John the presbyter. Papias distinguishes John the apostle from John the elder, although he lists them both (along with Aristion) among the disciples of the Lord. Eusebius distinguishes the two 'Johns' buried at Ephesus by referring to one as the apostle and the other as the presbyter.

Errors by critical scholars tend to include the following: a) assuming that a preference for the living Word rather than the written word implies a disparaging of the Johannine written Gospel; b) assuming that a failure to mention a connection with the Apostle John implies a disregard for his contribution, thereby discounting the possibility of his witness being historic or

---

14. Other questions also persist with the Papias tradition: a) He does not always distinguish between 'disciples' and 'elders'. Therefore, whether John the 'presbyter' is distinguished from the disciple John becomes a factor of debate. b) His disparagement of Matthew (or at least portions of it), claiming it had first been written in Hebrew and had then been translated with difficulty by others, has raised questions as to his knowledge. c) His description of Mark as Peter's companion and as having gotten down his teachings in the wrong order has seemed problematic to some. d) His attributing of embellished teachings found in apocryphal writings (2 Bar. 29.5) to the Apostle John's teachings of Jesus is problematic from a historicity standpoint. e) Eusebius refers to him as a man of limited intelligence (with reference to his millenarian perspective – counter to that of Eusebius), although his works are also referenced extensively by the same. f) Papias is credited *wrongly* with references to the early martyrdom of the Apostle John by Philip of Side and George the Sinner; they included John's martyrdom as fulfilled with that of James (Mk 10.38-9), although *neither* suggests they were killed at the same time or early. The point of the latter is that after his martyrological exile on Patmos, John returned to a martyr's death as predicted by the Lord. g) While Papias does not claim to have met any of the Apostles of the Lord (presumably including John), he is associated with the tradition that John the apostle and John the elder were both buried at Ephesus, and some later interpreters confused his speaking of the Presbyter as references to the Apostle.

significant; c) interpreting the references to the martyrdom of John along with James by Philip of Sides and George the Sinner implied an early death of John the apostle (the emphasis is made here that John's martyrdom was *after* the reign of Domitian as the last of the surviving Apostles);[15] and d) inferring that because Eusebius questions his intelligence, this proves what he had to say was of no historical worth.[16] These are some of the reasons why even competent scholars have differed in their assessments of Papias' testimony on matters Johannine.

While the authority of the Fourth Gospel gets significant treatment by such figures as Montanus, Heracleon and the author of the Apocryphon of John, one of the first orthodox direct references to John's being the author of the Fourth Gospel comes from Theophilus, Bishop of Antioch, whose apology was directed against Marcion.[17] Explicit connections between John the apostle and the Fourth Gospel include the Muratorian Canon, where a tradition surfaces declaring that the fourth of the Gospels was written by John, one of the disciples, who was encouraged to write down his own impression of what was revealed to his fellow disciples and bishops about the ministry of the Lord. This tradition accounts for the differences between John and the Synoptics as a factor of inspiration. In addition, Polycrates, who was engaged with second-century debates over the celebration of Easter, is cited by Eusebius as referring to the disciple who leaned against the breast of the Lord explicitly as 'John' (*Hist. Eccles.* 5.24).

By far the most explicit and controversial second-century witness to the connection between the Fourth Gospel and the Apostle John is Irenaeus, Bishop of Lyons. Irenaeus also sought to challenge the work of Marcion. A particular concern was to challenge Marcion's disparagement of Matthew, Mark and John, due to his preference for Luke. As a countering of this move, Irenaeus advocated the four-fold Gospel. There were four winds, four corners of the earth, four creatures of the Apocalypse and therefore four Gospels (*Adv.*

15. A closer look at the Papias Fragments along these lines will make it clear that neither Philip nor George (in the fourth and seventh centuries, respectively) imply anything about an early martyrdom of John, and George even emphasizes John's having returned from Patmos after the death of Domitian. It could be that John died in 44 CE, but it *cannot* be said that there is any evidence for it, or even any substantive suggestion of it, in early church history. It is not until the Modern era that such shaky inferences became foundational for 'critical' studies – but inadequately so.

16. When Eusebius' comment about Papias' intelligence is considered in its context, it becomes apparent that he is expressing frustration with his millenarian approaches to the end of the world – views that Eusebius strongly opposed. It is wrong to infer a negative judgement regarding Papias' historical sensibilities otherwise. Again, they may have been wrong, but Eusebius' pejorative statement cannot be used for such an inference, and it should be noted that Eusebius cites Papias more frequently than any other second-century historiographer – always with deference to his authority.

17. Alan Culpepper credits him with being the first orthodox writer to identify John as the author of the Fourth Gospel (2000, p. 122).

Haer. 3.11). Irenaeus then asserted their apostolic authorship, either on a first- or a second-generation basis. Matthew and John were thus accorded to apostles and eyewitnesses of the Lord, and Luke and Mark were accorded to followers of Paul, with Mark having been an interpreter and recorder of Peter's preaching to the churches.

While Irenaeus appears to be constructing his argument on solid traditional bases, three primary questions have been raised by critical scholars. First, the fact of his anti-Marcionite agenda raises a question as to whether his work should be considered historical or rhetorical. Second, the appeal to four winds and creatures of the apocalypse – and thus a perfect number of 'four Gospels' – is not exactly the stuff of historical 'proof' when it comes to determining the authentic number of canonical gospels. Third, the interest in connecting these four Gospels with apostolic or sub-apostolic personalities – given his apparent distortion of the Papias testimony on his having been a disciple of John the apostle – raises a question as to whether he may have committed an error here and elsewhere. Nonetheless, Irenaeus carried the day within the church, and by the fourth and fifth centuries Church Fathers commonly came to refer to Papias as a disciple of John the apostle, thus embellishing the connections between Papias and the first-generation apostles. Nonetheless, Papias' connection with John the presbyter remains unchallenged,[18] and despite his not having been one of the Twelve, but the author of the Johannine Epistles, Papias still regards him as a disciple of the Lord, which coheres with the eyewitness appeals of 1 Jn 1.1-3.

Aside from mistaken inferences that John the son of Zebedee died an early death along with James, therefore excluding him from authorship consideration, the majority opinion embraced a selection of the following tenets found in Eusebius:

Table 1.1

Eusebius on John

- Citing Clement, after the ascension of Jesus, Peter, James and John did not claim preeminence in church leadership, but they chose James the brother of Jesus to be the head of the Jerusalem church (*Hist. Eccles.* 2.1).

---

18. Martin Hengel argues convincingly for the connecting of the Johannine Elder with the final authorship of John (1989), and according to Papias, he may also have been an eyewitness. This would account for the 'we' language in 1 Jn. 1, where eyewitness authority is claimed by the Johannine community. Nonetheless, the view of B.H. Streeter (1929) is not altogether unlikely that '…John the Elder was "ordained" by John the Apostle' (p. 97), accounting for the two Christian leaders named 'John' at Ephesus.

- After the destruction of Jerusalem and Palestine by the Romans (66–70 CE), apostles and disciples of Jesus were assigned to different sectors of the Christian movement, and John was assigned to Asia, where he remained until his death at Ephesus (*Hist. Eccles.* 3.1).
- During the reign of Domitian (81–96 CE), John the apostle and evangelist was sentenced to confinement on the island of Patmos, where he wrote the Apocalypse (according to Irenaeus, *Hist. Eccles.* 3.18, 21), and he returned to Ephesus after the death of Domitian.
- John remained at Ephesus until Trajan's time as a true witness of what the apostles taught; and stories developed about his pastoral care, loving concern for the flock, the challenging of heretics such as Cerinthus, and his raising of a dead man at Ephesus (*Hist. Eccles.* 3.23, 29; 4.14; 5.18).
- As the Gospels of Matthew and John were alone considered memoirs of the ministry of Jesus, John's Gospel had the benefit of the other three, complementing the others by including reports of the *early* ministry of Jesus (the events *before* John had been thrown into prison – baptizing near Aenon near Salim – Jn 3.23-24), by providing an alternative to the single-year-of-ministry presentation of the Synoptics, and by converting oral tradition into a written one. Whereas Matthew and Luke had produced human genealogies of Jesus, John produced the spiritual (pre-existent) genealogy of Jesus as the greatest of the four Gospels (*Hist. Eccles.* 3.24).
- From Polycrates, Bishop of Ephesus, John is said to be the one who leaned against the Lord's breast. He also argues that John became a sacrificing priest, a witness and a teacher, and he also refers to him as sleeping (buried) in Ephesus (*Hist. Eccles.* 3.31; 5.24).
- From Papias' five volumes (*The Sayings of the Lord Explained*), he claims to have listened to John and to have been a companion of Polycarp. Papias lists John the apostle and John the presbyter as disciples of the Lord (*Hist. Eccles.* 3.39), explaining also that this testimony addressed the fact that the two tombs in Ephesus bearing the same name belonged to different persons: John (the evangelist) and John the presbyter – the latter of which is claimed to have been his personal tutor. Papias also claims to have reproduced the teachings of both in his writings (*Hist. Eccles.* 3.39).
- According to the presbyter John, Mark, who had never heard or met Jesus, served as Peter's interpreter, writing down Peter's stories, but not in the correct order. Peter had adapted his teaching according to the needs of the church without making a systematic (*or* chronological?) ordering of them, so Mark was justified in preserving everything he had heard and representing it faithfully as he had received it, taking care to not leave anything out (*Hist. Eccles.* 3.39).
- Irenaeus claims personal contact with Polycarp, who claims to have had personal contact with the Apostle John and others who had seen the

Lord, and Polycarp is reported to have recited their words about the Lord: his teachings and miracles, and things that had been heard from 'eyewitnesses of the Word of Life' (*Hist. Eccles.* 5.20). Irenaeus also declares that the Johannine teachings of Polycarp were 'in complete harmony with Scripture'.

- The authority of John who leaned against the breast of the Lord is garnered by one of the leading bishops of Asia (according to Polycrates' letter to Victor and the Roman church) with reference to keeping the 14th of Nissan as the beginning of the Paschal festival (the churches of Asia Minor had begun to celebrate Easter on the 14th of Nissan regardless of the day of the week; see Jn 12.1, 12). Upon citing the Petrine logion of Acts 4.19 and 5.29, however ('We must obey God rather than men'), Victor of Rome responded by attempting to cut off all the bishops of Asia Minor (*Hist. Eccles.* 5.24).
- Origen's commentary on John is also mentioned, including his belief that John was the Beloved Disciple (*Hist. Eccles.* 6.25).

In addition to perspectives on John contributed by Eusebius, other Patristic testimony continued to play a role in later discussions. Especially Origen's commentary on John and his trip to Palestine – tracing out the steps of Jesus' ministry and identifying 'Bethabara' as the place of John's baptism (Jn 1.28) – caught on and found its way into later discussions. Augustine's treatments, of course, moved toward a spiritualization of John's content, and later discussions of John's presentation of Jesus were primarily theological, even through the Reformation. The emphases of Zwingli, Luther, Calvin and Wesley all primarily had to do with theological interpretations of John, and it was not until the rise of Jesus studies and the emergence of historical- and literary-critical methodologies that the basic historicity of John came to be questioned.

At this point, the impressive contribution of Friedrich Schleiermacher is difficult to categorize. On one hand, his contribution makes him the father of modern theology; intellectual rigour of theological analysis characterizes his work, and the Christian faith has never been the same since. Regarding his approach to Jesus, however, he believed that the Johannine perspective on the Jesus of history was superior to that of the Synoptics based upon literary analysis. He believed that the Johannine Gospel was not only written by John the apostle, but that it also conveyed a profound and intimate sentiment regarding the spiritual life of faith. In that sense, Schleiermacher casts the Jesus of history in enlightenment terms as one who came to bring revelation and God's saving love to humanity as its central hope for life. It was that sentiment that also provoked the disdainful reaction of Strauss and others, marking the turn of an era in Johannine and Jesus scholarship.

2) *Modern Challenges and Advances – From Bretschneider to Bultmann*
The historical study of Jesus did not really get going until the late eighteenth and early nineteenth centuries, but when it did, things changed on many levels.

With the rise of historical Jesus studies, precipitated by the unpublished work of Hermann Samuel Reimarus in 1778, the Gospel of John came under critical scrutiny on matters of historicity.[19] Reimarus made several compelling observations that moved the discussions further after his death. He noticed that the Gospels spiritualized the presentation of Jesus and asked whether the actual goal of Jesus may have been more akin to the first-century messianic prophets, who sought to deliver Israel from the occupation of Rome. Given this likelihood, the theological presentation of Jesus in the Gospels came into question as to whether their origins were religious or historical. Especially the miracles of Jesus and his resurrection were suspect among naturalistic approaches to historiography, and such concerns are understandable.

During the ensuing discussions, Karl Gottlieb Bretschneider[20] surmised that John's Gospel could not possibly be authentic because it appears 'concocted' in contrast to the threefold witness of the Synoptics. Citing a number of difficulties with the Johannine text and rendering of the Jesus story, Bretschneider's work was written in Latin so as to engage the academic world primarily, but it still evoked considerable reactions. One of these was that of Friedrich Schleiermacher,[21] who constructed a life of Jesus rooted primarily in his analysis of the Gospel of John. Schleiermacher observed correctly that much of the Synoptic tradition appeared to be composed of disparate units of tradition that had been brought together by editorial and compilation processes. John's pervasive unity of style and form, though, presented evidence of the integrity of the Johannine tradition, bolstering the view that John provides a superior window into understanding the purposes and activities of Jesus.

With the opposition of Schleiermacher by David Strauss, however (1835–6), the place of John within the historical-Jesus investigations was eroded considerably, and as a rationalist challenge to supernaturalistic presentations in the Gospels, the origin of John's material was ascribed to mythological origins rather than historical ones. Strauss, however, continued to assume a 3-against-1 approach to the Synoptic/John question (versus Schleiermacher's 1-against-1 approach, assuming wrongly, however, Matthean priority), and the central obsession of his later book (1865) was largely consumed with proving

19. Extended discussions of the history of historical Jesus quests may be found elsewhere (Borg, 1994; Powell, 1998; Anderson, 2000a).

20. In this book, Bretschneider (1820) questions several features of John as being inauthentic: namely, the three Synoptics against the singular John, John's elevated and theological presentation of Jesus, the non-Jewish character of John's Christology, purported errors in the Johannine text, and challenges to the traditional view.

21. According to Jack C. Verheyden (Schleiermacher, 1975), 'In a way, Schleiermacher agreed with Bretschneider's point that the critic must choose between the Synoptics and John, but Schleiermacher chose the latter rather than the former' (p. xxxii).

Schleiermacher's analysis inadequate.[22] F.C. Baur bolstered the work of Strauss (his former student) with his own contributions, and by the middle of the nineteenth century, John's ahistoricity was well on the way to being established as the 'revisionist' view among many critical biblical scholars. This view asserts that because John is different from the Synoptics, and because John is distinctively theological and spiritualized, John must be regarded as ahistorical, rendering its material irrelevant – and even misleading – for the critical investigation of the historical Jesus.

Despite many problems with the revisionist view, it continues to be assumed by many scholars despite considerable evidence to the contrary. For instance, with the eventual emergence of Markan priority, the 3-against-1 denigration of John falls flat. If Mark rendered things one way, and if Matthew and Luke followed its lead, this would confirm the basic approach of Schleiermacher over and against that of Bretschneider. Strauss also began to reverse several of his anti-Johannine judgements in the preface to his third edition, not so much as an indicator of renewed confidence in John, but as a reflection of growing doubts regarding the certainty of his earlier negative conclusions.[23] In order to account for the origin of John's material, Strauss argued that contemporary mythological parallels formed the moulds within which Johannine renderings of Jesus' teachings and ministry were cast.

The work of F.C. Baur (1847) located John in the late middle second century (around 170 CE), and this required a fuller development of a History-of-Religions approach to explaining the origins of gospel material if it were not connected to an eyewitness or an independent tradition. In addition, the projection of the Prologue's Logos theology over the rest of the Johannine

---

22. In this book-length critique of Schleiermacher, Strauss puts the matter polemically: 'But in criticism of the Fourth Gospel, Bretschneider is the strong man of science, and Schleiermacher the man of frail religious-aesthetic partiality.' (1977, p. 41) As evidence, Strauss cites Schleiermacher's tendencies to speak of John's representing first-hand information in contrast to the Synoptics' representing second-hand and disparate material as superficial and uncritical. In several ways, however, Strauss does not appear to have understood Schleiermacher's treatment of John fully; he is unable to separate the faith claims of the Fourth Evangelist and Schleiermacher's theological interests from John's text-critical realities and Schleiermacher's exegetical observations. On that matter in particular, especially given the dialectical character of the Fourth Evangelist's thought, Schleiermacher's observation is *closer* to the 'science' of epistemological inquiry and literary criticism than Strauss recognizes.

23. Interestingly, in the preface to the third edition of his *Life of Jesus* (1972, p. lvii), Strauss confesses that he has become more doubtful of his doubts regarding John's historicity, and in that sense, his change of thought tracks entirely with the critical thrust of the present study (see below, Part II). It is precisely the critical evaluation of the doubts themselves that raises doubts about the de-historicization of John as a direct factor of critical inquiry. Strauss goes on to credit his earlier polemical zeal (and blindness) as a factor in his earlier countering of John's 'adverse and unfavorable side', while the other side of John has had a chance to grow on him. He later went back to some of his more critical views regarding John, however, due in part to the influence of his former teacher, F.C. Baur.

narrative evoked the extensive inference of mythological origins of John's distinctive material rather than having an origin in anything historical. Further elaborations upon the Hellenistic origins of Johannine theology, combined with naturalistic aversions to the wondrous, played major roles in removing John from the canons of historical narrative. Wellhausen, Schwarz and others,[24] however, attempted to locate the origins of the Johannine tradition as rooting either in earlier sources or more primitive layers, allowing a later finalization to have been built upon earlier material. It is these works, as well as those of Spitta and Wendt,[25] that Bultmann later employed in constructing his monumental source-critical synthesis. With the epoch-changing effect of Albert Schweitzer's *Quest for the Historical Jesus*, however, a new set of issues emerged.[26]

Schweitzer's application of critical analysis to critical investigations of Jesus' life exposed the subjectivity of so-called 'objective' historical studies. His work demonstrated, as none had hitherto done, how closely scholars' outcomes were to their personal investments. This caused a great deal of questioning as to whether we could *ever* know what the historical Jesus might actually have said or done. This being the case, the forward strides made during the first half of the twentieth century explored the history of traditional material, and headway was made in two particular directions as far as Johannine studies are concerned.

The watershed event in post-Schweitzer Johannine research involved the commentary of Rudolf Bultmann (1971). Published in German in 1941, this impressive work promised to explain the historical origin of the Johannine Gospel's material, while at the same time explaining the epistemological origins of its theological tensions.[27] Building on the works of scholars who had preceded him, and engaging the spectrum of available primary extra-canonical literature (especially emerging Gnostic literature), Bultmann's genius lay in his remarkable ability to combine theological perceptivity with linguistic deftness. Not only did he infer at least four other major sources underlying and overlaying the contribution of the Fourth Evangelist, he also inferred distinctive history-of-religions origins of each and claimed to be able to distinguish them on the basis of stylistic, contextual and theological evidence. As well as

24. Julius Wellhausen not only championed a documentary approach to the Pentateuch; he also laid out a documentary approach to the Gospel of John (1907). Eduard Schwartz also developed an intricate approach to John's 'aporias' (perplexities), laying out his analyses in four major critical essays published from 1907–08.

25. Friedrich Spitta actually believed that the identification of sources underlying John could provide historical information about Jesus (1910), as did Hans Heinrich Wendt (1902). It was their contributions among others upon which Bultmann constructed his impressive source-critical synthesis.

26. See now John Bowden's new complete translation, published in 2001.

27. An extensive treatment of the literary, historical and theological aspects of Bultmann's approach to John is developed elsewhere (Anderson 1996, pp. 33–169).

accounting for the origins of John's material as rooted in Hellenistic and Jewish mythic narratives and discourses, Bultmann also showed how John's major Christological and theological tensions originated from a set of literary dialogues between three sources, the evangelist and the redactor.

With the adumbration of Bultmann's approach for English-speaking audiences by D. Moody Smith in 1965 and its translation into English by George R. Beasley-Murray and others in 1971,[28] Bultmann's work began to command an international hold on Johannine scholarship.[29] In essence, most developments in Johannine studies over the second half of the twentieth century were formed in response to (both positively and negatively) his epoch-making commentary. Within that period, source theories came and went, traditionalist advocates targeted Bultmann as the adversary, composition and situation history theories abounded, and new literary studies emerged.

Regarding Jesus studies over this same period of time, Bultmann had also made his mark. Assuming that nothing could be known about the historical Jesus, following Schweitzer, Bultmann developed an extensive analysis of the Synoptic tradition (1963a) in which he outlined a history-of-religions and a form-critical analysis of the Synoptics. Of course, Bultmann argued that because history-as-such had little bearing on saving faith, the only hope for humanity was to respond in faith to the proclaimed Word. Therefore, he was willing to ascribe the bulk of gospel narrative to contemporary mythological origins, seeking instead to preserve the existential core of Jesus' teachings and the theological commitments of the evangelists. A reaction against Bultmann's de-historicizing platform, however, was championed by his former student, Ernst Käsemann. In his 1953 lecture, calling for a fresh investigation into the life and teachings of Jesus, Käsemann argued that something of the ministry of Jesus could be distinguished from gospel traditions, especially if it sounded significantly different. Another Bultmannian scholar, Gunther Bornkamm (1960), argued that even if the Gospels gave us something like a religious understanding of the historical Jesus, this was still worthy material on which to build a historical appraisal of Jesus of Nazareth. With the reporting of these fresh calls for a renewed historical investigation into the life and ministry of

---

28. An excellent service provided by Smith (1965) was to outline the sorts of materials comprising each of Bultmann's five different sources, explaining also the reasons Bultmann made the sorts of source-, rearrangement- and redaction-critical moves that he did. Smith's work deserves credit for Bultmann's work becoming accessible to English-speaking scholarship, even before it was translated into English.

29. See Bultmann 1971. Says Ernst Haenchen (Vol. 1, 1984, p. 34):

...like a mighty tree, it appeared not to permit anything strong and important to prosper in its shadow. This effect did not set in immediately, but once it began, it became clear that Bultmann's commentary on the Gospel of John decisively dominated an entire generation.

With the evidentiary failure of Bultmann's platform, though (Anderson, 1996, pp. 33–169), bringing back into play some of the leading critical works Bultmann's monograph displaced seems an important venture to consider.

Jesus, James Robinson inaugurated officially 'the New Quest' for the historical Jesus (1959).

While the renewed quest for the historical Jesus did not set out to marginalize the Gospel of John, it did result as a factor of the desire to begin with that which was most certain and proceed to that which was less, the Synoptics. In addition to Markan studies, Q studies also emerged as an academic discipline, and this led to the yoking of the Gospel of Thomas with Jesus sayings. Building upon the view that a hypothetical Q source may have been gathered as early as two decades after the ministry of Jesus, some scholars came to view Thomas as a later form of the material underlying primitive Q, thereby suggesting at least its partial primitivity. This claim for Thomas has especially been argued by the Claremont School, and the voting of participants in the Jesus Seminar has shown a pattern that endorses a higher valuing of the Gospel of Thomas than the canonical Gospel of John. What this has meant is that the Gospel of John, for all practical purposes, has been considered off-limits for any who are doing serious Jesus studies, and the impasse has been nearly a complete one.

The pinnacle expression of this modernistic tendency is displayed in the two volumes on the words and works of Jesus resulting from the investigations of the Jesus Seminar.[30] Between these two volumes, the only saying attributed plausibly to Jesus in John is the reference to the prophet not receiving honour in his homeland (Jn 4.44), and the only actions receiving the status of plausible or probable confidence are the inferences that Jesus was a follower of John the Baptist (and that his disciples had also been John's followers, Jn 1.35-42), that Jewish leaders accused Jesus of being uneducated (Jn 7.15), that Annas was the father-in-law of Caiaphas (Jn 18.13), from whose home Jesus was taken to the Governor's residence (Jn 18.28), and that Jesus was beaten and turned over by Pilate to be crucified (Jn 19.1, 16, 18).[31] It must be acknowledged, however, that archaeological research has not been noted as a primary factor in such studies, and one wonders what a more comprehensive historical investigation of John might produce. Given the empirical proclivity of the modern mind, this is an astonishing feature of this particular venture, claiming to use the tools of modern historians in arriving at its judgements. It seems as though the fact of Jesus' elevated presentation in John has displaced the scholarly regard for any of John's other historical material (such as archaeological and

30. See the works edited by Funk and others (1993, 1998), as well as his own monograph (1996) on the subject, for an excellent overview of their findings. See also Marcus Borg's survey of leading models for interpreting the historical Jesus (1994).

31. An excellent clarification is made by Marcus Borg in his *QRT* response to the question of whether 18% of Jesus' sayings within the Gospels does justice to their historicity. According to Borg, 'at least' 18% of them being authentic is very different from 'only' 18% being authentic, and he affirms the former is the way he and most members of the Jesus Seminar understand their work (2002, pp. 23–4).

topographical detail), even when it might be superior to the presentations of Jesus in the Synoptics. As a culminating expression of the New Quest, it should be questioned whether the results of the Jesus Seminar give us a portraiture of the 'historical' Jesus or the '*modernistic*' Jesus. At the dawn of the post-Modern era, the two may be considered very different realities.[32]

Over the last three decades or so, interdisciplinary studies – especially from the social sciences – have also been applied to Jesus quests, and Tom Wright has appropriately called this trend 'the third quest' for the historical Jesus. Within this venture, modernistic categories of thought are supplanted by the endeavour to appreciate how people would have perceived things in the first-century Mediterranean world. Sociology, religious anthropology, psychology and newer literary-critical methodologies have been applied to the classic issues seeking to understand what sort of narratives the Gospel traditions represent and how they might be read more profitably in the interest of casting fresh light on Jesus and his ministry. Seeing Jesus as a transformer of Judaism (*not* advocating a radical break with it), challenging purity laws in the name of divine love, considering the political and economic aspects of Jesus' prophetic work, and fitting Jesus with emerging constructs of first-century charismatic leaders are all examples of the benefits of these sorts of studies.[33] For Johannine studies, a new wave of incisive literary-critical approaches to the text has given new life to many aspects of reading the Fourth Gospel, and in combination with emerging theories of the Johannine situation, rhetorical devices in John are sometimes effectively combined with inferences as to the intended audiences. While some details in the Johannine narrative indeed served the rhetorical interests of the evangelist, ascribing *all* of them to that origin – including all of John's archaeological content – moves beyond the evidence. Therefore, even within the third quest for the historical Jesus, as with the earlier ones, John's historical-type material remains a problem deserving to be addressed.

3) *Critiques of Modern Hypotheses – From Neander to Blomberg*
While Schleiermacher mounted a rigorous opposition to Bretscheider, his work was not published until 1864, after his death. Other critiques of Bretschneider, however, caused him to soften his critical claims against John,

---

32. This question emerges helpfully from the dialogue with Marcus Borg in the 2002 issue of *QRT* (Borg, 2002; Anderson, 2002b). If the criteria for determining historicity are particularly modernistic, and if the work is constructed on the modernistic platforms of Strauss, Baur, Bultmann and Perrin (rather than employing, say, first-century Mediterranean criteria for determining historicity, or other methodologies, including Cognitive-Critical methodologies and socio-religious analyses), the 'historicity' analyses must be contextualized rather than absolutized. The quest for the 'historical Jesus' may indeed differ from the quest for the 'modern Jesus'.

33. See especially the 1980 monograph by John Riches on the ways Jesus sought to transform Judaism toward its better expressions, rather than supplant it.

although the impact of Strauss, Baur and others became something of the established critical view. Nevertheless, a multiplicity of attacks was raised against the critical view of John's historicity, only allowing the briefest of mention here. In 1837, Johann August Wilhelm Neander challenged Strauss, armed with de Wette's contribution and much of Schleiermacher's work (Kealy 2002, pp. 399–400). His arguments favoured the historicity of John's accounts of the life of Christ, including an early Temple cleansing and a pre-Passover last supper. He argued that John's presentation of Jesus as the Christ casts light upon his ministry from the perspective of eternity. Assaults upon and defences of the critical approach to John continued for the remainder of the nineteenth century.

Several decades later, in Britain a set of vigorous counter-assaults upon the modernist attacks on John's authorship and historicity was launched by three scholars of note: Westcott, Lightfoot and Hort. Their work largely carried the day among many British scholars for the first half of the twentieth century, and they argued for the historicity of John on the basis of textual character-istics and apostolic authorship. In particular, Westcott (1908) worked his way toward Johannine authorship concentrically, from the least unlikely toward the centre of his thesis. By his mounting of internal and external evidence, the Johannine evangelist deserves to be regarded as: a) a Jew, b) of Palestine, c) who was an eyewitness and member of the Twelve, and finally, d) John the apostle. Preceding the commentary of R.H. Lightfoot (1956), a collection of essays by Joseph Barber Lightfoot (1893, pp. 1–198) posed a considerable challenge to the de-historicization of John in arguing for the 'authenticity and genuineness of John's Gospel' on the basis of internal and external evidence. His authority as a Patristic scholar carried over into his investigation of New Testament historicity, and this work became formative for other treatments of the subject, as well.

During the early twentieth century, several defences of John's apostolic authorship and historicity were produced (Askwith 1910, Headlam 1948, Higgins 1960, Mussner 1966, J.A. Robinson 1908, P.V. Smith 1926), to the extent that Archbishop William Temple was able to declare at the beginning of his commentary on John that any scholar whose work on John did not begin with an apostolic premise stood 'self-condemned' from the start (1939). Other challenges to the Modern critical view of John performed analyses of critical scholarship (especially in Europe), and the literature reviews of Sanday (1872) and Howard (1931) fulfil this role. From the critical side, the literature review of Bacon (1918) takes its place with an apologetic thrust of its own.

Within this set of discussions, internal and external bases of evidence were amassed, and the most extensive of these was C. H. Dodd's 1963 monograph: *Historical Tradition in the Fourth Gospel*. In its own epoch-making way, Dodd's two-volume contribution to Johannine studies (1953, 1963) first assessed the sociological and religious background of John, and then analysed the character historical tradition in the Fourth Gospel by focusing first on the Passion narrative, and moving from there to the works and words of Jesus as presented in John. Not only did Dodd identify many non-identical parallels between John's and the Synoptics' renderings of events, but he argued for an inference of independence as an individuated perspective on the ministry of Jesus. The work of John A.T. Robinson (1985) argued for the priority of John (rather than its posteriority), and the works of Morris (1969, 1995), Carson (1991) and Blomberg (2002) pose vigorous defences of John's historicity and apostolic authority. As with the other categories, these studies are only suggestive of a much larger current of investigative inquiry.

4) *The Autonomy and Development of the Johannine Tradition – From Gardiner-Smith to Smith*

As a factor of seeking to infer the character, origin and development of the Johannine tradition with less of an apologetic interest for or against modernist or traditionalist perspectives, a significant thrust of twentieth century Johannine studies has explored the Johannine tradition as an autonomous development whether or not anything can be known in particular about its authorship. Within this venue, the highly significant work by P. Gardner-Smith (1938) demonstrates John's pervasive independence from the Synoptic gospels. This short book demonstrates with impressive clarity that at every turn, where John overlaps with the Synoptics, John also departs from the Synoptics. Unless one is prepared to adopt a view of pervasive contrariness, John must be considered largely independent from the Synoptic traditions.[34] Upon this approach many other analyses of John's tradition were developed, although the works of a significant number of scholars (notably Barrett, Neirynck, Brodie and others) argued for some form of Johannine dependence upon Mark.

During the second half of the twentieth century, however, major commentaries and studies affirmed the autonomy of the Johannine tradition. Typical of the tendency to forfeit the discussion on authorship for the sake of establishing positive headway on the question of the character of the Johannine tradition, Raymond Brown declared his move away from an earlier assertion of the Fourth Evangelist being the son of Zebedee in favour of his being an anonymous eyewitness, who was a Christian leader, but not a member of the Twelve (1979, 2003). Brown thus inferred the Johannine tradition as having had an apostolic source, but not necessarily one that would have come from the inner ring of the apostles. This would have thus allowed for the independent character of John's tradition, as it developed within its own Palestinian and Asia Minor trajectories. Robert Kysar crowned this inference with the lucid description: *John, the Maverick Gospel* (1993).

C.K. Barrett (1978) and Barnabas Lindars (1972) had also speculated that the Johannine evangelist could indeed have been an independent eyewitness

---

34. This is also D. Moody Smith's conclusion after examining the issue critically for a period spanning four decades, articulated clearly in the addendum to the second edition of his *John Among the Gospels* (2001): 'John, an Independent Gospel', pp. 195–241.

without having been John the son of Zebedee, and Rudolf Schnackenburg moved to an agnostic stance on the question of authorship between his earlier and later work, as well.[35] What can be seen in the major critical commentaries of the second half of the twentieth century is a move toward affirming the historicity of the Johannine tradition as a factor of its own developmental history. Characteristic of these approaches is the inference of early oral tradition, produced in written forms, crafted into an earlier edition, followed by further preaching and the finalization of the Johannine Gospel. Building also on the insights of J. Louis Martyn (2003), that history and theology deserve to be considered in evaluating the Johannine narrative, greater emphasis has been placed on the history of traditional development than on the historical character of that tradition, itself. The problem is that not all of John's narrative can be explained as a factor of developing context, so at least some affirmation of traditional historicity is made along the way. For this reason, the authoritative work of D. Moody Smith (2001) on John's independent relation to the Synoptics still carries the day. John's tradition is autonomous, representing an individuated perspective on the ministry of Jesus – *whoever* the author might have been.

Given the explosive character of historical-critical impasses, some scholars have employed new literary-critical methodologies while leaving open the historical-critical issues – moving more toward narrative criticism and reader-response analysis. Having investigated the Johannine 'school' in his earlier work, Alan Culpepper wrote an epoch-changing book considering the Gospel of John simply as a literary work with a plot, characters, dialogues and other features designed to engage the reader with the subject and progression of the text. *The Anatomy of the Fourth Gospel* applied the latest literary tools of analysis to the Johannine text, allowing the reader to derive excellent inferences as to the meaning of the text regardless of the historical character of the material – or the lack thereof. Jeff Staley pioneered work on John from the perspective of reader-response analysis, and he fully engaged the reader as a direct partner in the making of meaning. In addition to these studies, the last decade of the twentieth century and beyond has seen an avalanche of studies exploring such subjects as characterization, new historicism, irony and rhetorical analysis.

The great advantage of the new literary paradigms for interpreting John is that serious and profitable critical analysis of the text can be conducted regardless of one's levels of certainty regarding authorship, differences with the Synoptics, composition and historicity. Of course, the Jesus of history plays no direct role in such analyses, as the narrative is treated as would be any fictive

---

35. Brown calls attention to his having moved to this position independently-yet-concurrently with Schnackenburg in his introduction to *The Community of the Beloved Disciple* (1979), and yet he seems to overstate Schackenburg's movement. Less than certain, however, is different from being of the opinion that such an identification was mistaken or disproven.

literary composition. The problem is that the Johannine narrative has many features (let alone, its own direct claims) that call for some sort of historical analysis. Whether challenging the traditional view with the marshalled weight of scientific authority, or sidestepping historicity issues altogether, this is at least some of the story of the de-historicization of John, resulting in the de-Johannification of Jesus.

B. *Modern Paradigms and Their Adequacy*

While the present essay cannot develop fully the critical analyses of alternative options evaluated elsewhere,[36] the findings of earlier works become the foundations of further research. Not all of these issues are treated directly here, but they are indeed discussed elsewhere for those interested in considering the issues further.[37] As approaches are analysed, however, even partially convincing results are nonetheless beneficial for pointing ways forward. Questions may still be valid even if particular answers are insufficient, and every critical analysis done properly casts new light on related matters. Therefore, a critical assessment of paradigms and their adequacy serves scholarship most effectively when it sympathetically employs learnings from the analysis of failed models as well as successful ones. These elements, then, contribute fresh building material for a new synthesis.

1) *The 'Traditional' View: John's Apostolic Authorship*
The traditional view, that the Fourth Gospel was written by an apostle, John the son of Zebedee at the end of his life, bears with it considerable problems. First, the writer of John 21 claims *another* person is the author – the Beloved Disciple who leaned against the breast of Jesus at the supper – and this suggests *at least one other hand* in the composition process if one takes the text literally. Also, the 'explanation' of the death of the Beloved Disciple suggests apparently that he has died by the time of the finalization of John. Further, John shows signs of editing, suggesting a redactor has indeed added his hand to the construction and/or finalization of John. This set of facts poses serious problems for the view that a particular disciple wrote all of John on his or her own.

A second problem is that John's material is considerably different from the Synoptics, making it difficult to imagine that 'the historical Jesus' is all that well represented in the Fourth Gospel. While apostolic reflection may indeed have been a part of the Johannine tradition, the Fourth Gospel is also very

36. See the engagement by five scholars in the inaugural issue of *Review of Biblical Literature* 1, 1999, pp. 39–72); see also Anderson, Ellens and Fowler (2004).

37. Fuller treatments can be found regarding a) the history of the Johannine situation (1991, 1996, 1997), b) the agency schema (1999a), c) cognitive-critical analyses (2004b), d) rhetorical analysis (2000b) and e) Johannine-Markan relations (2001).

different from the Synoptics, and the verdict of Bretschneider nearly two centuries ago – that in contrast to the Synoptic Gospels, John's presentation of Jesus was concocted – has largely won the day among New Testament scholars. This suggestion has been embellished by scholars who also misappropriate Clement's statement that the Synoptics recorded the 'facts' about Jesus' ministry (*ta somatika* – the bodily content) and that John conversely wrote 'a spiritual gospel' (Eusebius, *Hist. Eccles.* 6.14). This conjecture by Clement of Alexandria, of course, proves nothing about Synoptic facticity or Johannine ahistoricity. It simply reflects a conjectural attempt to reconcile the differences of approach and content between John and the Synoptics. John's 'spiritual' approach, for instance, may imply first-order connectedness to and reflections upon events rather than merely distanced theologization.[38] Upon this fallacious conjecture many theories of Johannine composition have faltered.

Likewise, conjectural fallacies have abounded regarding how an apostolic author would or would not have operated. Do we really know, for instance, what an octogenarian would have thought and how he would have operated as a transmitter of tradition, eyewitness or otherwise? Advocates and critics of the traditional view alike have based their arguments unreflectively upon opinions of what an 'eyewitness' would or would not have thought or said, and these opinions have rarely ever been rooted in psychological or anthropological research. Therefore, 'scholarly' views of John's non-authorship have become every bit as entrenched as alternative views were a century ago, but with little more than opinion backing them up. What if the redactor's claim, 'And we know his witness is true', (Jn 19.35) was primarily making an ideological or theological claim, rather than a factual one? Have extended arguments for John's non-authorship been constructed on solid exegetical work, or upon shaky foundations? If understood more adequately as a defence of an antidocetic presentation of Jesus' suffering (Jn 19.34-5), or as an emphasis upon the challenging of Petrine eschatological or ecclesial perspectives (Jn 21.15-24), the advocating and challenging of the 'traditional view' of John's authorship might well have had a different history of development.

2) *The 'Critical' View: John's Employment of Alien (non-Johannine) Sources.* For much of the twentieth century great promise was held regarding the view that John was composed of several sources, and source-critical hypotheses served the function of explaining the origins of John's material as well as the epistemological root of the Fourth Gospel's theological tensions. Bultmann's elaborate posing of three sources (a *sēmeia* source, a Revelation-sayings source and a Passion narrative), which were used by the evangelist to construct a gospel, which in turn was disordered (for 'external' reasons) and then

---

38. See especially the Cognitive-Critical analyses (Anderson, 1996, 2001, and 2004b).

reordered by the redactor (who also added sacramental, futuristic and Synoptic-like material) was the greatest flower of New Testament *Religionsgeschichtlich* speculation in the Modern era. However, it could not have been written in the same way two decades later, after the discovery of the Dead Sea Scrolls, whereupon Jewish and Hellenistic distinctions have become largely obsolete. Even the extensive programme of David Strauss was fabricated upon this flawed foundation, and given the demise of Jewish/Hellenistic bipartite speculation, a new paradigm must be established.

The greatest problem with Bultmann's great scheme, however, lies not with its conception but with its evidence. It would indeed be significant, theologically and otherwise, if John *were* composed of at least five distinct sources. However, when Bultmann's own evidence for distinguishing sources – stylistic, contextual and theological – is applied in other parts of the Gospel, they show themselves to be representative of the Fourth Gospel overall, rather than smaller components of it. This can especially be seen in John 6, when Bultmann's own evidence for sources is tested throughout this chapter. The results are not only inconclusive; they are *non-indicative*. Likewise problematic are disordering and reordering hypotheses. For there to have been 10 disorderings of the material found in John 6 precisely in between sentences (at 80 Greek letters per sentence) would have required a ratio of $1:80^{10}$ (or 1:10 quintillion odds). A rationalist must thus baulk at such proposals, even if they are theoretically conceivable. The more elaborate one's diachronic theory of composition grows, the more tenuous it becomes. It is true, however, that such a theory allowed Bultmann to restore the 'original' order of the Johannine text, thereby exposing the poetic and supposedly Gnostic character of the distinctive sayings of Jesus in John. John's tradition, however, is as much unitive as it is disunitive, and beyond inferring the hand of an evangelist and an editor, not much can be said in favour of Bultmann's elaborate programme.

On the other hand, Bultmann noticed subtle turns in the text and special nuances of meaning appearing to escape other interpreters, to their peril. Bultmann did indeed identify theological tensions in the text and contextual oddities that deserve to be addressed by later theorists. He picked up astutely on apparent tensions between John's Christocentric soteriology and non-Johannine instrumentalistic sacramentology, high and low Christological elements, and theological tensions with regards to Jesus' miracles, forcing interpreters to grapple centrally with the classic Johannine riddles.[39] In these and other matters, Bultmann points the way forward. For instance, his inference that the redactor may have been the author of the Johannine Epistles is right

---

39. Indeed, the Christological tensions in John are real; see Appendices I–VI: 'John's Exalted Christology', 'John's Subordinated Christology', 'Johannine Signs as Facilitators of Belief', 'Johannine Signs and the Existentializing Work of the Evangelist', 'Realized Eschatology in John' and 'Futuristic Eschatology in John' (Anderson, 1996, pp. 266–71).

on target, and his work contributes helpfully to other composition approaches as well. Stylistically, however, John is a basic unity, albeit with several aporias and rough transitions along the way.[40] John thus betrays largely a synchronicity of authorship and a diachronicity of composition over an extended period of time.

3) *Markan-Dependence Theory*

In partial response to growing scepticism regarding source-analytical explanations for the origin and development of the Johannine tradition, several scholars have explored once again the theory of John's dependence upon Mark. In less nuanced ways, for instance, Thomas Brodie (1993) has assumed that all connections between John and any other traditions imply Johannine dependence on the rest. This approach is well meaning, but it fails to develop convincing criteria for assessing source dependence in either direction. It fails to account, for instance, for the possibility that John's tradition may have been early as well as late, and that other traditions may have drawn from Johannine material as well as the other way around. C.K. Barrett, while agreeing that if John has employed Mark it has been a very different utilization than Matthew's use of Mark, still seeks to explain John's similarities with Mark on the basis of Markan-dependence inferences. The Fourth Evangelist would have been far less concerned with following a written text, and he would have been more interested in spiritualizing the meanings of events and details narrated in Mark, according to Barrett.

A close analysis of John 6 and corollaries in the Synoptics, however, appear to confirm the basic directions of P. Gardner-Smith and C. H. Dodd.[41] John's tradition appears to have its own independent origins separate from the Synoptic traditions, and yet, the contacts with Mark are intriguing. Within John 6 alone, 24 contacts exist with Mark 6, and 21 contacts exist with Mark 8.[42] *None* of these contacts, however, are identical ones, absolutely disconfirming any theory of John's close dependence upon, or spiritualization of, written Mark. Consider these similar-and-yet-different details:

---

40. The degree of perplexity between these aporias is not equal, however, and the most perplexing lend themselves most favourably to a two-edition hypothesis, as approached most fruitfully by Barnabas Lindars (1972, pp. 46–54).

41. See analyses in D. Moody Smith (2001) and Anderson (1996, pp. 90–109, 167–93).

42. See *Table 7:* 'Similarities *and* Divergences between John 6 and Mark 6' (Anderson, 1996, pp. 98–99), and see *Table 8:* 'Similarities *and* Divergences Between John 6 and Mark 8', (pp. 101–2).

Table 1.2

Similar-yet-Different Details in John 6 and Mark 6 and 8

- *Grass:* grass is mentioned in both Mark and in John; but it is 'green grass' in Mark and 'much grass' in John (Mk 6.39, 44; Jn 6.10).
- *200 denarii:* the disciples ask if they should buy 200 *denarii* worth of loaves for the crowd in Mark; but in John Philip exclaims that 200 *denarii* would not be enough for everyone even to have a little (Mk 6.37; Jn 6.7).
- *The appearance of Jesus on the lake:* in Mark Jesus is perceived as a phantom who was about to float by the disciples in the boat; but in John Jesus is coming toward them (Mk 6.49-50; Jn 6.19).
- *The loaves:* in Mark 6 and 8 loaves are produced by the disciples; in John Andrew finds a lad who has food to share (Mk 6.38; 8.5; Jn 6.8-9).
- *The result of the feeding:* in Mark 6 and 8 (and in *all three* of the other Synoptic feeding narratives) the result of the feeding is described as the crowd 'ate the loaves and were satisfied'; in John Jesus rebukes the crowd the next day for not having seen the signs but being interested in him because they 'ate and were satisfied' (Mk 6.42; 8.8; Jn 6.26).
- *Peter's confession:* Peter's confession in Mark is 'you are the Christ'; while in John it is 'you are the Holy One of God' (Mk 8.29; Jn 6.69).

These persistent examples of similarities-and-divergences in the material closest between Mark and John, other than the Passion narratives, suggest some sort of contact, but *not* the Johannine borrowing from written Mark. Obviously, the sorts of contacts unique to John and Mark involve by definition the Markan material omitted by Matthew and Luke. Interestingly, though, many of these details are telling in their own way regarding the character of the Markan and Johannine traditions. Two primary sorts of material omitted by both Luke and Matthew include non-symbolic, illustrative details and theological asides.[43] For whatever reason, this sort of material is most characteristic of the Markan and Johannine traditions, and whether or not these characteristics reflect oral traditions employed by these two evangelists, they possess precisely the sorts of material left out of a written source (Mark) by its two known users: Matthew and Luke.

Implications of these issues are as follows: first, there do appear to have been contacts during the early stages of the Markan and Johannine traditions, but

---

43. See *Table 10:* 'Non-Symbolic, Graphic Detail Distinctive to the Johannine Tradition (Jn. 6.1-25)', *Table 11:* 'Marcan Detail (Mk 6.31-52) Omitted by Matthew *and* Luke', *Table 12:* Marcan Detail (Mk 6.31-52) Omitted by Matthew Alone', *Table 13:* 'Marcan Detail (Mk 6.31-52) Omitted by Luke Alone', *Table 14:* 'Interpolations Added by Matthew (Mt. 14.13-33)', and *Table 15:* 'Interpolations Added by Luke (Lk. 9.10-17)', (Anderson, 1996, pp. 187–90).

these do not seem to have the same sort of a derivative relationship as between Mark and Matthew and Luke, that is, if the Matthean and Lukan redactions tell us anything about how gospel writers may have operated. Second, what appears likely is that at least some of the Johannine/Markan contacts occurred during the oral stages of their traditions. Third, if this were so, it cannot be claimed that the influence went in just one direction; rather, an 'interfluential' set of relationships is a more likely assumption. Put otherwise, the distinctive contacts between Mark and John reflect traces of orality which were characteristic of the sorts of details preachers used in narrating their accounts of the ministry of Jesus, and this material is precisely the sort of material omitted by Matthew and Luke.

4) *Midrashic-Development Approaches*

According to Peder Borgen,[44] at least some of the material in John originated from Midrashic developments of Old Testament motifs. In particular, Borgen argues at some length that John 6 is a unity, and that it represents a homiletical development of Exod. 16.4, where it is mentioned that God gave them bread from heaven to eat. Borgen argues that Jn 6.31-54 shows the development of these biblical themes, building on a proem text and expanding the presentation to include the rest of the material in John 6. Borgen bases his work on the treatments of manna in Philo and the Babylonian Midrashim and correctly identifies similar Greek words and patterns existent in these other treatments of the manna theme. In this way Borgen demonstrates Jn 6.31-54 to be a basic unity against Bultmann's inference of at least three different sources within this section, and yet his analysis falls short in two ways. First, he fails to note the fact that when the manna motif is considered in its most pervasive use within Philo and the Midrashim, it appears most frequently as a secondary text drawn in as a 'proof text' to support another theme or interpretation.[45] This means that most of the Jewish uses of manna do not employ Exod. 16.4 as a proem text to be developed homiletically, but rather, they develop another text or theme primarily, drawing in the manna motif as a secondary support text. This is also the way it functions in John 6.

The second observation follows from the first: namely, the material developed in John 6 is not a Hebrew Scripture text, exposited midrashically and Christologically from verses 32–54. Rather, we have in John 6 a Christocentric development of the meaning of the feeding miracle by Jesus, employing the Jewish manna motif and its midrashic associations as part of the development. In other words, the origin of the traditional material in John 6 was *not* the Jewish Midrashim upon the manna motif, but it was an independent Johannine reflection upon the meaning of the feeding and its

---

44. See especially Borgen's significant monograph (1965).

45. See *Table 1:* 'The Rhetorical Use of Manna Pattern in Ancient Jewish Literature' (Anderson, 1996, p. 59); see also Appendix VII, 'Philo's Use of Manna as a Secondary Text' (pp. 272–3).

related discussions. More specifically, after the feeding, the crowd comes to Jesus asking for more bread, and upon his de-emphasis on the physicality of the sign they press their main point by means of employing standard Jewish manna rhetoric. Jesus overturns their exegesis, not with his own rapier skill, but by pointing to God, the eschatological source of both the earlier manna and the present Bread, which Jesus gives and is.[46] In that sense, Jesus challenges exegesis with eschatology. Again, the epistemological origin of John's tradition here seems to be an independent reflection upon the feeding events that was parallel to the traditional memories of Mark 6 and 8. In fact, many of the elements disbursed between these two Markan traditions are more unified in John, suggesting the integrity of the Johannine rendering.

5) Historicized-Drama Hypotheses

A common theory of accounting for the origin of the Johannine tradition involves the conjecture that John is written novelistically and that the historical-type detail has been added as a means of making the narrative more believable. Bultmann certainly claims this to have been the case, assuming it is in keeping with ancient narrative practice, and this is the explanation he poses to account for the prolific detail and geographical material in John. Two major problems, however, confront such a view. First, when Matthew's and Luke's redactions of Mark are analysed, they appear to do the opposite of the 'common practice' inferred by Bultmann and others. Rather than adding non-symbolic, illustrative detail to make a story more engaging and 'realistic', this is precisely the sort of detail they – the two closest writings to John other than Mark – leave out! So, if John operated like *other* first-century writers, especially other gospel writers, the adding of such detail would have been uncharacteristic. Among second-century pseudepigraphal gospels and writings some of this is done, but these writings show little, if any, similarity to the Gospel of John on this and many other matters.

Also, John may be novelistic, but John is not written as an ethereal fiction. John's Gospel narrative assumes an actual ministry of Jesus, including his death, burial and resurrection. The characters and events have indeed been dramatized, but such a possibility does not rule out a historical connection. This judgement is all the more likely when such otherwise unmotivated details are included prolifically in John, such as the number of years it has taken to build the Temple until then (46 years), the mentions of 200 and 300 *denarii*, actual measurements regarding the boats' distances from the shore (Jn 6.19; 21.8), the numeration and identification of specific days (Jn 1.29, 35, 43; 2.1; 5.9; 6.22; 11.53; 12.12; 19.14, 31, 42; 20.1, 19) and the time of day (Jn 1.39), and especially the unlikely number of the great catch of fish: *153*

---

46. See 'Manna as a "Rhetorical Trump" in Ancient Judaism and John', (Anderson, 1997, pp. 11–17).

(Jn 21.11). While much of John is highly theological in its explicit function, many of John's details do not appear to serve intentionally symbolic functions, and many of these may indeed represent proximity to the real events being narrated rather than stabs at realism interjected by a later writer hoping to make the text more engaging. As a means of furthering this interest, the Fourth Evangelist more characteristically employs irony and the characterization of misunderstanding discussants. Thus, John is more of a dramatized history than a historicized drama.

6) *Two Editions of John*

The most convincing of all the theories of John's composition is that of Barnabas Lindars in his posing of two editions of John. While not all of Lindars' proposals are equally convincing,[47] his theory makes the best sense of the continuities and discontinuities in the Johannine text with the least amount of speculation.[48] Independently, John Ashton also came to accept most of Lindars' proposals in his two-edition hypothesis, although he accepts John's use of sources more readily than critical analysis would merit (1991). The most perplexing aporias in John, requiring composition explanations, include the following:

Table 1.3

Major Literary Aporias in John

- The relation of the poetic form of the Prologue to the baptistic narrative in v. 6–8, 15 and 19–42.
- The Galilee / Jerusalem / Galilee / Jerusalem sequence between chapters 4, 5, 6 and 7, in which debates over the healing on the Sabbath in John 5 are resumed again in chapter 7.

47. See discussions of composition in Anderson (1996, pp. 33–47). Lindars believes the evangelist himself has finalized the Fourth Gospel, adding his own material to an earlier edition, but the fact that rough transitions are left in (Jn. 14.31; 6.71; ch. 21, etc.) implies the conservative hand of an editor, seeking not to disrupt the authoritative work of another. The third-person references to the ascribed author in chs 21 and 13 suggest the hand of the editor, *not* the evangelist, in the finalization process. Unconvincing also is Lindars' view that the original placement of the Temple cleansing was at the end of Jesus' ministry, and that it was moved early to make way for the Lazarus narrative. Chapter 11 seems to have been anticipated by the exclamation of the steward in Jn 2.9-10, and the late ordering of the Temple cleansing by the Synoptics may be conjectural as easily as chronological in its Mark-determined location. The Johannine Temple cleansing is also reflected upon in John 4 and implied in John 5, which erodes speculations regarding its relocation or being placed where it was for 'theological' reasons.

48. Unconvincing, for instance, are the parts of Pierson Parker's two-edition theory (1956), where he assumes John 4 and 2.1-12 were included in the second edition of John. Nonetheless, he does place John 6 and 21 in the later edition of material and points out ten parallels between these two chapters.

- The abrupt ending in Jn 14.31, which appears to have flowed directly into chapter 18 originally.
- The apparent original conclusion of the gospel at Jn 20.31, which is followed by further material in John 21 and concluded with another ending seeming to imitate the first.
- Third-person references to the acclaimed evangelist as the 'Beloved Disciple', or an eyewitness, added by a later hand.

In accommodating these major perplexities, it may be inferred that a first edition of John was probably produced around or shortly after 80 CE, and this edition was produced to show that Jesus was the authentic Jewish Messiah (Jn 20.31). The preaching ministry of the evangelist continued, however, and after his death this material (Jn 1.1-18, chs 6, 15-17 and 21) was added by the redactor, whose work also appears remarkably similar to the work of the presbyter, the author of the Johannine Epistles. Finally, the Fourth Gospel was finalized and circulated around the turn of the century as the witness of the Beloved Disciple, 'whose testimony is true'. This being the case, the Johannine Epistles were written before and after the Johannine Gospel.

7) *The History of the Johannine Situation*
At least seven crises, or extended sets of dialogical relations, can be inferred within a hypothetical reconstruction of Johannine Christianity.

a) *North–South Tensions.* While the early history of Johannine Christianity is less discernible, several aspects of it can be inferred. It apparently did develop within a northern Palestinian (either Galilean, Samaritan or possibly even trans-Jordan) setting for some time, and ambivalent relations with Judean religious leaders are apparent. During the early period of the Johannine tradition's formation an independent Jesus tradition developed in its own trajectory, and parallel to the pre-Markan and Q traditions, the Johannine preaching on the works and teachings of Jesus represented the evangelist's application of Jesus' ministry as an extension of his own ministry. Jesus' teachings came to be put into the evangelist's own paraphrastic style of discourse, but the Johannine rendering also developed with an explicitly Christocentric focus, which accounts to some degree for its individualistic presentation.

b) *Dialogues with Adherents of John the Baptist.* Also within the early stages of the Johannine tradition, encounters with followers of John the Baptist are evident. John the Baptist's insistence that Jesus is the Messiah, not he, served acute needs within the developing Johannine tradition, at the latest within the first three decades after the death of Jesus (consider Jn 3.5, for instance, in the light of issues related to the followers of Apollos in Acts 18-19). It may have been during this period that the Johannine preaching came into contact with oral deliveries of the pre-Markan tradition. As individuated and parallel traditions, the Johannine and pre-Markan preaching posed alternative presentations of Jesus' ministry as indicative of varying emphases, even between apostolic traditions. There never was a time when there was a singular Jesus tradition from which later trajectories departed. Some differences went back to the earliest stages of gospel traditions.

c) *Tensions with Leaders of the Local Synagogue.* During the middle period of the Johannine tradition's development, we see a set of crises with local Jewish authorities. Perhaps connected with the destruction of Jerusalem by Rome in 67–70 CE, the Fourth Evangelist moved to one of the mission churches in Asia Minor or elsewhere to assist in the strengthening of the movement, and in the attempts to evangelize local Jews with the news that Jesus was the Jewish Messiah, the evangelist forged some of the signs material, the I-Am sayings, and the controversy dialogues into more programmatic patterns. The first-edition of John is rife with these attempts to put forward a convincing view that Jesus was indeed the prophet like Moses, anticipated in Deut. 18.15-22, and the importance of his being sent from the Father is codified in Martha's confession (Jn 11.27), 'Yes, Lord, I believe that you are the Messiah, the Son of God, the one coming into the world'. The concluding statement at the original ending of the first edition (Jn 20.31) confirms this apologetic thrust, although it appears to have met only with partial success. Either before or after the Jamnia marshalling of the *Birkat ha-Minim*, Johannine Christians were put out of the Synagogue, several followers of Jesus remained behind cryptically, and some Johannine community members may even have been recruited back into the Synagogue by the appeals to the religious certainty and ethnic identity of Judaism (1 Jn 2.18-25).

d) *Emerging Pressures from Rome.* A second crisis during this middle period may be inferred, as pressures to offer public emperor worship arose during the reign of Domitian (81–96 CE). 'Persecution' may not be the best way to describe this harassment, but having been put out of the Synagogue, followers of Jesus would have been hard-pressed to argue effectively for receiving a monotheism dispensation, which members of Judaism received. Thus, they would have been expected to offer public Emperor laud, especially during the stepping up of the practice under Domitian. As indicated by the correspondence between Pliny of Bythinia and Trajan (ca. 110 CE), the penalty for not doing so was customarily death.[49] This led, then, to the later stages of the Johannine situation involving struggles with Gentile Christians and the opposing of docetizing developments.

e) *Docetism as an Internal Threat.* In response to Roman harassment and oppression around matters associated with the emerging Emperor Cult, opposing such a practice would have been the most difficult for Gentile Christians. Gentile members of Asia Minor were accustomed to worshipping the king or emperor as a matter of political loyalty, and they would not have

---

49. See Richard Cassidy's convincing argument on this crisis in the background of the Johannine situation (1992).

seen it as a spiritual offence in quite the same way that the monotheistic Jewish-Christian leadership would have. The primary argument against assimilation would have been the suffering example of Jesus, and such was precisely the teaching to which the docetizing leaders objected. The primary attraction to the teaching was not simply that it fit into a Hellenistic world-view, but it was the implications that made it most attractive. If a non-human Jesus neither suffered nor died, his followers need not be expected to do the same. The material added to the final edition of John has within it most of the incarnational material in John (Jn 1.14; 6.51-8; 15.18–16.2; 19.34-5; 21.18-23), and this is no accident. It was preached and written to oppose docetizing inclinations among Gentile believers, and the same sequence of issues can be seen clearly in the epistles of Ignatius and the Epistles of John.[50]

f) *Intramural Dialogues with Rising Institutionalism.* A final intramural crisis to be inferred in the Johannine material relates to dialectical tensions with institutionalizing Christianity within the late first-century church. It is doubtful, for instance, that the organizing work of Ignatius and others like him was experienced as problem-free, and tensions with Diotrephes and his kin (3 Jn 9-10) may be inferred in the juxtaposition of Peter and the Beloved Disciple in John. Notice that the Elder has written to the *ecclēsia* about Diotrephes, perhaps an institutionalizing centre of the Christian movement (the only uses of *ecclēsia* in the Gospels are in Mt. 16.17-19 and 18.15-20), whence Diotrephes is deriving his hierarchical authority. Notice that he not only refuses to welcome the Johannine *philoi*, but Diotrephes also expels members of his own fellowship who are willing to take them in. Analyses assuming the issue to be merely inhospitality overlook the larger issue, which is the infelicitous wielding of positional authority by Diotrephes, even within his own community, as the singular precipitator of the inhospitable reception of Johannine Christians. But why was Diotrephes threatened by Johannine Christians? While Käsemann's view that it was incipient Docetism is overly conjectural, a more likely possibility is that he was threatened by Johannine egalitarianism and familial ecclesiology – and well he should have been, for their influence – especially in the name of a competing apostolic tradition – would have dismantled his very attempt to hold his church together by means of proto-Ignatian monepiscopal hierarchy, with himself at the top. Thus, his 'loving to be first' was not a factor of selfish ambition, but a claim to primacy, after the model of emerging Petrine hierarchical models of church organization. In response to this and other evolutions in ways structural, the

---

50. See, for instance, the anti-docetic emphases of the second and third antichristic passages in 1 Jn. 4.1-3 and 2 Jn. 7. They emphasize opposing Docetist teachers versus the Jewish-Christian tensions alluded to in 1 Jn. 2.18-25 (see Anderson, 1996, *Table 21:* 'Three Acute Intramural Crises Faced by Johannine Christianity', pp. 245–8; and Anderson, 1997, 'Four Acute Crises Faced Within Johannine Christianity As Implied by John 6', pp. 24–57).

Johannine Elder finalized the witness of the Beloved Disciple and circulated it as a manifesto of radical Christocracy: the effectual means by which the risen Lord continues to lead and direct the church.[51]

g) *Dialogues with Synoptic Traditions.* A seventh crisis is actually a set of dialogues that spanned all six of the previous ones, and in that sense represents a running engagement with parallel Gospel traditions regarding the meaning and memory of the story of Jesus. From the first period to the last, John's tradition appears to have been commenting on the meaning of Jesus' signs, the character of the Kingdom, Christian leadership and its effectiveness, the return of Christ, and other themes where John's and other traditions intersect. These dialogues, however, need not have been engaging a particular written gospel for them to have been in effect. Sometimes primary or secondary orality would have been a sufficient occasion to engage in an inter-tradition dialogue, and several signs of such engagement can be seen at various places within the Johannine text.

Each of these crises was probably somewhat overlapping-yet-largely-sequential within the history of Johannine Christianity. Obviously, a fair amount of conjecture is involved in developing any theory of Johannine history, but all of the above projections are rooted in plausible evidence. Common fallacies involve assuming Johannine Christianity stayed only in one place over 70 years, or that it only struggled only on one front. Living communities rarely enjoy the luxury of facing only one set of issues over several generations, and a theoretical history of Johannine Christianity must account for the apparent dialogical factors suggested by internal and external evidence. These crises and dialogues also accounted for some of the theological emphases in John, with Jewish-Christian dialogues pushing Christological motifs higher, and anti-docetic tensions evoking incarnational motifs. Whatever the case, John's relations to the other gospel traditions must be considered within a plausible projection of the history of Johannine Christianity.

8) *Cognitive Criticism and Traditionsgeschichte*
Gospel traditions were not disembodied sets of ideas floating abstractly from sector to sector within the early church. No! They were human beings, who reflected upon experiences in the light of perceptions and religious understandings. The unreflective notion that religious typological ideas were simply taken over by Gospel traditions, thus explaining the epistemological origin of the events narrated in the Gospels, is too simplistic. Religious typologies and mythic constructs indeed were applied to interpretations of Jesus' ministry, but they were employed *because* they made sense to either an understanding of what Jesus said and did, to an evangelist, to audiences along the way or any

---

51. For further developments, see Anderson 1996 (pp. 221–251, especially *Table 20:* 'Matthew 16.17-19 and its "Christocratic Correctives" in John', p. 240) and 1991.

combination of the above. This being the case, quests for the historical Jesus must inevitably engage the histories of the periods between Jesus' ministry and the finalization of the Gospels, and human factors in the conveyance of the material included the experiences, perceptions, hopes, frustrations and disappointments of these human vehicles through which the traditions were passed from one setting and generation to the next. The scientific analysis of this set of reflective processes is what I call 'cognitive criticism'.

Differences between Gospel traditions, and in particular Mark and John, should not be lumped too readily, therefore, into disjunctive categories of 'historical' versus 'theological', or 'authentic' versus 'concocted', as though historicity itself were unrelated to subjective determinations of value. *All* the gospel traditions were theological, and they were all historical, in the sense that they sought to connect meanings of important events in the past with the perceived needs of the eventual present. In these ways, Papias' view that Mark's tradition included the preaching of Peter, which was crafted, at least in part, to address the emerging needs of the church, may also be assumed for all the gospel traditions – apostolic and otherwise. What cognitive criticism allows is the scientific analysis of the dialectical relationship between perception and experience and its impact upon the emerging theological content within the various gospel traditions, and even between 'apostolic' interpretations.

Some differences between Mark and John may even reflect radical differences of first impression rather than later divergences rooted in emerging understandings alone.[52] Others, such as the valuation of miracles (including explanations of their subsequent relative dearth), betray the faith development of different formers of gospel traditions as their preaching ministries addressed the needs of the early church. One of the most promising aspects of cognitive criticism is that it examines the relation between the ministries of the purveyors of Jesus and their presentations of Jesus' ministry. Such approaches to gospel traditions help to account not only for differences between the Gospels, but they also provide insights into historical developments between the ministry of Jesus and the finalization of those accounts in the written Gospels to which we have access.

C. *The 'Dialogical Autonomy of John' – A New Synthesis Advanced*

While various components of this synthesis are argued elsewhere (some are developed in Parts II and III, below), presenting them together as a larger set of theories will serve the present analysis well. Individual components of the

---

52. See the analysis of these possibilities using the religious anthropological models of James Loader (1981) and James Fowler (1981) in *Christology* (pp. 137–169) in Anderson, ch.7, 1996; see Fowler's response (2004).

larger synthesis are based on their own sets of evidence, but they also inter-relate to each other, and the stronger aspects of one approach will impact the others. Within this synthesis, critical approaches to the enduring Johannine issues, including literary, historical and theological matters, are combined into a workable whole. The autonomy and independence of the Johannine tradition, however, does *not* imply isolation and seclusion. Rather, its dialogical development also must be considered in Cognitive-Critical perspective, integrating the most compelling of composition, literary and historical-development theories into a workable whole.

1) *An Autonomous and Developing Tradition*
Because the evidence for alien sources underlying John is unconvincing on the basis of evidence, and because none of John's similarities with Mark are identical, John *cannot* be said to be a derivative work. Rather, John is an autonomous tradition, representing an independent reflection on the ministry of Jesus that has developed in its own distinctive set of ways.[53] While independent, this does not mean, however, that it is *isolated* from other tradi-tions. Rather, several levels and forms of dialogue may be inferred within the Johannine tradition, and critical analysis profitably identifies particular features of development, making profitable use for meaningful interpretation.

2) *The Dialectical Thinking of the Evangelist*
One of the primary sources of John's theological tensions is the dialectical thinking of the evangelist.[54] As a conjunctive thinker, he often presents things from one side, and then from another, as a means of exploring the complexity of an issue. It is also a fact that John's composition history shows some dialogue between earlier impressions and later experiences – causing new understandings and discoveries. In the evangelist's reflection upon his tradition, he can be observed to be making meaning out of earlier perceptions, and in the light of new experiences, new openings are suggested. Understanding the dialectical character of the thinking of the evangelist is essential for effectively interpreting the theological content of John – complete with all its tensions, but it is also central to understanding the sort of historical narrative that John represents, as well.

3) *The History-of-Religions Origin of John's Human-Divine Dialectic*
Contrary to Bultmann and others, the history-of-religions origin of the Johannine revelational structure is *not* the Gnostic redeemer-myth, but the

---

53. The conclusion of P. Gardner-Smith (1938) is still compelling, that John's stance with relation to the Synoptics is essentially independent, and Moody Smith's conviction on this matter (2001) still stands. 'Autonomy', though, is preferable to 'independence'.

54. Here the work of C.K. Barrett (1972) is compelling: the Fourth Evangelist is a dialectical thinker, and applying the cognitive-critical works of James Loder and James Fowler suggest how this mode of dialectical thinking may have emerged.

prophet-like-Moses agency schema.[55] Jesus' sense of mission is rooted in Deut. 18.15-22, and he is one with the Father precisely because he is totally subservient to the will of the one who sent him. Like the Mosaic prophet, Jesus says nothing on his own behalf, but only what the Father has commissioned him to say; humanity is called to hear him as hearing the divine sender; humanity will be held accountable to their response to the divine agent by the sender; the authentic prophet is judged to be authentic if his words come true; but the prophet who speaks presumptuously shall be put to death. Ironically, when Jewish authorities question Jesus as to the authenticity of his mission, they mistake his declaration of his divine commission as presumptuous speaking (connected also to Deut. 18.15-22), and this becomes a basis for their scriptural warrant to put Jesus to death.

4) *Dialogical Engagements in the Johannine Situation*
The Johannine tradition develops within its own situation, and it appears to have gone through at least three major periods – each having at least two crises within it. The *first period* (30–70 CE) shows evidence of Palestinian development. Within this period, north–south tensions with the Judean leadership in Jerusalem can be inferred, as well as engagements with followers of John the Baptist. The *second period* (70–85 CE) shows evidence of a Gentile setting – perhaps in one of the Pauline mission churches, such as Ephesus. Within this period, religious tensions with members of the local Jewish community can be inferred, and the requirement of Emperor worship under Domitian (81–96 CE) becomes a problem. The *third period* shows signs of the proliferating of neighbouring Christian communities, and during this period, tensions with docetizing Gentile Christians and with rising institutionalization within the church can be inferred. From beginning to end, a running dialogue with parallel gospel traditions can be inferred, so this seventh crisis runs from beginning to end across the history of the Johannine situation. This being the case, John's narrative can be seen to be engaging emerging audiences along the way (see Appendix II, below).

5) *A Two-Edition Theory of Composition*
Despite the Johannine tradition's having many signs of unity and synchronicity, it also bears a good number of literary perplexities suggesting at the very least a two-edition theory of composition. Based on the work of Barnabas Lindars, the completion of a first edition of John was followed by the evangelist's continuing preaching and ministry, and eventually, supplementary material was added to the earlier Gospel narrative. In contrast to Lindars' view, I believe

---

55. On this matter, the works of Jan-A. Bühner (1977) and others demonstrate a clear connection between the Mosaic Prophet schema rooted in Deut. 18.15-22 and John's *agency Christology* (see Anderson, 1999a).

John 11 was a part of the first edition material and that the Temple cleansing stood where it was in the first edition as well as the final edition. The outline is as follows (see also Appendix I, below):

Table 1.4

A Two-Edition Theory of Johannine Composition

- Following several decades of Johannine preaching (and perhaps some writing) a first edition of John was completed between 80 and 85 CE, to some degree as a response to Mark. This 'second' Gospel (chronologically) was not distributed widely, but it began with the ministry of John the Baptist (1.15, 19-42) and concluded with 20.31, declaring the evangelistic purpose of the Johannine Gospel.
- The teaching/preaching ministry of the Beloved Disciple (and possibly other Johannine leaders) continued over the next decade or two, and during this time (85–100 CE), the three Johannine Epistles were written by the elder (85, 90, 95 CE).
- After the death of the Beloved Disciple (around 100 CE) the elder compiled the Gospel, adding to it the worship material of the Prologue (1.1-18), inserting the feeding and sea-crossing narrative (Jn 6) between chs 5 and 7, and inserting additional discourse material (Jn 15-17) between Jesus' saying, 'Let us depart', (Jn 14.31) and his arrival with his disciples at the garden (Jn 18.1). He also apparently attached additional appearance narratives (ch. 21) and eyewitness/Beloved Disciple passages, and crafted a second ending (21.24-5) in the pattern of the first. Then, he circulated the finalized witness of the Beloved Disciple, 'Whose testimony is true!' as an encouragement and challenge to the larger Christian movement.

6) Aspects of Interfluentiality between John and Other Traditions
Given John's pervasive autonomy, John is not dependent on Mark or other traditions, but neither is John isolated from them. Based upon individuated analyses of all four Synoptic traditions (including Q) and their particular similarities and differences with John, distinctive inferences can be made regarding relationships between the Johannine and each of the Synoptic traditions. While this theory will be developed fully in Part III, John's relationship with Mark was interfluential, augmentive and corrective; John's relationship with Q was formative, and perhaps interfluential; John's relation with Luke was formative, orderly and theological; and John's relationship with Matthew was reinforcing, dialectical and corrective. These relationships, along with a two-edition theory of composition, are also sketched in Table 3.3, below, to show the relationships more clearly.

7) *Revelation and Rhetoric – Dialogical Modes of the Johannine Narrative*
As a means of engaging the reader in the narrative, several rhetorical devices
are employed. Several bases are put forward, designed to lead the reader into
a believing response to the divine initiative, and this involves the revelational
mode of dialogue within the Johannine narrative. The narrator also attempts
to engage the reader in an imaginary dialogue with Jesus by means of the
crafting of misunderstanding dialogues. Misunderstanding is always rhetorical
in narrative, and over 30 dialogues with Jesus in John function to correct the
shallow and flawed understandings of the reader, guiding him toward the way
of liberating truth.[56]

Findings

While the historicity of John was a foundational assumption of biblical scholarship before the Modern era, things changed toward the beginning of the
nineteenth century. Leading to one of the most vigorous and sustained debates
in theological studies, the removal of John from the canons of historical
narrative has been argued and countered with such energy and verve that it
has at times polarized critical and traditional scholarship. What John did for
polarizing theological discussions of Jesus as the Christ in the Patristic era, John
has also done for polarizing critical discussions of the historical quest for Jesus
in the Modern era. And yet, whereas restoring the dialectical tension to structures of belief in the fourth century provided a Johannine way forward, such
has not yet been the case regarding John and the quest for Jesus. The camps
are still divided. Over the last half-century, however, several improvements
have been made in terms of critical approaches to various aspects of the
Johannine problem. While some modern approaches to matters Johannine
have greater weaknesses than strengths, others are more worthy of serving as
a platform for further constructive work. In the light of the dialogical
autonomy of John, new possibilities emerge for investigating familiar
problems, and it is upon the best of those foundations that the present work
will seek to build.

56. Note the presentation of revelation and rhetoric, two dialogical modes within Johannine
narrative in Anderson (1996, pp. 105–7, 221–6; 1997, pp. 17–24).

PART II
ON PLANKS AND PLATFORMS –
A CRITICAL ASSESSMENT OF CRITICAL FOUNDATIONS
REGARDING JOHN, JESUS AND HISTORY

'It must be remembered that topography and chronology were among the least of the author's concerns. His head was among the stars. He was seeking to determine the place of Jesus in the spiritual universe and his relations to the eternal realities. These were the matters that interested and absorbed him, not itineraries and time tables, so that practical mundane considerations that might apply to Mark, Matthew, or Luke have little significance for his work.'

From Edgar J. Goodspeed, *An Introduction to the New Testament* (Chicago: University of Chicago Press, 1937, p. 310)

Jesus and gospel studies possess rich histories of analysis, and within those histories new findings and distinctive trends emerge. Few scholarly developments – in any field – have been as interesting, though, as the modernistic de-historicization of John and the de-Johannification of Jesus.[1] To a certain degree, each of these trends has bolstered the other, and the assertion of many a scholar claiming the authoritative weight of critical and scientific study is that 'the *one* thing we know for sure' is actually *two*: the Fourth Gospel is of *no* historical value, and historical Jesus research must be performed *untainted* by any Johannine influence.[2] The question is the degree to which either of these assertions is true – a solid platform upon which to base the frameworks of further studies. Negative claims are even more difficult to substantiate than positive ones, and surprisingly large numbers of scholars speak in terms of certainty along either or both of these propositions. Simply challenging a traditional view, however, does not confirm an alternative view, and the planks in these platforms deserve to be tested with the same critical scrutiny and rigour as those they have endeavoured to supplant. This is *why* this study is needed.

Obviously, John's ahistoricity goes against the traditional view that the Fourth Gospel was written by the Apostle John, connected inferentially with the redactor's claim that the Johannine evangelist was an eyewitness who leaned against the breast of Jesus at the last supper, was present at the crucifixion, and that 'his witness is true' (Jn 13.23; 19.26, 34-5; 21.7, 20, 24). Over half a century ago, Pierson Parker declared, 'If there was one "assured result of biblical criticism" for such scholars of the 1920s, 1930s and 1940s, it was that John, the son of Zebedee, had nothing at all to do with the writing of this gospel'.[3] Another scholar has even declared more recently that now the burden of proof is upon any who would challenge the purported scholarly consensus regarding John's patent ahistoricity.[4] This claim reflects an interest

1. See Robert Kysar's paper offered at the John, Jesus and History Consultation in Toronto, November 2002, 'The De-Historicizing of John'.

2. Can it be put any clearer than the introductory statement of Funk, Hoover and the Jesus Seminar (1998, p. 10)?

The first step is to understand the diminished role the Gospel of John plays in the search for the Jesus of history. The two pictures painted by John and the synoptics cannot be both historically accurate.... The differences between the two portraits of Jesus show up in a dramatic way in the evaluation, by the Jesus Seminar, of the words attributed to Jesus in the Gospel of John. The Fellows of the Seminar were unable to find a single saying they could with certainty trace back to the historical Jesus.

So much for the words of Jesus; the results of the Jesus Seminar's analysis of the actions of Jesus (Robert Funk and the Jesus Seminar, 1998) are equally sparse. *None* of Jesus' deeds in John are rooted in history, save the death of Jesus (pp. 433, 435), in this analysis.

3. Pierson Parker (1962, p. 35).

4. Robert Funk (1996, p. 127) goes on to say:

In the Gospel of John, Jesus is a self-confessing Messiah rather than a self-effacing sage. In John, Jesus seems to have little concern for the impoverished, the disabled and the religious outcasts.

in establishing the sort of 'critical orthodoxy' Bishop Robinson alluded to half a century ago.[5] Whereas the question in traditionalist circles used to be, 'Do you believe in the historicity of John?', the litmus test for the modernist biblical scholar has come to be, 'Do you believe in the ahistoricity of John?'. Because a scholar's livelihood and career may hinge upon distinguishing oneself as a hard-minded scientific scholar rather than a soft-hearted traditionalist one, the stakes are high indeed. Further, no scholar wants to come across as embracing a naively traditionalistic view; and yet, the present critical question remains: 'Is the ahistoricity of John an open-and-shut case – on critical grounds?' If so, fine. Scholars may build on a solid platform, conducting further studies upon an established foundation. However, if the modernist platform fails to stand up to critical analyses, or if parts of it are found to be less solid than others, critical scholarship at the dawn of the post-Modern era demands an alternative. This is why this study is needed *now*.

Before continuing with analysis, however, two points deserve to be made before acknowledging a scholarly consensus exists at all on the matter. First, many, perhaps even most, of the leading Johannine scholars over the last two centuries would not have agreed to John's patent ahistoricity; so, if any 'consensus' exists, it must be regarded as one that is purported among a group that excludes many of the keenest experts in the field. One need only consider the works of Schleiermacher, Lightfoot, Westcott, Sanday, Robinson, Hoskyns, Dodd, Brown, Schnackenburg, Barrett, Lindars, Carson, Beasley-Murray, Morris, Hengel and many others to realize that many of the great Johannine scholars of the Modern era stood or would have stood against the purported 'consensus'. As Raymond Brown says (1965, p. 271),

> ...We are not always to assume facilely that the Synoptic Gospels are recording the historical fact and that Jn has theologically reorganized the data. In the cases we have studied, an interesting case can be made out for the basic historicity of the Johannine picture and for theological reorganization on the part of the Synoptic Gospels. We are coming to realize more and more that the critics have played us false in their minimal estimate of the historicity of the Fourth Gospel.[6]

Although John preserves the illusion of combining a real Jesus with the mythic Christ, the human side of Jesus is in fact diminished. For all these reasons, the current quest for the historical Jesus makes little use of the heavily interpreted data found in the Gospel of John.

5. While Robinson's essay (1959) called for a 'New Look at the Fourth Gospel', his monograph on the 'priority of John' (1985) claimed too much by equating early tradition with early finalization. A more plausible approach would connect primitivity of tradition with its development and later finalization.

6. In another essay on John's historicity (1962), Brown argues that the Johannine rendering of the last supper on Thursday seems more plausible historically. Arguably, the Synoptics have stylized it as a Passover meal to conform with emerging Christian worship practices – a judgement bolstered by the criterion of dissimilarity. Brown further develops and refines his belief in John's historicity in his revised and expanded introduction to John (2003, pp. 90–114).

A second fact, however, is that even some of the most sceptical of scholars have had to express reservations over the degree to which certainty about John's ahistoricity can be assumed. A telling example of such a turnaround may be found in David Strauss' introduction to his third edition of his *Life of Christ*. In response to criticisms regarding his earlier marginalizations of John's historicity, he had to reverse himself, as follows:[7]

> The changes offered by this new edition are all more or less related to the fact that a renewed study of the Fourth Gospel, on the basis of de Wette's commentary and Neander's *Leben Jesu Christi*, has made me again *doubtful of my earlier doubt* concerning the authenticity and credibility of this Gospel. It is not that I have become convinced of its authenticity, merely that I am *no longer certain of its inauthenticity*. From among the peculiarly striking and frustrating features of credibility and incredibility, of proximity to and distance from the truth, which exist in this most remarkable Gospel, I had emphasized in the first composition of my work, with one-sided polemical zeal, only what seemed to me the adverse and unfavorable side. In the meanwhile the other side has gradually come into its own for me (emphases added) ...

Ironically, many scholars aligning themselves with the revisionist view outlined by Strauss, Baur and others have failed to balance their critical views with reflective nuance. Just as a traditionalist arguing for the eyewitness historicity of everything in John based upon shallow assumptions is flawed, so is an unreflective arguing of a critical view. For some reason, while the Gospel of John possesses the most extensive and explicit claims to representing a first-hand narration of Jesus' works and ministry, it has ceded place to the Gospel of Thomas and other second-century apocryphal narratives in some recent Jesus studies. The question is whether those exchanges are warranted and whether a distorted presentation of Jesus is being constructed by those who claim to know. On the other hand, there are good reasons for scholars to question John's historicity and contribution to understanding Jesus and his ministry, so the bases for these platforms deserve fresh critical consideration. Such is the critical interest of the present investigation.

A. *Planks in Platform A: The De-Historicization of John*

John's claims to historicity are problematic. In many ways John's presentation differs significantly from those of Matthew, Mark and Luke, and the Johannine Jesus is clearly crafted in the image of the evangelist's own convictions. Further, the Fourth Evangelist's presentation of Jesus is a spiritualized one, so this fact raises questions as to the motives for particular aspects in the construction of the Johannine narrative. As the main planks in the platform

---

7. David F. Strauss (1864, 1972, p. lvii) here goes on to describe his need to hold the negative and positive aspects of critical study together in tension; he later changed his mind.

of John's de-historicization are analysed, including an assessment of strengths and weaknesses, the bases for this judgement will be better ascertained. Fresh considerations of classic problems also may lead to other ways forward not yet considered, but such can only be envisioned at the end of such an analysis.

1) *John's Differences with the Synoptics*

A great and puzzling fact of biblical studies is that John is *very* different from the Synoptics. Rather than a birth narrative, John's story begins with the advent of the eternal Logos. Rather than ministering for one year, three Passovers are mentioned in John. Rather than cleansing the Temple at the end of Jesus' ministry, John's Temple incident is at the beginning, and John mentions two miracles that were the first ones performed in Cana of Galilee. Rather than ministering exclusively in Galilee, the Johannine Jesus goes to and from Jerusalem, and he performs three Judean miracles. Rather than teaching pervasively about the Kingdom of God and doing so in parables and in short pithy sayings, the Johannine Jesus speaks in long I-Am discourses, engaging the Kingdom motif only in two passages. In contrast to the Synoptic Jesus, John's Jesus performs no exorcisms but knows what is in the hearts of humans and escapes capture in knowing ways. And, rather than celebrating the last supper as a Passover meal where the Eucharist is instituted, the Johannine rendering omits the words of institution and presents the event as happening the day before the Passover meal would have taken place. These are just some of the facts that contribute to preferring the Synoptics' presentation historically over the Johannine.

a) *Strengths:* John's ahistoricity seems confirmed if one assumes a 3-against-1 majority with John being the lone Gospel out. This indeed was the argument of Bretschneider, who in 1820 argued that because of the threefold witness of the Synoptics, they could not possibly have concocted their view, while the same cannot be claimed for John.[8] Rather, he argued the historical probability of material in John should be considered low, and a generation later Strauss levied this argument against Schleiermacher's preference for John's historicity over and against the Synoptics, designating Brettschneider to be the true man of science on the matter.[9] Indeed, Jesus could have cleared the Temple more

---

8. Karl Gottlieb Bretschneider (1820) questions several features of John as being inauthentic: namely, Jesus' speaking with exalted self-references, his knowing the hearts of others, his claiming to represent God, and all of his miraculous deeds. By hastily excluding all of John's wondrous reports and themes from his perceived categories of naturalism, Bretschneider expels John from the canons of historicity in the name of modest, scientific inquiry.

9. Strauss (1965, 1977, p. 41) fails, however, to appreciate much of the critically significant work conducted by Schleiermacher, such as his extensive observations about the fragmented character of the Synoptic narratives in contrast to the more unitive Johannine narrations.

than once, but John's presentation, because it is out of step with the majority, calls for explanations on grounds other than historical ones. Likewise, in the presentation of Jesus' teachings, the Synoptic presentation of Jesus' use of parables seems far more reliable as a guide to Jesus' teaching ministry than the more elevated revelatory discourses in the Johannine I-Am sayings. These are some of the good reasons for questioning John's historicity on the basis of major differences with the Synoptics.

b) *Weaknesses:* If Luke and Matthew used Mark, however, viewing John's differences with the Synoptics as a 3-against-1 minority must be reconsidered. Critically, scholars in the nineteenth and early twentieth centuries who took this view did so before Markan priority was established but failed to make the appropriate self-correction along the way. If Mark got it wrong here and there, so did Matthew and Luke. If John and Mark are worthy of being considered the bi-optic Gospels, as several recent studies have argued,[10] this means that the door must be held open in ascribing greater or lesser degrees of historicity to the Johannine and Markan traditions. For instance, John may be more realistic in presenting a Jesus who travelled to and from Jerusalem, like most observant Jews would have done during his time. This being the case, John's three-year ministry also seems more realistic than Mark's one-year presentation, perhaps locating all the Jerusalem and judgement material at the end for the purposes of a narrative climax rather than reflecting chronological knowledge. Indeed, Mark's gathering of Jesus material and ordering it into a progressive narrative must have involved some conjecture, and the killing of Jesus due to a Temple disturbance is far more likely to have been inferred ('concocted', to use Bretschneider's language) than the unlikely-to-have-been imagined 'threat of the risen Lazarus' in John.

Was this a factor in the second-century opinion of Papias (few scholars if any have noted that he cites the Johannine elder as the source of this opinion!), that while Mark preserved Peter's preaching effectively, he got it down in the *wrong order?* If such were the case, one of the motivations for producing the 'second gospel' (John's first edition was completed around 80–85 CE, before the Gospels of Luke and Matthew) might have been to set the record straight.[11]

---

10. See Part III, below, especially Table 3.3; see also Anderson (2001 and 2002b).

11. Of all the theories of John's composition, the most compelling is the two-edition theory of Barnabas Lindars (1972), inferring a first edition emerging around 80, to which the editor added supplementary material after the death of the Beloved Disciple around 100 CE. Here I agree with Bultmann, however, that the compiler may likely have been the author of the Johannine Epistles, rather than the evangelist himself (contra Lindars), thus leading one to believe that the Epistles were plausibly written *between* these two editions. I concur with Lindars that material added to the final edition included the Prologue (Jn. 1.1-18), chs 6, 15–17 and 21, and Beloved Disciple and eyewitness passages. Contra Lindars, evidence for the translocation of the Temple cleansing making space for the Lazarus narrative seems weak.

John should thus be reconceived at least in part as a complementary presentation for readers and hearers of Mark,[12] and some of John's contrasts to Mark may have been intentional. Indeed, Matthew and Luke eventually did the same, as did the editor who added the second ending of Mark. With these issues in mind, the fact of John's differences with the Synoptics does not force a 3-against-1 overruling of John's account. We have two individuated perspectives between John and Mark, the bi-optic Gospels, and any assumptions about how early Christian narrators would have gathered and presented their material must also be subjected to critical scrutiny. The case is thus still open, and exploring these distinctive presentations analytically may yet lead to some new ways of approaching long-standing New Testament riddles.

2) *Synoptic Omissions in John*
One of the strongest arguments against an apostolic origin of John's material is that leading themes and events in the Synoptics, especially those at which the sons of Zebedee are reported as being present, are missing. First, the calling of the Twelve is not found in John, nor are more than eight disciples mentioned. Second, the Transfiguration is not mentioned in John, nor is it reported that Peter, James and John had gone with Jesus to the Garden of Gethsemane. Third, if the Beloved Disciple really had been leaning against the breast of Jesus at the last supper, how could he have missed the institution of a meal of remembrance? That would certainly have been an unlikely event to have forgotten or omitted. Fourth, Jesus' having spoken in parables about the Kingdom of God is terribly conspicuous as a pervasive omission in John; and fifth, Jesus' exorcisms are not mentioned at all in John. These facts pose major problems for anyone arguing that the Synoptic and Johannine presentations of Jesus are both historically reliable.

a) *Strengths:* Indeed, if the Apostle John were in some way connected to the purveying of the Johannine witness, it seems odd that at many of the points at which we might expect an event to have been embellished or expanded, we have pervasive silence. How could the son of Zebedee, for instance, have omitted the calling of the Twelve, the Transfiguration, the words of the institution, and the anguish of Jesus at Gethsemane, if he were indeed both present at those events *and* the traditional source of the Fourth Gospel? These facts pose major problems for the traditional view of John's authorship, and they are one of the key reasons critical scholars reject it. A further problem is that the sons of Zebedee are referred to as *Boanergēs* (sons of thunder) in Mk 3.17, and elsewhere they are reported as wanting to call down fire from heaven (Lk. 9.54). The reflective character of the Fourth Gospel

---

12. The relation between John and Mark as the two 'Bi-Optic Gospels' is developed elsewhere (Anderson, 2001 and 2002b).

seems to betray a very different personality type, to say the least. Beyond these particulars, the omission of Jesus' parables, major teachings on the Kingdom of God, and exorcisms make it very difficult to reconcile an apostolic or eyewitness origin of John's material, even if the author was not the son of Zebedee. For these reasons, one can understand why critical scholars might find the traditional view of John's authorship problematic.

b) *Weaknesses:* On the other hand, the Markan presentation of the disciples, including the sons of Zebedee, might not have been completely untainted by subjectivity when considering its historicity. The ambivalent presentation of the sons of Zebedee would certainly have furthered the personal interests of someone like Peter if he or anyone like him were indeed a source of Mark's tradition. For instance, their having been included along with Peter here and there might reflect a Petrine co-opting of their authority, whereby the inclusion of Peter within an inner ring (the sons of his employer) would have served his own interests as a narrator, let alone the interests of those wanting to preserve his memory. Note that it was Peter who in Acts 1 is presented as wanting to preserve 'the Twelve' and who called for a successor to Judas. Certainly, the presentation of the sons of Zebedee as desiring precedence among the disciples is rejected by the Markan Jesus – just as Peter's failure to comprehend servanthood is presented graphically in John 13 and 21. Note that the martyrdom of the sons of Zebedee is predicted by Jesus in Mark (Mk 10.38-9), whereas the martyrdom of Peter is predicted by Jesus in John (Jn 21.18-19). Was the labelling of James and John as thunderheads a sober, historical judgement, or was it a factor of Petrine projection?[13] The point here is not to argue for particular personalities under-lying gospel traditions; the point is that making too much about what can and *cannot* have been true regarding particular disciples, based upon a few terse comments in Mark, overreaches the bounds of historical demonstrability from the Synoptic side. Motive-criticism may be the more appropriate tool here, rather than historical-criticism. Therefore, the grounds for excluding *anyone* from Johannine authorship based upon Synoptic presentations of Jesus' followers are weak.

Another weakness of making too much out of Johannine omissions of the Synoptic presentations of Jesus' ministry is that it fails to account for more plausible explanations. For instance, if the Fourth Evangelist were familiar with at least parts of Mark, it could be that parts were left out because of a desire to be complementary.[14] A primitive witness poses that John filled out the

---

13. Neither is the point being made here that Peter, or John, or any other *particular* person lay behind these trajectories. Impressive, though, is the fact that from the earliest stages of gospel traditions to the era following their finalization one can infer distinctively 'Petrine' and 'Johannine' *trajectories* (Anderson, 1996, pp. 153–60, esp. notes 22–6) on at least seven different themes.

14. The impressive 1998 Ph.D. thesis of Ian Donald MacKay on John 6 and Mark 6 and 8 changed my mind on this score (published 2004). I now see John's independence from Mark as *non-dependence* rather than *isolation*.

earlier parts of Jesus' ministry,[15] and this might explain the emphasis upon the wedding miracle and the healing of the official's son being the first two signs performed in Galilee. The point may have been setting the record straight over and against the Markan presentation of the exorcism of the demoniac and the healing of Peter's mother-in-law in Mark 1. Likewise, the other three miracles in the first edition of John[16] are all three Judean miracles, perhaps filling out the almost entirely northern ministry of Jesus in the Synoptics. Therefore, if the Fourth Evangelist were intentionally seeking to complement and augment Mark, this would have explained why much of Mark's material was left out. Matthew and Luke built *upon* Mark; John built *around* Mark.[17] The likelihood that John 6 was added as part of the final edition of John throws the augmentive function of John's first edition (probably between 80 and 85 CE) into sharper relief. If the five signs in John's first edition fill out the earlier and the Judean aspects of Jesus' ministry as a complement to Mark, John's omissions of most of Mark's material are not scandalous but understandable.

A further point deserves to be made here. The omission of the Transfiguration scene in John is more likely to have been related to the Johannine distinctive presentation of Moses and Elijah than an oversight. In Mark, the roles of Moses and Elijah are fulfilled in two ways: they appear at the Transfiguration (in keeping with the prophecy of Mal. 4.4-5), and they are present in the ministry of John the Baptist. In John, however, the Baptist *denies* that he is either the Prophet (Moses) *or* Elijah (Jn 1.19-27). Here Johannine augmentation of Mark moves to correction. The Baptist explicitly denies these associations in John, clearing the way for both typologies' being fulfilled in *Jesus*. Not only does Jesus perform the same sort of signs as Elijah had performed (in the Johannine feeding, even the same word is used for the barley loaves that Elijah had reproduced – *krithinou* – see 2 Kings 4.43, LXX), but he is explicitly hailed as the prophet like Moses predicted in Deut. 18.15-22 (Jn 6.1-15). It is no exaggeration to say that the entirety of the Johannine Jesus' sense of agency is cast in the form of the Mosaic prophet,[18] and this may have played a role in John's omission of the Markan Transfiguration scene. Jesus, not the Baptist, fulfils the typologies of Elijah *and* Moses in John.

---

15. Note the comment in Eusebius, *Hist. Eccles.* 3.24.7-13 to this effect. The connecting of the first two signs in Cana of Galilee with a chronological augmentation interest casts at least part of the Johannine evangelist's purpose into sharp relief with reference to Mark in particular.

16. A flawed assumption is that because the Johannine evangelist fills out the Judean ministry of Jesus this 'proves he must have been' a southerner rather than a Galilean (see, for instance, Parker, 1962). Of Parker's 21 points, *none* of them is compelling – individually or collectively.

17. See Part III, below.

18. See the many connections between the Septuagintal rendering of Deut. 18.15-22 and the Johannine Father-Son relationship (Anderson, 1999a).

A strict 'omission of Synoptic material' view of John, however, must be tempered by noticing the many non-identical similarities between the two traditions. Many of John's miracles are similar to Synoptic ones (a healing of a royal official's servant/child, the healing of a paralytic, the healing of a blind man, the raising of someone from the dead, etc.), but other than the feeding and the sea crossing, they do not appear to refer to the same events. Likewise, Synoptic-like sayings have long been noted in John, but they have not been thought of as authentic aphorisms by recent historical-Jesus studies. The characteristic agrarian metaphors associated with the Synoptic Jesus – presented in terse, aphoristic form – appear to have been displaced by long revelatory discourses in John. A closer look, however, shows that these sorts of sayings are far from missing in John. Indeed, Jesus' revelatory discourses do develop themes in ways quite distinctive from sayings in the Synoptics, but it cannot be said that agrarian images are missing from John, or that short, terse Jesus-sayings are absent from the Johannine text. A factor in their having been missed is their placement within dialogues and within the body of larger discourses. They are *not* absent from John, and one cannot say that their presence in John simply marks Synoptic derivation. Several agrarian wisdom aphorisms are found in distinctively Johannine settings, and these sayings conform very closely to the criteria used to distinguish historical-Jesus sayings otherwise. If they were found in Mark or Thomas, rather than John, few scholars would be questioning their authenticity. Consider, for instance, the great number of Synoptic-like aphorisms in John 4 and 12 alone:[19]

Table 2.1

Synoptic-like Aphorisms in John

- 'I have "food" to eat you know nothing about'. (4.32)
- 'My "food" is that I might do the work of the Having-Sent-Me-One and might accomplish his work'. (4.34)
- 'Do you not say, "It will take about four months for the harvest to come?" Look, I say to you, lift up your eyes and see the fields because they are already white with harvest'. (4.35)
- 'The one reaping receives wages and gathers grain unto eternal life in order that the sower might celebrate together with the reaper. For in this the saying is true, that "one sows and another reaps". I sent you to harvest what you have not worked for; others have laboured, and you have enjoyed the benefits of their hard work'. (4.36-8)
- 'Unless a wheat kernel dies by dropping into ground, it remains alone; but if it dies it bears great quantities of wheat'. (12.24)

19. See below the over six dozen aphorisms in John detected by Drummond (1904) and Bridges McKinnish (1987).

- 'The one loving his life will lose it; but the one hating his life in this world will keep it for eternity'. (12.25)
- 'If anyone serves me, let him follow me, and where I am there will my servant be. If anyone serves me, my Father will honour him'. (12.26)
- 'The time for the judgement of this world has now arrived: the ruler of this world shall now be cast out; and I, if I be lifted up from the earth, will draw all to myself'. (12.30-1)
- 'You only have the light among you for a short time. Walk in the light you have lest darkness overtake you; because the one walking in darkness does not know where he is going. While you have light, believe in the light, that you may become children of light'. (12.35-6)

The Johannine omission of Kingdom sayings, parables and exorcisms is more problematic. John does have two 'Kingdom' passages in John 3 and 18, but they are both corrective rather than elucidative. The Kingdom is *not* this, but that. Then again, while John has no Synoptic-like parables, Jesus' disciples report being troubled by his speaking in riddles (*paroimia*, Jn 10.6; 16.25-30) and celebrate his speaking plainly. This harkens back to the Markan presentation of parables as wedges dividing insiders and outsiders rather than being means of clarification (Mk 4.11-12, 33-4). Of course, John's I-Am sayings are highly metaphorical, as are the Synoptic parables, but they are presented in a distinctively Johannine form. Why the exorcisms of Jesus are omitted from John is difficult to explain, other than to point out that all of the Synoptic miracles were omitted from the first Johannine edition. Then again, an incidental Markan detail is interesting to consider. The particular disciple who was uncomfortable with other exorcists in Mark, and who reported to Jesus that they had asked them to desist, was none other than John, the son of Zebedee (Mk 9.38).[20] If these disciples, or people like them, might have had anything to do with any stage of the Johannine presentation of Jesus' ministry, discomfort with exorcist ministries may have played a factor in John's omission of Jesus' exorcisms. Because of the vulnerability of making too much out of John's omissions of Synoptic material, especially with relation to who could and could not have been connected to the Johannine tradition, the critical scholar should exercise caution before de-historicizing John too readily.

---

20. While the discovery of a hitherto overlooked first-century clue to Johannine authorship might not make much of a difference to scholars convinced of John's non-apostolic authorship (Anderson, 1996, pp. 274–7), it challenges the view that Irenaeus was the first to make such a connection. Peter and John are presented as speaking in Acts 4.19-20 in two characteristic statements: one Petrine, and the other Johannine (see Acts 5.29 and 11.17 for the first and 1 Jn. 1.3 and Jn. 3.32 for the second). Luke's even unintended connecting of the Apostle John with a characteristically Johannine phrase – a full century before Irenaeus – approximates a fact, calling for critical consideration of the implications.

Unlike Mark, John contains only two sections that develop the Kingdom motif, and rather than being illustrative they are antithetical. They suggest what the active reign of God is like in contrast to alternative understandings of it. In contrast to Nicodemus' religious understanding of the Kingdom of God, Jesus emphasizes the need to be born from above, using the powerful effect of the invisible wind as a metaphor (Jn 3.1-21). And, with reference to Pilate's political understanding of power, Jesus declares the Kingdom's reign is one of truth (Jn 18.33-8), explaining that this is why his disciples do not fight or resort to force. In these two passages one could infer a Johannine contrasting of the reign of God to two primarily worldly spheres: the religious and the political. Does this mean, though, that the teachings of Jesus on the *basileia tou theou* are pervasively missing in John, or do we have a Johannine representation of the essential Kingdom teaching of Jesus, even as represented in the fuller Synoptic accounts? After all, the spiritual workings of God's active and dynamic reign are indeed contrasted to the human scaffoldings of the religious quest in the Synoptics, and the truthful and penetrating activity of God's present-and-ultimate reign is contrasted to all worldly powers – political and otherwise. In that sense, rather than leaving out Jesus' teachings on the Kingdom, it could be said that John summarizes them. When considering *basileic* language in John, though, it is not entirely void. John has a considerable number of *basileic* references, but they focus largely on the *basileius*, Jesus, rather than on the *basileia*, the Kingdom.[21] On the face of it, one could consider John's dearth of Synoptic-like Kingdom parables and teachings as evidence of disconnectedness from a Jesus tradition, but this misreads the evidence. John's *basileic* presentation of Jesus as a king is even more pronounced than those of the Synoptics, and the source of those differences more likely resides in an alternative emphasis and the individuated development of the Johannine tradition itself.

While major Synoptic themes and features are omitted from John, the default inference of John's ahistoricity is naive and simplistic. Other motives and factors are more compelling in explaining these facts. Such interests as 'building around' Mark in non-duplicative ways, reserving the Moses and Elijah typologies for Jesus (not John the Baptist), preferences against exorcisms (especially when rendering a narrative in a Gentile setting), and a practice of paraphrasing Jesus' teachings in Johannine forms of delivery, cause a rethinking of the larger issues. It is also a fact that much Synoptic-type material is present in a distinctively Johannine form, so 'total absence' is often *not* the case; rather, an alternative presentation is. A classic case in point is the

---

21. Consider, for instance, these references to Jesus in Johannine *basileic* terms: Jesus is acclaimed as the King of Israel (Jn 1.49; 12.13), he is embraced as a king like Moses (Jn 6.15), he fulfils the kingly prophecy of Zechariah 9.9 (Jn 12.15), he is questioned and affirmed as a king (Jn 18.37; 19.12), and he is presented and disputed as the King of the Jews (Jn 18.33, 39; 19.3, 14, 15, 19, 21). John's is a Christocentric basileiology.

way the Lord's Prayer can be said to be found in embellished form in John 17.[22] Finally, as argument from silence is an extremely tenuous basis on which to build, it cannot be said that this is a very sturdy plank, able to support much interpretive weight.

3) *Johannine Omissions in the Synoptics*
Considering the material distinctive to John, many of Jesus' sayings and deeds are among the most memorable among the four gospels. The great I-Am sayings (I am the bread of life, light of the world, resurrection and the life, good shepherd, true vine, and the way, the truth and the life) in John are certainly rich with content and of great importance Christologically. Five of John's miracles (the wedding miracle, the healing of the official's son, the healing of the Jerusalem paralytic, the healing of the blind man, and the raising of Lazarus) are nowhere mentioned in the Synoptics. The oddity here is that *if* these sayings and events really happened, how could they *not* be mentioned or closely replicated in the other three Gospels? Other distinctively Johannine events also stand out, such as Jesus' dramatic dialogues with the likes of Nicodemus, the Samaritan woman, the Jewish leaders, Pilate and Peter. And, Jesus is portrayed in John as having visited Jerusalem at least four times during his ministry, whereas in the Synoptics he visits Jerusalem *only once* – the time when he was crucified. Given their absence in the Synoptics, the inference is that much of John's material must have originated in some way *other* than historicity, requiring alternative explanations.

a) *Strengths:* Obviously, the raising of Lazarus would have been considered one of the greatest miracles of Jesus by all who knew about it, and its absence from the Synoptics strongly suggests that it was not known of by their writers. Put otherwise, if the raising of Lazarus were indeed to have happened, how could it *possibly* be confined to a minority report of one gospel narrative?[23] Because the Johannine signs clearly serve the rhetorical purposes of the Fourth Evangelist, presenting evidence that Jesus was indeed the Jewish Messiah, the distinctive Johannine signs indeed could have had an origin other than public historical events in the presence of Jesus' disciples. The same can be said of the wedding miracle – by no means a private or secluded event. Likewise, the I-Am sayings must be considered the most theologically significant statements uttered by Jesus about himself anywhere in the four canonical Gospels. If Jesus were indeed to have uttered them, how could they not also have been included in the Synoptics? Conversely, the language and diction of Jesus in John is nearly identical to that of John the Baptist (see Jn 3.31-6) and the

---

22. C.F. Evans builds this case in his provocative essay (1977), making one wonder if the Johannine prayer is an expansion, or the Q prayer of Jesus is an abbreviation.

23. While the so-called secret Gospel of Mark might betray an independent account of a resurrection narrative very much like the account in John 11, its existence is itself in doubt, thus offering little or no corroboration of the Johannine Lazarus narrative.

Fourth Evangelist. In that sense, the Johannine Jesus' discourses probably reflect the evangelist's paraphrase of Jesus' teachings rather than a historical rendering of such teachings. Further, they are far more self-referential than the Kingdom sayings of the Synoptics and the Markan Messianic Secret, and one can understand how John's presentation of Jesus would call for explanations *other* than historical ones.

b) *Weaknesses:* As with the former issue, one of the primary weaknesses of questioning the origin of the distinctive Johannine material is that it also argues from silence. Such arguments can only be tenuous, and by definition, they elude certainty. To argue that everything significant said or done by Jesus would be included in the Synoptics, or even in all of the Gospel records, is likewise fallacious. The conclusion of John explicitly declares intentional selectivity (Jn 21.24-5), and the same was probably true of Mark and the other Gospels. It is also problematic to argue that Mark would have had access to *all* of Peter's preaching material (or whatever Mark's primary source might have been), let alone other narrative sources that might have been connected to particular geographical regions.[24] Further, if the patterning of the Johannine miracles in chapters 2, 4, 5, 9 and 11 seems to be crafted so as to augment the Markan narration of Jesus' ministry, the Cana miracles apparently fill out the early part of Jesus' ministry, and the other three contribute Judean miracles to the mix – perhaps reflecting the sentiment that Mark's rendering was incomplete. In that sense, the distinctive Johannine signs appear to have been presented as a means of filling some of the gaps left by the Markan project, and the final words of the first edition of John allude to that possibility. The evangelist is apparently aware of other signs reported that 'are *not in this* book...' (in other words, 'Yes, I *know* Mark is out there, and I *know* I'm leaving things out, so stop reminding me...') '...but *these* are written that you might believe...' (in other words, '...but the above material has a purpose *beyond* what Mark sought to accomplish...') Jn 20.30-1.

   While the Johannine Jesus clearly speaks in the language of the evangelist, this is not to say the Johannine paraphrase has no root in the ministry of the historical Jesus.[25] Indeed, the Markan Jesus also delivers several I-Am sayings, although they are not as fully developed as those in John.[26] What one cannot say is that Jesus' I-Am sayings are absent from, or insignificant in, Mark.

    24. A.J.B. Higgins raises significant questions about John's topography in his third chapter: 'Is John the Fourth Gospel?' (1960, pp. 63–82). See also Kundsin (1925).
    25. Franz Mussner (1966), shows how the Johannine memory and paraphrastic work may have developed in distinctive, gnoseological terms.
    26. See, for instance, Jesus' response to the High Priest in Mk 14.61-4, where, when asked if he were the Christ, the Son of the Blessed, Jesus declared, '*I Am*! And you shall see the Son of Man seated at the right hand of power and coming with the clouds of heaven'. At this, the High Priest tore his garments and called for the blasphemy to be penalized. See also the words of Jesus at the sea crossing: *Egō eimi; mē phobēsthe* ('It is I; fear not.' Mk 6.50), which are identical to the words of Jesus in John 6.20, despite contextual differences.

Table 2.2

Similar Egō Eimi Sayings of Jesus in Mark and John

- *Egō eimi! Mē phobēsthe!* An epiphany (Mk 6.50 – It is not a ghost; *It is I!*) / a theophany (Jn 6.20 – *I Am!*) on the Lake.
- An I-Am association with the burning bush, Abraham and Exod. 3.14-15 is declared by Jesus before Jerusalem leaders (Mk 12.26 – *eimi* understood; explicitly declared in Jn 8.58).
- I-Am claims are mentioned regarding alternative Messiah figures (Mk 13.6 – *false* Messiahs will say 'I am the Christ' / Jn 1.20 – John the Baptist confessed, 'I am *not* the Christ!').
- A Christological claim in response to Pilate's question (Mk 14.62 – Are you the Christ, the Son of the Blessed? *I am!* / Jn 18.37 – Are you a king, then? You say that *I am* a king.).

One could also argue that the I-Am sayings in John making use of the predicate nominative are similar in their metaphorical character to the parables of the Synoptics (especially the shepherd/sheep/gate imagery, truth and way emphases, the light-of-the world motif, the vine/vineyard theme, the resurrection and life themes, and the bread and subsistence motif), although they clearly are not couched in the same parabolic form as the Synoptic teachings of Jesus. While it could be argued that Synoptic developments were constructed upon themes present in John, it is more likely to see the Johannine discourses as Christocentric developments of plausible Jesus sayings. What *cannot* be said is that the Johannine I-Am metaphors are at all missing in the Synoptics.

Table 2.3

Johannine I-Am Metaphors in the Synoptic Jesus' Teachings

- *Artos* – Jesus is tempted to turn stones into *bread* (Mt. 4.1-4; Lk. 4.1-4), and he feeds the multitudes with *bread* (Mt. 14.13-21; 15.32-9; Mk 6.32-44; 8.1-10; Lk. 9.10-17).
- *Phōs* – Jesus' disciples are the *light of the world* (Mt. 5.14-16).
- *Thura* – The (narrow) *gate* is emphasized (Mt. 7.13-14 and Lk. 13.24) as the way to *life*.
- *Poimēn* – The parable of the *shepherd* and the sheep (Mt. 18.10-14; Lk. 15.3-7) emphasizes the care of Jesus for his fold.
- *Anastasis* – Debates over the *resurrection* arise between Jesus and Jewish leaders (Mt. 22.23-33; Mk 12.18-27; Lk. 20.27-40), and the raising of Jarius' daughter (Mt. 9.18-26; Mk 5.21-43; Lk. 8.40-56) brings life out of death.

- *Hodos* – The '*way* of righteousness' (Mt. 21.28-32) is advocated over 'the *way* that leads to destruction' (Mt. 7.13-14).
- *Alētheia* – The way of God in *truth* is what Jesus teaches (Mt. 22.16; Mk 12.14, 32; Lk. 21).
- *Zōē* – The narrow way leads to *life* (Mt. 7.14), and Jesus discusses what it means to inherit eternal life (Mt. 19.16, 23-30; Mk 10.17, 23-31; Lk. 18.18, 24-30).

Even some of the associated clusters of I-Am metaphors can be found together in Jesus' teaching in the Synoptics. Indeed, while much material thought to be characteristic of Jesus found in the Synoptics is not found in the same way in John, it cannot be said that it is altogether missing. Some of it is situated in a different set of contexts and forms. John's tradition reflects a distinctively Christocentric rendering of Jesus' teachings, but that does not imply a radical disconnection from the Jesus represented by the Synoptics. If these and other Johannine aphoristic sayings in John would have been found in Mark, or even in the second-century Gospel of Thomas, it is doubtful that they would have been passed over in the selection of Jesus-sayings material.

4) The Johannine Jesus Speaks and Acts in the Mode of the Evangelist

One of the great puzzlements of John's witness is that the Johannine Jesus speaks with the voice of the evangelist. Then again, so does John the Baptist. The ending of John 3 is notoriously difficult when trying to ascertain who is speaking the last six verses. It appears the Baptizer is continuing into a monologue, having moved into it from a dialogue with his own followers about Jesus' being the Messiah. Then again, it sounds a great deal like the climactic Christological declaration of Jesus in Jn 12.44-50, so one may be tempted to infer a resorting to the words of the Lord in Jn 3.31-6 without having marked narratologically a change of voice.

Or, is it the evangelist's way of inserting the core of his own theological beliefs into the narrative, thereby granting the Baptist a pedestal on which to declare the evangelist's own theological convictions? After all, William Loader has shown effectively that these two passages comprise the 'central structure' of John's Christology, and that they provide a valuable lens for viewing the Son's saving mission from the Father and his ambivalent reception in the world, rife with implications (1984, 1989). However, if indeed it is the case that the evangelist has imbued the Baptist's climactic witness to Jesus' mission with his own theological framework and terms, why not infer the same for the declaration of Jesus at the climax of his ministry and elsewhere in John? Especially when the language of John's Jesus is so dissimilar to that of the Synoptic Jesus, this makes it extremely difficult to imagine the *ipsissima verba* of the historical Jesus coming to us through the Johannine text. The words (and deeds) of Jesus in John betray such an obvious projection of the Johannine rendering that considerable caution must be exercised before attributing too much of the Johannine Jesus' teaching to the Jesus of history, proper.

a) *Strengths:* First, the Johannine witness comes to us explicitly from the perspective of post-resurrection consciousness. Several times the point is made that the disciples did not 'understand' the action or words of Jesus at the time, but later, after the resurrection, they understood fully what he was getting at (Jn 2.22; 12.16). Likewise, Jesus himself emphasizes that their comprehension will be fuller in the future, as mediated by the Holy Spirit, and this prediction is borne out in the perceptions of the Johannine narration (Jn 7.37-9; 13.7, 19-20; 14.25-31; 15.26-16.4; 16.12-16). From this perspective, the Johannine memory is pervasively influenced by later discovery, and this perspective by its own admission presents the past in the light of future valuations. In that sense, a 'what really happened back then' mode of historicity is less important to the evangelist than the connecting of 'what happened' to 'what it really meant...*and means now*' form of narration.

A second question relates to the connections between the language and thought forms of the Johannine Jesus and those of the Johannine evangelist. As mentioned above, the Johannine Jesus speaks in the language of the evangelist, and impressive similarities can be observed between the corporate Johannine situation reflected by the Prologue, the witness of the Baptist, the interpretive work of the evangelist, the words of Jesus and the narration of Jesus' works. In contrast to the Gnostic redeemer-myth as the central history-of-religions origin of the mission of Jesus in John, its similarities are much closer to the prophet-like-Moses agency schema of Deut. 18.15-22. Indeed, many of these features can be found throughout the Fourth Gospel, and it is indeed the case that the evangelist's understanding of Jesus' ministry has been subsumed into this agency schema. Therefore, aspects of historicity must be read through such a missional and theological lens.

Table 2.4

The Mission of Jesus in John

- No one has seen God at any time, and only by the saving/revealing initiative of God can humanity be 'drawn' to the Father.
- Jesus comes to the world as the agent of God, revealing God's love and truth to the world.
- The world's reception of the revealer is ambivalent; some believe, but some do not.
- Those who know God receive the revealer, but those who challenge the authenticity of Jesus' mission expose their spiritual condition.
- Jesus affirms his speaking and doing only what he has seen and heard from the Father, attested by his words and works.
- The world is therefore invited to respond believingly to the Father's agent as responding to the Father (Deut. 18.15-22).
- Those who believe receive life and further light; those who reject the revealer seek to preserve the 'comfort' of their darkness.

Nearly all of these seven themes may be found in each of the above five portions of the Johannine Gospel, showing the degree to which the evangelist's presentation of the ministry of Jesus and the witness of the Baptist had become integrated within his own ministry. This set of connections leads to a third question: to what extent does John's presentation of Jesus' teachings reflect the teaching of the historical Jesus as opposed to the evangelist's teaching within the evolving history of his situation? Certainly, the above outline reflects at least two levels of history (using Martyn's construct): the mission and reception of Jesus and his message, and the mission and reception of the evangelist and his message. Indeed, nearly everything claimed for Jesus (he came unto his own and his own received him not, but as many as received the gospel are given the power to become the children of God, Jn 1.12) can also be claimed for the evangelist and the Johannine leadership. At least four crises within the Johannine situation can be inferred in the narration of the feeding and the sea crossing in John 6, not just the one in John 9.[27] In that sense, because John's narration addresses the evolving needs of the Johannine audience and represents the teaching ministry of the evangelist, its being a reliable guide to the historical Jesus comes into question.

b) *Weaknesses:* The cardinal weakness, of course, of assuming interpretive relevance completely eclipses originative history is that it simply is not true. Historicity is not limited to the irrelevant, and to assert such misjudges the character of historiography itself. Every historical project distinguishes events of greater significance from their alternatives, and that implies subjectivity of judgement. Mark's narrative also distinguishes important events from others, so the question is better put as to whether the *Markan* selection of historically significant content is closer to the historical Jesus than that of the Johannine rendering. Further, to assume that an independent gospel tradition either did not accommodate to Jesus' teachings, or that it did not adapt Jesus' teachings to its own content needs, is fallacious and unrealistic. Given the fact that the Johannine Jesus' teachings are rendered in the modes of the evangelist's own teaching ministry, the following features must be taken into consideration.

First, despite distinctively Johannine characteristics, there are dozens of aphorisms in John sounding very much like the sort of thing the historical Jesus would have said. Those mentioned above are only some of the most distinctive ones; others have been identified in analyses not noted by so-called historical-Jesus studies. For instance, Wilbert Francis Howard lists no fewer than 60 (Jn

---

27. Note that: a) the desire for more loaves corrects Synoptic-type valuations of the feeding (*not* a *semēia* source); b) the Jewish leaders' request for manna as Moses gave reflects debates over the authority of the Torah (Deut. 8.3); c) the disciples' being scandalized over eating and drinking the flesh and blood of Jesus is aimed at docetizing Gentile believers; and d) Peter's figurative 'returning the keys to Jesus' corrects the proto-Ignatian tendencies of Diotrephes and his kin (these four crises behind John 6 are developed further in Anderson, 1997).

1.51; 2.16, 19; 3.3, 6, 8; 4.14, 21, 23, 31, 34, 44, 48; 5.14, 17, 19, 23, 30, 40, 44; 6.27, 33, 35, 44, 63; 7.7, 17, 24, 37; 8.12, 26, 32, 34, 36, 51; 9.4, 39, 41; 11.25; 12.24, 25, 26, 32, 36, 44, 47; 13.15, 20, 34, 35; 14.1, 2, 6, 9, 15, 21, 27; 17.1; 18.36, 37) aphorisms in John,[28] and Linda Bridges isolates 26 aphoristic sayings in John (Jn 1.51; 2.19; 3.3, 5; 4.14, 35, 38; 5.19; 8.12, 34-5; 9.4-5; 11.25-6; 12.24-5, 35-6; 13.16, 20; 14.6; 15.13, 16, 20; 16.20-1, 23; 20.23; 27b, 29).[29] About half of those identified by Bridges are also selected by Drummond and Howard. Given the prolific inclusion of aphoristic sayings in John, it is extremely difficult to imagine why these sayings have gone unnoticed by Jesus scholars preferring instead the mid-second-century Gospel of Thomas with its Gnostic proclivities over the Gospel of John in terms of historicity.[30] An explanation of that fact may lie in the tendency to analyse Johannine discourses as longer units, therefore missing aphorisms embedded within the larger contexts. Many of the above sayings, though, are not found in larger discourse sections, so their being overlooked entirely comes across as a striking oversight among otherwise critical scholars.

A second mistake in judgement is to infer that because the historical Jesus spoke in characteristically terse, pithy aphorisms, he therefore did not deliver *any* longer discourses. Here, a meaningful criterion for inclusion becomes used inappropriately as a measure of exclusion, which is faulty logic. Given that set A (aphorisms) overlaps with set B (Jesus' characteristic style of teaching), it does not follow that set C (longer discourses or alternative diction) cannot have had any overlap with set B. Put otherwise, how did Jesus hold the attention of multitudes for more than a few minutes at a time? If he were to have held the attention of crowds for hours on end at times (as the feeding narratives and other sections in all four Gospels suggest), he must have delivered longer discourses as well as short aphorisms. Thus, aphoristic sayings were probably included in these longer discourses, but it is difficult to imagine that they were the only content or form delivered. Another variable also presents itself: were Jesus' teachings delivered to his disciples identical to those addressed to the multitudes? Probably not. Therefore, to assert that Jesus' teachings cannot be represented in the distinctively Johannine presentation cannot be maintained critically.

A third fallacy is the assertion that a Johannine paraphrase of Jesus' teachings cannot represent the content or character of the teaching of the historical Jesus. Earlier impressions are not necessarily more authentic than

---

28. W.F. Howard (1931, p. 267) cites these verses as examples given by J. Drummond (1904, pp. 17–19). He also says, 'Many more can be found, particularly in chaps. xiii–xvii. One of the most striking is xx. 29.'

29. See Appendices A and B in Linda McKinnish Bridges (1987, pp. 253–8).

30. Indeed, the Jesus Seminar's according of authentic Jesus sayings is more prolific in Thomas than all the canonical gospels put together (see Anderson 2000a) – a surprising judgement for such a clearly Gnostic second-century collection!

distanced reflections, nor are historical presentations more authentic when not interpreted or paraphrased. Franz Mussner's intriguing monograph on the historical Jesus in the Gospel of John takes for granted a spiritualized reflection underlying the Johannine 'memory', but he performs upon that premise a critical analysis of how the Johannine tradition might have developed as *anamnesis*.[31] In his analysis of key Johannine vocabulary terms ('gnoseological terminology'), Mussner applies the terms: 'to see', 'to hear', 'to come to know', 'to testify', 'to remember' (and to have brought to remembrance) to a realistic estimation of how the 'historical reason' of the evangelist might have developed. While Mussner's investigation is motivated by the desire to reconcile historicity with inspiration, he makes a significant set of phenomenological contributions. First, he acknowledges the distinctive features of Johannine spirituality and memory. Second, he describes how such memory from a distance really might have been experienced as a factor of the work of the *Paraklētos* calling to present earlier content for the needs of the emerging Johannine situation. Third, rather than seeing such developments as a historical disjunction with a more primitive Jesus tradition, he shows how continuity between earlier experiences and later perceptions may have emerged within the Johannine circle of leadership. In that sense, he gives us an alternative model for historical investigation within a distinctive situation such as the Johannine.

While the Johannine Jesus clearly speaks in the language of the evangelist, so does John the Baptist, and so do others in the Fourth Gospel. This being the case, however, it cannot be said that aphoristic sayings of Jesus are totally absent. No fewer than 70 to 80 have been identified, and yet their being embedded within longer sections may explain why they have been missed by some scholars. Nor can it be claimed that Jesus' characteristic aphorisms comprised the totality of everything he ever said. While paraphrases of Jesus' teachings are a given in John, this is not to say, though, that they are completely truncated from the teaching ministry of the historical Jesus. This plank rests upon a significant problem, but it cannot be said to solidly support a total divorce between historical sayings of Jesus and later Johannine renderings. As Mark's source (and thus Matthew's and Luke's) rendered Jesus' sayings meaningfully for the needs of emerging audiences in the church, so did the Johannine narrator, and in some ways the Johannine paraphrase may have been closer to original teachings of Jesus than scholars have thought.

31. Mussner's question, 'Who is really speaking here?' is a good one (1966). Throughout the course of his analysis, he is able to show how both the historical Jesus *and* the paraphrastic evangelist might have been implicated together.

5) *The Johannine Material is Rendered in Response to the History of the Johannine Situation*

Because much of John's material shows evidence of development within the history of the Johannine situation, at least two levels of history must be considered in assessing the historical character of the Johannine material. In reality, *all* gospel narrative is historical; the only question is, 'What aspect of history is represented regarding a particular passage or detail?' As well as historical origins in the ministry of Jesus and within the influence of history-of-religions background, at least six or seven crises can be inferred within the Johannine situation. In the earlier period, the Palestinian period (30–70 CE), the first two crises appear. The first betrays tensions between northern Galileans and Samaritans and their southern neighbours, the Judeans, with the issue here appearing to have related to centralizing pressures and the rejection of northern perspectives by the Jerusalem-centred authorities. The second crisis betrays an interest in emphasizing that John the Baptist was not the Messiah, and it probably reflects dialogues seeking to convince Baptist adherents that Jesus was. In the middle period, the Asia Minor I Period (70–85 CE), the Johannine Christians faced two more crises. The third crisis involved tensions with local Synagogue over the orthodoxy of the Jesus movement and their attempts to convince Jewish family and friends that Jesus was the Jewish Messiah. The fourth involved hardship experienced at the hand of the local Roman presence under the reign of Domitian (81–96 CE) as residents of the Empire were forced to offer emperor laud or suffer the consequences. Later, the Asia Minor II (85–100 CE) period, saw the emergence of multiple communities in the Johannine situation. The fifth crisis stemmed directly from the attempts of Gentile Christians to diminish the effects of required Emperor laud. They taught a message of assimilation, legitimated by a non-suffering and docetic Jesus. The sixth crisis reflects intramural tensions with rising institutionalism within the Christian movement, as the Johannine tradition calls for more egalitarian and familial approaches to church governance. The first edition of John was probably finalized around 80–85 CE, and the Johannine Epistles were probably written in the interim between that time and the gospel's finalization around 100 CE (Table 2.5 and Appendix II, below). A seventh set of dialogues that spanned all six of the above crises involved dialectical interaction with other gospel traditions. Within these evolving issues – largely sequential, but also somewhat overlapping – the Johannine presentation of Jesus was formed in response to the needs of the churches, as were the Markan and other gospel traditions.

Table 2.5

An Outline of the Johannine Situation in Longitudinal Perspective

- Period I: The Palestinian period (ca. 30–70 CE)
  Crisis A – Dealing with north/south tensions (Galileans/Judeans)
  Crisis B – Reaching followers of John the Baptist
     (The oral Johannine tradition develops.)

- Period II: The Asia Minor period I, the forging of community (ca. 70–85 CE)
  Crisis A – Engaging local Jewish family and friends
  Crisis B – Dealing with the local Roman presence
     (The first edition of the Johannine Gospel is prepared.)

- Period III: The Asia Minor period II, dialogues between communities (ca. 85–100 CE)
  Crisis A – Engaging docetizing Gentile Christians and their teachings
  Crisis B – Engaging Christian institutionalizing tendencies (Diotrephes and his kin)
  Crisis C – Engaging dialectically Christian presentations of Jesus and his ministry (actually reflecting a running dialogue over *all three* periods)
     (The Epistles are written by the Johannine Elder, who then
     finalizes and circulates the testimony of the Beloved Disciple
     after his death.)

a) *Strengths:* Strict objectivity in historiography, as such, is of little value to interpreters. For instance, weeks and months of flat-line seismograph readings are objectively historical, but they are far less significant than the punctuating measures of seismic activity, even if they last for only moments. The relevant recording of the past always hinges upon inferred meanings for later generations, and in that sense, the subjective inference of original significance is always determined in the light of an account's eventual impact and relevance. That being the case, many aspects of the Johannine memory appear to have been formed on at least two levels of history. What happened 'even back then' (Jn 9.22; 12.42; 16.2) is brought to bear on 'what's happening now'.

Regarding crisis one, a crisis involving hegemonic actions and attitudes of Jerusalem-centred Judaism would have affected the preservation of material within the northern situation of the evangelist. Whether he lived in Samaria, Galilee or the trans-Jordan (Galilee seems the most plausible), the presentation of the *Ioudaioi* and leaders of Jerusalem, who reject the northern prophet and are scandalized by Jesus' healing on the Sabbath and claiming divine agency, would have borne resonance with the experience of northern Jewish populations travelling to Jerusalem for festivals and worship several times a year. In that sense, the relevance of the northern prophet being rejected by the Judean authorities (Jn 4-5, 7-8) would have matched the experience of Galilean and Samaritan populations seeking to worship authentically as children of Israel. With relation to the second crisis – still in the early period – the evangelist takes great pains to connect the Baptist's testimony with the authenticity of Jesus as a means of reaching either Baptist adherents, or as a means of cashing in on his authority in respect to his apologetic interests (Jn 20.30-1). The Johannine tradition is distinctive in this matter, and it may even be the case that some of the Johannine leadership might originally have been followers of the Baptist, who left him and followed Jesus. Indeed, John 1 even portrays Jesus' first disciples as being such. Therefore, the vested interest of the evangelist should be kept in mind regarding the baptistic material in John.

The middle period of the Johannine situation appears to have involved the movement of the evangelist to one of the mission churches, probably in Asia Minor, and several details bear witness to such a possibility. First, the explanation of Jewish customs interprets the story of Jesus for a Gentile audience. Second, the translation of Aramaic words into Greek connects the original language of the Lord with later Hellenistic audiences. Third, tensions with Jewish and Roman leaders in the earlier period of the Christian movement find resonance with what is happening in the fifth and sixth decades of the Johannine situation. With the destruction of the Temple in 70 CE, religious authority in Judaism shifted from the cultic religion of Jerusalem to scriptural religion practiced more broadly. As the emphasis upon Jewish biblical faith continued to collide with Jesus adherents claiming his divine agency and status rooted in Deut. 18.15-22 and Christian worship (Jn 1.1-18), local religious authorities understandably sought to retard the Jesus movement. The *Birkat ha-Minim* of the Jamnia Council codified some of the threats of expulsion that were already at work in Asia Minor and elsewhere, and the Johannine historical project connected religious hostility in the past with the impending crisis of the present. 'Even back then' believers were put out of the Synagogue for confessing Jesus openly, and this historical marker connects earlier memories with present experience. In that sense, it reflects the emerging process of self-identification, as Johannine Christianity individuates away from its Jewish origins. The second crisis within this period involved the hardship received at the hand of the local Roman presence, intensifying the requirement to express loyalty to the empire by requiring public Emperor laud. Domitian (81–96 CE) even required his Roman subjects to refer him as 'Lord and God' thus providing a backdrop to the confession of Thomas and the presentation of Pilate in John 18-20. Against these probable Jewish and Roman historical backgrounds, the Johannine narration must be read as reflecting a contextual history of delivery rather than an originative history alone. It was probably at the end of this phase in the history of the Johannine situation that the first edition of John was written.

The later period of the Johannine situation brought with it two more crises (85–100 CE) – the crisis of having to confront docetic tendencies among

Gentile Christian teachers advocating a doctrine of assimilation with Rome, and the resultant remedy to Docetism: the emergence of proto-Ignatian hierarchies within the Christian movement. As a result, the emphasis on water and blood flowing from the side of Jesus (Jn 19.34-5) emphasizes the physicality of his having suffered, and this antidocetic emphasis is the acute occasion for asserting the eyewitness origin of the Johannine tradition. Indeed, nearly all the incarnational and antidocetic material in John can be found in the supplementary material added to the first edition (including Jn 1.1-18, chs 6, 15-17, 21 and eyewitness and Beloved Disciple passages).[32] Likewise, the juxtaposition of Peter and the Beloved Disciple speaks with relevance to issues surrounding emerging institutionalization in the late first-century church. Here investigations of the 'historical Peter' and the 'historical Beloved Disciple', seeking to prove or disprove John's historicity, miss the point entirely. The seventh set of dialogues was less of a crisis and more of a running dialogue with alternative Synoptic traditions. This being the case, at least some of John's presentation of Jesus-history emerges in dialogue with alternative perspectives. Historiography is itself a rhetorical venture, and the primary historical interest involves unpacking the meaning of these figures' authority being yoked to the addressing of needs within the historical Johannine situation.[33]

In these and other ways, the Johannine memory is thoroughly engaged in history, but the question is: '*Which* history?' All of John relates to history; the question is whether particular material reflects originative history in the ministry of Jesus, the religious history of ideas and typologies attached to Jesus narratives, the history of the Johannine tradition itself, or an echo of the historical Johannine situation evolving from one period to another. The fact that audiences in the history of the Johannine situation were being addressed by the Johannine narration raises serious questions about the degree to which the Jesus of history is being presented here as opposed to John's Jesus simply being a projection of the emerging needs of the Johannine historical situation.

b) *Weaknesses:* Again, like many of the previous issues, some merit is granted the concern, but the fallacy comes when an overly reductionistic approach to the Johannine tradition displaces other plausible aspects of Johannine historicity. Two points deserve to be made here. First, the Johannine tradition is not the only gospel tradition crafting the words and deeds of Jesus to later needs of the Johannine audience. Mark too, according to Papias, preserved the preaching of Peter, which itself was reportedly crafted to meet the needs of the church. One might infer several 'craftings' of Mark's Jesus tradition to address the needs of the early church: the Way of the Cross and costly discipleship, anticipations of the return of Christ, the Messianic Secret as an antidote to Messianic

32. See Table 1:4 above and Appendix I below.
33. Kevin Quast develops this view (1989), as structure and charisma complement each other within the Johannine narrative and situation.

embellishments, and exhortations to be faithful in following Jesus regardless of apparent outcomes. Likewise, Matthew's tradition crafted a Jesus relevant to the teaching needs of Matthean sectors of Christianity, demonstrating Jesus as the authentically Jewish Messiah, and Luke constructed a portrayal of Jesus presenting him as a just and righteous man as a way of minimizing Roman criticisms or concerns about the Jesus movement. In these ways the Synoptic traditions also applied originative histories of Jesus to emerging histories of their respective situations, so John is not alone in such a venture.

A second point to emphasize is the fallacy of assuming that because John's narration shows signs of later developments, it cannot have represented anything historical about the events in Jesus' ministry. The inference of a history of tradition development does not demonstrate the absence of originative history. Put otherwise, eventual relevance in itself does not negate historical origination. Indeed, the emerging Johannine narrative certainly evolved into its eventual form, but arguing that its originative history was *not* rooted in events or reflections upon them is impossible to demonstrate or maintain. This is especially the case when several aspects of John's presentation of Jesus square very closely with the basic historic elements of the Synoptic tradition, despite not having been dependent upon them.

First, Jesus' cleansing the Temple is included in John as well as the other Gospels, and while John's rendering is at the beginning rather than the end of Jesus' ministry, this independent narration probably goes back to an originative incident. Second, Jesus' teaching on the love of God in John is parallel-with-though-not-dependent-on the presentation of the same theme in the Synoptics. While the Abba-Father language of Mark is probably closer to the language of the historical Jesus than the Johannine Father-Son relationship, the two are nonetheless close and can be said to reflect consonance with each other as windows into the sort of relationship Jesus probably described. Third, Jesus' healing on the Sabbath and challenging religious authority is presented as clearly in John as it is in the Synoptics, despite its many distinctive features. Fourth, the Passion narrative in John is very similar to those of the other Gospels, and yet John's rendering is also different enough to evince derivation. Just because the sequence is the same between the entry, the supper, the garden scene, the arrest, two trials (one Jewish and one Roman), the crucifixion and death of Jesus, and his resurrection and appearances, this does *not* imply common source dependence. Try rearranging the order of *any* of these elements in the stories. It does not work. The trial cannot come after the death, nor can the garden scene come after the arrest, neither can the supper come after trials. A more plausible explanation is that the Johannine and Synoptic traditions represent parallel narrations of a common set of events impressed upon the memories of different traditions, and this is why even Bultmann had to infer a Passion source underlying John.[34] The Johannine narration cannot be explained

---

34. See Anderson (1996, pp. 33–6) for further details.

adequately on any other basis. For these and other reasons, while the historical development of the Johannine situation must be considered when analysing John's historicity, it cannot in and of itself negate any theory of Johannine origins, whether it be rooted in a reflection upon the ministry of Jesus or in an imaginary novelization of later Christian beliefs.

6) *The Johannine Evangelist Spiritualizes and Theologizes According to his Purposes*

The distinction made by Clement, that while the Synoptics wrote about the bodily aspects of Jesus' ministry, John wrote a 'spiritual gospel', has provided a heuristic key for de-historicizing the Johannine witness. Based upon this inference, differences between John and the Synoptics have been largely ascribed to Synoptic factuality versus Johannine theologization. When considering the message of Jesus, the Johannine paraphrase of Jesus' teachings and the spiritualization of how he was received (both positively and negatively) bolster this move. When considering the ministry of Jesus, his signs are clearly discussed symbolically and theologically, and the revelatory function of the signs – including their pointing to the mission of Jesus – becomes their primary interpretive value in John. And, when considering distinctive aspects of chronology or narration in John, such as the timing of the Temple cleansing and the last supper, 'the theologizing work of the evangelist' receives attribution as the basis for Johannine peculiarities. 'John does not present a historical challenge to the Synoptic tradition,' scholars explain these differences; 'John's presentation reflects *theological* interests rather than *historical* ones.' The question is the degree to which this thesis holds.

a) *Strengths:* Indeed, the Fourth Evangelist is the most spiritualizing and theologizing among the four canonical gospel writers, and since the second century CE, he has simply been called 'the theologian'. In John, the theological import of Jesus' teachings – highlighted by the I-Am sayings and the Son's relation to the Father – form the basis for most of the Christological debates within the history of Christian theology. And, as mentioned above, the origin of that work must be credited as including centrally the theologizing work of the evangelist. Likewise, the presentation of the theological significance of Jesus' miracles also roots in the reflective process of the evangelist's thinking. Even the emphasis upon the existential value of Jesus' signs betrays the theological engagement of the evangelist's thinking, operating on a Stage-5 level of faith (Conjunctive, according to James Fowler's approach) contrasted to less dialectical and more conventional ones.[35] On theologizing explanations of John's distinctive chronology, the 'Paschal theology of the evangelist' gets

---

35. See cognitive-critical approaches to biblical analysis in Anderson (2004b and 1996, pp. 136–65) as well as in Anderson, Ellens, and Fowler (2004).

credited with the placing of the Temple cleansing early and the locating of the last supper on Thursday, the day the Paschal lambs were slain. These moves preserve the 3-against-1 approach to the Johannine/Synoptic problem, alleviating historical embarrassment from the Johannine distinctives. If John's differences of presentation were rooted in theological interests rather than historical differences, the four canonical Gospels can more easily be harmonized. The theological valuation of John's witness thus displaces apparent historical incongruities, and Clement's dictum finds its destined modernistic application.

b) *Weaknesses:* While Jesus' teachings and deeds are indeed spiritualized and theologized in John, however, Clement was not declaring John to be historically inferior. The word translated 'facts' (as in, the Synoptics preserved the 'facts' in contrast to John) is actually *somatika* – referring to the *bodily aspects* of Jesus' ministry as contrasted to the *spiritual perspective* of John. In that sense, it is a mistake to interpret Clement as making a historical judgement about John *or* the Synoptics. Clement was not a modern positivist. He was simply declaring, nearly a century after the four Gospels' completion, his inference of their tone and approach, not respective degrees of historical reliability. Therefore, to employ Clement's dictum as a licence for de-historicizing the Johannine witness falls flat from a critical perspective. It was nothing of the sort originally, but it came to be used in the Modern era as a means of bolstering a 3-against-1 marginalization of John before Markan priority was established. In the light of a bi-optic approach to the Johannine/Markan analysis, the spiritualistic discounting of John's distinctive presentation no longer holds.

A second problem emerges when seeking to explain John's chronological differences on the basis that the evangelist's 'Paschal theology' caused the moving of the Temple cleansing early and the location of the last supper on a Thursday rather than on a Friday. The first fact to consider is that the evangelist cannot really be said to have much of a 'Paschal theology' to begin with. Indeed, John the Baptist declares at the beginning, 'Behold the Lamb of God, who takes away the sin of the world!' (Jn 1.29, 36), but the Lamb of God theme occurs nowhere else in the rest of the Gospel. The Johannine Apocalypse culminates with Christ as the victorious Lamb, but it is a mistake to connect the Johannine Apocalypse and Gospel too closely together, as though one can be read through the other. John has no explicit Paschal theology other than the witness of the Baptist in the first chapter, so this cannot be said to have been a pervasive interest or investment of the evangelist. It could be argued that the interpretation of Caiaphas' willingness to 'sacrifice' Jesus instead of risking a Roman onslaught as an economy of violence reflects a Johannine atonement theology (Jn 11.45-57), but the thrust of the larger passage is more political than theological. Of the Paschal imagery present in John, Jesus is more clearly portrayed as the good shepherd – the true shepherd – who lays down his life for the sheep. The pastoral image of Christ as shepherd in John is far stronger than the presentation of Jesus as the Lamb, so it thus is not a strong basis upon which to build any sort of a heuristic platform. Further, as the outline of John's central Christological structure above shows, it centres not around atonement theology – that is more properly Pauline – but around *revelation*. Imputing Pauline or Synoptic atonement theology into that of the Fourth Evangelist is itself an unfounded move.

A third weakness with this particular approach is that it assumes an absence of otherwise historical factors in the location of the Johannine Temple cleansing and last supper. Indeed, rhetorical interests are present in the construction of all narratives, historical and otherwise, but to assert that no historical-type awareness or motivation is evident in the Johannine ordering and presentation of these events simply is not true. Regarding the Temple cleansing the following apparently historical associations are present: a) First, the unit (Jn 2.12-25) is hemmed by chronotopic markers. The beginning of the passage bears three chronological details: *meta touto* ('after this') is a general reference – not necessarily a chronological one – as is *kai ekei emeinan ou pollas hēmeras* ('and there [in Capernaum] they remained just a few days' v. 12). The next statement, though, is more particular. *Kai egnus ēn to Pascha tōn Ioudaiōn* ('And the Passover of the Jews was near') locates the event at a particular festival time, although which Passover season is meant may be debated.[36] The end of the passage also bears with it chronological references, again mentioning the Passover feast and the *sēmeia* ('signs') he had been doing (Jn 2.23). Whether the evangelist used these references with particularly chronological meanings in mind, and even if they were wrong, it cannot be said that historical-type details are entirely missing. They are present at least in general ways.

b) A second fact is that it cannot be claimed that the Temple cleansing unit has no references to the narration of events before and after. First, the way to Jerusalem (via Capernaum, Jn 2.12) again draws in the mother of Jesus who had just been mentioned in Jn 2.1-5. While she is not mentioned as being present in Jerusalem, Jesus' disciples are. At the beginning of John 3, though, Nicodemus makes reference to Jesus' 'signs', and this statement (in addition to Jn 2.23) appears to include the Temple cleansing as a *sēmeion*. These references, of course, are not necessarily made with the Temple cleansing in mind, but in John 4 Jesus appears to be travelling from the south to the north (thus having to pass through Samaria), and the events in John 5 are inexplicable without Jesus having been to Jerusalem before. Already in Jn 5.18 the

---

36. The question of *which* Passover festival this may have been is relevant here; if indeed the reference were to the same Passover mentioned in Jn 11.55, a theory of transposition would be required. Such is the view of Barnabas Lindars, for instance. In addition to these references, a third mention of the proximity of the Passover is found in Jn 6.4, but in none of them is an explicit connection made with the Paschal atonement theology. The unwitting prolepsis of Caiaphas in Jn 11.50 is a response to a reference to Roman violence and destruction, and this theme of impending political violence is more closely associated with *engus to Pascha* in John than an inferred Pauline atonement motif (see Anderson, 1996, pp. 172–3).

Jerusalem-based leaders are presented as wanting to kill Jesus, and if the only thing he had done in Jerusalem up until that time were the healing of the paralytic, this extremely hostile reaction is hard to explain. The desire to put Jesus to death is again mentioned in Jn 7, and without an early Temple cleansing in the mind of the narrator it is difficult to imagine why these references would have been mentioned during the early ministry of Jesus. Again, the point is not to argue John's chronological veracity; it is to challenge the often-made assertion that the early placement of John's Temple cleansing bore no chronological/sequential associations with it.

c) A third difficulty with the current 'consensus' is that several aspects of the Markan locating of the Temple incident at the end of Jesus' ministry do not appear to be ordered by 'factual' knowledge or information. For one thing, Mark locates *all* the Jerusalem events at the end of Jesus' ministry, as though he only visited the city *once* during his entire ministry. John's presentation of several visits to Jerusalem indeed seems more plausible than the Markan singular visit. Mark also locates nearly all the judgement and apocalyptic teachings of Jesus as happening on that eventful visit to Jerusalem, but such could simply be a factor of conjecture or climactic narration, clumping material together at the end, rather than motivated by factual information. And, Mark only mentions one Passover, the one at which Jesus was killed, implying that Jesus' ministry and opposition were all mounted within a relatively short period of time rather than over a period of several years. This could have been the case, but John's rendering here seems more plausible. Another oddity is that Mark's presentation of the events narrated in the Johannine rendering of the Temple cleansing are more fragmented than they are in John. For instance, the mention of the event itself is in Mk 11.15-17 (cf. Jn 2.14-17), while the challenging of Jesus' authority comes in a return visit in Mk 11.27-33 (cf. Jn 2.18-22). Still less integrated are two references to Jesus' declaration that he would raise up 'this temple' in three days, the first made by those who stood before the chief priests and the Jewish council (Mk 14.58) and then made by those who observed him hanging on the cross (Mk 15.30). Interestingly, while both of these statements assert that Jesus had made this declaration, he is only portrayed as having done so in Jn 2.19. Because the material in Jn 2.13-25 is more integrated, and the parallel material in Mark is more disintegrated and diffuse, it cannot be said that the best explanation for the differences is Mark's factuality at the expense of John's.

d) A fourth problem with the 'scholarly consensus' that Mark's rendering is rooted in objective fact and John's is rooted in spiritualizing fancy is that John's presentation correlates with several aspects of historicity. First, the reference to 46 years it had taken to reconstruct the Temple locates the event around the year 27 CE, toward the beginning of Jesus' ministry, as Herod had begun the construction of the Temple around 19 BCE.[37] Further, this particular

---

37. See Higgins (1960, pp. 44–6) and Josephus (*Antiquities* XV.xi.1).

detail in Jn 2.20, declared on behalf of the Jewish leaders, is not explicable on the basis of numerology or semeiology; it simply is mentioned as an 'innocent' objection to the three-day reconstruction reference. Second, the mention of the disciples' having remembered later his word, after the resurrection (Jn 2.21-2), appears to have involved considerable passing of time rather than just a few days. Again, John's presentation could have been wrong, but it cannot be said that the Synoptic/Johannine differences are simply due to factuality versus spirituality. A third fact is also interesting here; Papias' opinion that Mark preserved Peter's teaching favourably – but in the *wrong order* – is attributed to 'the Elder' (*Hist. Eccles.* 3.39.15). Was this the Johannine Elder, reflecting a second-century opinion that Mark's conjectural ordering of events deserved to be set straight? If so, John's presentation may have been a corrective in the name of a *historical* opinion in opposition to the Markan rendering. For these reasons at least, the Temple-cleansing differences between John and Mark cannot be said to confirm a 'factual' Mark in opposition to a 'spiritual' John. John too is *somatic* (Origon, *Comm.* 1.9).

But what about the dating of the last supper? Would not Mark's presenting the event as a Passover meal have been a more likely timing than John's rendering of the event on Thursday night? After all, Mk 14.12-16 records that the last supper was being prepared on the day the Paschal lambs were killed, the Day of Preparation, making it a more formal Passover meal. Supposedly, John's locating the event on the eve of the Day of Preparation (Jn 19.14, 31, 42) would have been motivated by 'the Paschal theologizing interests of the evangelist' over and against the 'superior chronology' of Mark. Two major problems accompany this view. First, if the Passover were observed on the Sabbath that year, it seems highly unlikely that Jesus' crucifixion would have happened on the Sabbath, and if Mark's rendering in ch. 14 were correct, this would have been the case. John's reporting the sense of urgency that the bodies needed to be removed from the crosses before the Sabbath seems far more likely. Another problem with the Markan rendering is that Mark presents the appearance narratives as happening on the 'first day', the day after the Sabbath (as does John), which would have meant that Jesus was only in the tomb overnight (Mk 16.1-2, 9). Given Mark 14 on its own, to allow three days in the tomb, the Johannine rendering is required. And yet, Mk 15.42 claims that Jesus was actually crucified on the Day of Preparation, thus contradicting the earlier Markan passage that the meal was on the same day. This is not just a matter of John against Mark; it also is a matter of Mark against Mark. Then again, if the Passover were held the day before the Sabbath that year, the above could be more easily harmonized. Another fact is that 'eating the Passover' would not necessarily have been confined to one day; it could have involved a week-long set of celebrations. The problem for such a move is that Jn 19.31 declares that the Sabbath was a 'high day' that year, implying the Passover and the Sabbath were on the same day.

A second problem with preferring a Passover meal setting over a less formalistic meal in John is that the former too easily can be explained as an adapted meal conforming to evolving Christian cultic practice. John's assertion that Jesus did not baptize (Jn 4.2) and the omission of the words of the institution of the Eucharist in John 13 cannot be explained on the basis of 'spiritualization' or the representation of evolving cultic practice. Indeed, John goes against those cultic developments within the broader Christian movement, but the Markan rendering supports them. For these and other reasons, the primary examples used for explaining Synoptic/Johannine differences on the basis of factuality versus spiritualization fall way short of a compelling critical argument.

The 'theological interests of the evangelist' is one of the most inexact and carelessly used explanations given among scholars who do not otherwise know what to do with a particular Johannine feature. Rarely is its use subjected to critical assessment, and seldom are the bases for its use laid out clearly. The de-historicizing treatment of the above issue is a telling example. First, despite John's making no mention of the Paschal lambs' being killed, this distinctively Markan theme (Mk 14.12) is carelessly imputed into the Fourth Evangelist's motives despite the relative dearth of Paschal theology in John.[38] Second, the issue is set up as John versus Mark, when Mark too disagrees with Mark. Third, the more cultic Passover meal and institutionalizing rendering in Mark gets precedence over John's more innocent presentation, against the criterion of dissimilarity. And fourth, these specious moves are amassed as critical evidence illustrating a prime case of Johannine ahistoricity, functioning to deconstruct other apparently historical Johannine material. If these same sorts of moves were made in favour of John's historicity or apostolic authorship, critical scholars would certainly raise objections – and yet, as challenges to its historicity, it appears they are given a critical pass.

A final fallacy also accompanies this discussion: namely, the assumption that theologization and spiritualization necessarily imply ahistoricity. Indeed, the spiritualization of earlier events calls into question the memory of purported events, and evolving narrations may have supplanted earlier renderings, but to say that symbolization, spiritualization or theologization displaces originative history is terribly flawed as a historiographic procedure. Apply the premise to any subject, and the extent of its fallacious character becomes evident. Does the phenomenon of 'war-story embellishment' prove a war never happened, or that there was no connection between originative events and later reflections? Do symbolized expansions upon traumatic experiences prove that they never happened? The embellishment of events does not negate their ontology. Indeed, the case can be made that dialectical processes of thought and reflection betray a first-order level of encounter rather than second-order reasoning. For these and other reasons, equating John's spiritualization of

---

38. The witness of the Baptist, 'Behold the Lamb of God, who takes away the sin of the world!' (Jn 1.29, 36), is more fittingly a reference to Isa. 53.7, where it is the suffering and faithfulness of Israel as the Suffering Servant of Yahweh through which the world is redeemed, than a Paschal atonement theme.

events in the ministry of Jesus cannot be considered a solid proof of its ahistoricity.

In summary, of the various planks in the platform contributing to the de-historicization of John, none of the strengths of these positions are compelling. Problems indeed are inferred, and ones that need to be addressed critically, but John's aspects of historicity are as disruptive for the purported consensus as obstacles to John's historicity were to the traditionalist view. Therefore, a flat appraisal of John's ahistoricity is devoid of nuance, and it fails to account for dozens of exceptions to its claims. For this reason the genuinely critical scholar cannot be satisfied with the purported critical consensus.

B. *Planks in Platform B: The De-Johannification of Jesus*

Attempting to employ the Gospel of John for Jesus studies is indeed problematic. A Jesus who possesses sole control over his future, and who 'knows' what is in the hearts of humans, is hard to be equated with the Incarnation. Likewise, it is difficult to know how to square the Logos, who was with God in the beginning and through whom all was created, with the historical Jesus who suffered and died under Pontius Pilate. John's historicity seems to have been subsumed into John's Christology, and therefore, John is felt to provide very little insight into what the historical Jesus may have been like. After John is removed from the database used to reconstruct the 'historical' Jesus, criteria are established which function to separate John further from historical-Jesus quests. The problem, however, is that this move is circular in its conception and its exercise. This being the case, the planks in the platform of the de-Johannification of Jesus must also be assessed critically to determine whether John's marginalization from Jesus studies is warranted or not.

1) *John's Similarities with the Synoptics – Especially Mark*
An obverse problem of John's differences from the Synoptics is the fact that John is also very similar to them. Many similarities between John and Mark can be found, and despite the sustained objections of P. Gardner-Smith, Raymond E. Brown and D. Moody Smith, such scholars as C.K. Barrett, Franz Neirynck and Thomas Brodie[39] have inferred John's spiritualized use of Mark. The significance of this inference as it relates to Jesus, John and history is that if John were a spiritualization of Mark, this would account for a major

---

39. When comparing the theories of Gardner-Smith (1938), Brown (2003) and Smith (2001) with Barrett (1978), Neirynck (1977) and Brodie (1993), the weaknesses of Markan-dependence theories appear greater than independence theories.

factor in the origin of John's tradition. On one hand, if John is seen as an expansion upon Mark, this would bolster interests in securing a historical basis for John. On the other hand, dependence upon Mark casts John in a derivative relation to Mark rather than having an original claim to its own tradition. Whatever the case, the many differences from Mark continue to pose difficulties for a Markan dependence view, and this fact comprises one of its major vulnerabilities.

a) *Strengths:* The hypothesis that John is derivative from Mark has several strengths to it, although it by no means is embraced by the majority of Johannine scholars. The first strength involves the similar beginnings and endings of Mark and John. Both begin (after the Johannine Prologue) with the beginning of the 'Gospel' and the ministry of John the Baptist, and both end with the Passion, death, resurrection and appearances of Jesus. A second strength is that similarities in the Passion accounts are impressive. They both begin with an acclaimed entry to Jerusalem, a last supper, prayer and arrest in the garden, two trials (a Jewish and a Roman trial), the crucifixion and death, the resurrection, and finally appearance narratives. Third, both have an impressive number of general similarities around the feeding of the multitude, the sea-crossing, further discussions of the feeding, and the confession of Peter. Fourth, multiple particular similarities (distinctive to Mark and John) exist regarding graphic detail (the mention of 200 and 300 *denarii*, the grass upon which the people sat, the use of 'the Holy One of God' as a Christological title, and the use of Isa. 6.9-10 to explain the unbelief of the Galileans. These similarities imply some form of contact between these traditions. Fifth, some aspects of John's witness show signs of being crafted for readers and hearers of Mark. The references to the adverse reception in Nazareth and the timing of the Baptist's imprisonment point to familiarity with the Markan witness,[40] as do the clarification of the first two signs performed in Galilee (Jn 2.11; 4.54) and the acknowledgement that other signs were performed by Jesus not reported in '*this* book' (Jn 20.30). For these and other reasons, some scholars have inferred the Johannine and Markan traditions to have implied a derivative relationship.

b) *Weaknesses:* The problem with such a view, however, is that despite all these similarities, *none* of them is identical. Mark has 'green' grass; John has 'much' grass. While 'Holy One of God' is used as a title for Jesus in both Gospels, in Mark it is uttered by the demoniac (Mk 1.24), while in John it is declared by Peter (Jn 6.69). In fact, of the 45 similarities between John 6 and Mark 6 and

---

40. Richard Bauckham's essay, 'John for Readers of Mark' (1998, pp. 147–72), raises the sort of possibility that Ian MacKay (2004) argues in greater detail. Johannine-Markan traditional contact, though, need not imply derivation.

8, *none* of them are identical.[41] Further, the Temple cleansing's being placed at the beginning of Jesus' ministry argues strongly against John's dependence upon Mark. After an extensive analysis of John's relation to the Synoptics, and in particular Mark, Moody Smith resolutely affirms the same conclusion that P. Gardner-Smith came up with in 1938. If the Fourth Evangelist were aware of Mark or the other Synoptics extensively, he disagreed with them at almost every turn.[42] Certainly if there were some contact or familiarity, the relation of John to Mark was nowhere near the much closer connections evidenced between Mark and the other two gospels. A further problem is that much of the Johannine archaeological and geographical detail is found only in John, so the Markan tradition cannot have been a source of the majority of the most likely-to-be-considered historical Johannine material. For these reasons, Johannine familiarity with Mark cannot be ruled out, but dependence upon Mark can. Therefore, John's independence from Mark should be regarded as non-dependence, or autonomy, rather than isolation.

2) *John's Composition: Diachronic or Synchronic?*

John's composition has been a considerable interest of Johannine scholars due to its many perplexities (*aporias*). First, formal and vocabulary differences exist between the Prologue (1.1-18) and the rest of John's narrative. The Prologue is poetic and stanza-based in its form (suggesting a worship setting in its origin), whereas the rest of John is prose. A second perplexity is that several odd progressions require attention: chapters 5 and 7 are in Jerusalem, while chapters 4 and 6 are in Galilee; after Jesus says 'let us leave' in 14.31, it takes three chapters for them to arrive at the Garden (Jn 18.1); Jn 20.31 seems to have been an original first ending with chapter 21 having been added at a later time; Mary is mentioned in ch. 11 as the one who anointed the feet of Jesus, but she does not actually do so until ch. 12; Jesus says 'none of you asks where I am going' in 16.5, and yet Thomas had just asked him about where he was going and how to know the way in 14.5; and finally, neither 5.4 nor 7.53-8.11 is found in the earliest Greek manuscripts of John. These perplexities raise more than a few questions about John's order and composition, and some scholars have advocated a diachronic history of John's composition. The relevant question here involves the degree to which John's narration represents a coherent presentation of Jesus or whether it represents a fragmented one, composed of alien material and disparate sources possessing varying degrees of historicity.

41. For the particulars, see Tables 10–15 in Anderson (1996, pp. 187–90).

42. After a thorough review of the literature D. Moody Smith sides with Gardner-Smith (2001), although with the move of Raymond Brown (2003) toward considering 'cross-influence' between John and other traditions, a theory of 'interfluence' deserves development.

a) *Strengths:* The greatest of Johannine diachronic composition schemes is the theory devised by Rudolf Bultmann. He argued for three primary sources from which the evangelist derived his gospel material, for the constructive work of the evangelist which then fell into a disordered state, and the reconstructive (and reordering) work of the redactor who prepared the Fourth Gospel into the perplexing state in which we find it today.[43] This being the case, a *sēmeia* source provided the distinctive signs found in John, a Gnostic revelation-sayings source availed the evangelist's distinctive I-Am sayings explaining their origin, and an individuated Passion narrative made it possible for John's distinctive material to have been gathered without the evangelist having been an eyewitness. Bultmann's source-critical inferences were based on stylistic, contextual and theological bases, and they accounted for several perplexing Johannine features. First, they accounted for the rough transitions in John, and even some smooth ones. Second, they explained the origins of John's Christological tensions, as these were due to dialogues between sources and evangelist and redactor. Third, they accounted for the inferred historical origins of John's material – it was derivative from other sources and from mythological origins from which a distinctive narrative was constructed. In so doing, John's distinctive presentation of Jesus was accounted for, and John's theological-rather-than-historical character was explained. Other diachronic schemes have abounded, but Bultmann's represents the zenith of modern Johannine diachronic reconstruction.

b) *Weaknesses:* Despite the brilliance of Bultmann's approach, it falls flat when tested on the basis of its own evidence. Regarding the differences between 'Hellenised Aramaic' and 'Semitising Greek', when all of Bultmann's stylistic evidence is gathered and applied to John 6 as a case study (the very place where four of his five sources should be discernibly present), its distribution is not only non-convincing, it is non-indicative. Other than the fact of a narrator's stylistic work being obvious (which does not imply the use of alien material), the rest of the features are evenly distributed throughout John 6.[44] Likewise, contextual reasons for inferring a disordering and a reordering of John's text are terribly weak. Bultmann misses the irony of Jesus' knowing response to the crowd's question about his arrival in Jn 6.26 (*when* did you get here...as in, *when's lunch?*) and infers instead a displacement of material. His inference of a disordered John 4, 6, 5, 7 makes better sense if seen as the insertion of John 6 into an earlier version of the gospel.[45] Theologically, John's

---

43. See especially the analysis of Bultmann's programme (1971) by Moody Smith (1965).

44 See an analysis of the viability of Bultmann's evidence on its own terms in Anderson (1996, pp. 70–136).

45. This is the view of Barnabas Lindars (1972, pp. 46–54); independently of one another, John Ashton and I came to the same favourable impressions of its prime viability (see Ashton, 1991, pp. 124–204), although he embraces a final editor along the lines of Brown, as do I.

Christological tensions should be viewed not as dialogues between sources and editors, but as a function of the dialectical thinking of the evangelist. In that sense, these tensions are internal to the thinking of the evangelist, rather than external. While Bultmann is happy to describe modern theologians as dialectical thinkers, he ironically fails to allow a first-century theologian the same privilege. With relation to the evangelist's subject, Jesus, this dialectical level of engagement may reflect proximity to Jesus rather than distance.

As mentioned above, the most plausible and least speculative of Johannine composition theories involves a two-edition theory of composition inferring that a first edition of John was finalized around 80–85 CE, while a final edition was compiled around 100 CE by the redactor after the death of the Beloved Disciple (implied in Jn 21.18-24). Material added to the final edition would have included the Prologue, chs 6, 15–17, 21, and Beloved Disciple and eyewitness passages. With Bultmann here, the editor appears to have added several sections that are quite similar to 1 John, so it is plausible to identify the author of the Johannine Epistles as the final compiler of the Johannine Gospel. This would explain the third-person references to the purported author and appeals to authority otherwise (1 Jn 1.1-3, etc.). If something like this two-edition process would have been the case, the Johannine Gospel would have been written *before-and-after* the Epistles (probably written between 85 and 95 CE). What can be inferred, then, in the first edition material is the concern to present Jesus apologetically as the Jewish Messiah in response to engagement with the local Synagogue presence, while the supplementary material shows signs of anti-docetic emphases on the suffering and humanity of Jesus.

3) *The Lateness of John and Historical Validity*
A central plank in the platform of arguing for the de-Johannification of Jesus results from the belief that John was finalized last among the canonical Gospels. Indeed, both the traditional view and the consensus of most Johannine scholars agree that John was finalized last among the four Gospels, and recent estimations locate John's finalization around 100 CE. While several scholars in recent years have argued for the chronological priority of John,[46] it is fair to say that most Johannine scholars go with the later date. Because of John's chronological 'posteriority' the case is made that earlier sources, such as Mark and hypothetical Q, provide a closer measure of what the historical Jesus may have been like.

---

46. Three leading studies arguing John's primitivity include J.A.T. Robinson (1985), Klaus Berger (1997) and Peter Hofrichter (1997). Their primary weakness is common; primitivity of tradition need not imply earliness of finalization. Despite the earliness of much of John's material (see E.R. Goodenough, 1945), it still seems to have later and more developed material in it as well.

a) *Strengths:* Indeed, the earlier the traditional material, the greater the confidence is that may be placed in its historicity. Given the high degree of plausibility regarding Mark's being the first Gospel to have been finalized, and given the likelihood that an early sayings tradition was drawn upon by Matthew and Luke (Q, or whatever it may have been), a portrait of the historical Jesus based upon Mark and Q should be accorded primacy over the more spiritualized and Hellenized John. Given that Luke and Matthew were also probably finalized before John likewise gives the Synoptic presentations of Jesus precedence over the Johannine. The Johannine Prologue betrays a cultic appraisal of Jesus rooted in the faith and worship of community experience. A Logos Christology, for instance, combined with a presentation of Jesus who has sole control over what happens to him, clearly betrays a more distanced and confessional reflection, challenging assertions of John's historicity. Likewise, the post-resurrection faith of Johannine Christians shows signs of superimposing the Christ of faith over the Jesus of history more so than in any of the other canonical gospels.[47] John's apparent addressing of docetizing tendencies within its audience also raises questions about Gnosticism and John – certainly reflecting later developments in Christianity. For these and other reasons, John's lateness accords it a secondary place among the Gospels with reference to historicity.

b) *Weaknesses:* John's relative lateness among the canonical Gospels, however, does not mean that John is late-and-only-late. Indeed, John also appears to contain a great deal of primitive tradition and material.

1) John operates in ways parallel to Mark in rendering Jewish terms in Greek ones, including such Aramaic words as *rabbi/rabbouni* (Jn 1.38; 20.16), *Messias* (Jn 1.41; 4.25), *Bethzetha* (Jn 5.2), *Siloam* (Jn 9.7), *Gabbatha* (Jn 19.13) and *Golgotha* (Jn 19.17). These terms appear to have served at the latest within the Palestinian period of John's tradition, and their 'translation' appears to have bridged primitive tradition with later Hellenistic audiences.

2) John explains Jewish customs to a Gentile audience. Such passages as Jn 2.6, 13; 4.9; 5.1; 6.4; 7.2; 11.55; 19.31, 40, 42 connect Palestinian Jewish worship practices and social customs with later non-Jewish audiences. If John were late-and-only-late, the presence of this material would be hard to explain.

3) John includes some of the most explicit archaeological and topographical references among all the Gospels. Particular places locating events are

47. While Maurice Casey (1996) argues for the 'profoundly untrue' character of John, he never clearly defines the meaning of 'true'. He then commits two simplistic and disjunctive errors. First, he forces a dichotomy between seemingly all of John and the Synoptics, requiring a choice to be made between them. Second, he insists upon a division between theology and historicity, denying the latter by affirming the former. Even his correct detection of theological content, however, is hindered by inadequate inferences of its meaning, equating the presentation of the *Ioudaioi* in John with anti-Semitism and racism, and thus pervasive historical error.

mentioned, including the places where John was baptizing (*Bethabara* beyond the Jordan, Jn 1.28;[48] *Aenon* near *Salim*, Jn 3.23; beyond the Jordan, Jn 3.26; 10.40) and places where Jesus performed his ministries are mentioned explicitly (other than Jerusalem, Galilee, Jn 1.43; 4.3; 6.1; 7.1, 9; Cana of Galilee, Jn 2.1-11; 4.46-54; Capernaum, Jn 2.12; 4.46; 6.17, 24, 59; Judea, Jn 4.3, 47, 54; 7.1, 3; 11.7; Samaria, Jn 4.4, 5, 7, 9; the Sea of Tiberias, Jn 6.1, 23; 21.1; Bethany, Jn 11.1, 18; and a village near Ephraim to which Jesus withdrew, Jn 11.54).

4) Also, places where people were from include the following: Philip, Andrew and Peter were from the town of Bethsaida (Jn 1.44; 12.20-1); Jesus, from Nazareth, saw Nathanael, an authentic Israelite, under a fig tree (Jn 1.45-8); Judas, son of Simon, was from Kerioth in Judea (distinctively the only disciple of Jesus from the south, Jn 6.71; 12.4; 13.2; while another Judas was *not*, Jn 14.22); Jerusalem leaders declare, 'How can the Christ come from Galilee?' (the Christ was to come from Bethlehem, David's village, Jn 7.41-52); Bethany was the home of Mary, Martha and Lazarus (Jn 11.1, 18-20; 12.1); the one the soldiers sought was 'Jesus of Nazareth' (Jn 18.7); Mary of Magdala and other women were present at the cross, and Mary was present after the resurrection (Jn 19.25f.; 20.1, 18); Joseph of Arimathea requested the body of Jesus (Jn 19.38); and Nathanael was from Cana of Galilee (Jn 21.2).

5) Explicit distances reported include the disciples setting off across the lake for Capernaum and rowing 25 or 30 *stadia* (Jn 6.17-19); Jesus' return with his disciples to Bethany, 15 *stadia* from Jerusalem (Jn 11.18); and the boat was about 200 *pēchōn* from the shore, where Jesus had built a fire (Jn 21.8-9). Likewise, spatial uses of *anabainō* ('ascend' or 'go up') are employed topographically in John (with reference to Jerusalem, Jn 2.13; 5.1; 7.8, 10; 11.55; 12.20; with reference to the Temple, Jn 7.14; and out of the water, Jn 21.11); as are uses of *katabainō* ('descend' or 'go down'; to Capernaum, Jn 2.12; 4.47, 49; into the water, Jn 5.7; into the boat, Jn 6.16). Spatial and topographic references appear to be used with intentionality in John.

6) Particular topographical details appear to be known by the narrator, including John's baptizing in Aenon near Salim, because there was plenty of water there (Jn 3.23). Jesus departed across the Sea of Galilee, that is, of Tiberias (Jn 6.1; 21.1). Jesus visited Jacob's well in Sychar of Samaria, having to go through Samaria between Jerusalem and Galilee (Jn 4.5); neither the

---

48. It is more likely to infer that 'Bethany' was added later than to infer that *Bethabara* or *Betharaba* replaced the more common place name. The speculation that because Bethany was not across the Jordan, and that the evangelist has thus made an inexcusable geographical mistake, is itself based upon a flawed assumption (cf. Parker, 1955). Leading archaeological investigations in Jordan are currently excavating a site east of the Jordan River (not far from Jericho), which have found both the remains of a village and a former tributary to the Jordan that had once formed pools of water – confirming the Johannine account.

mountain of Samaria (Gerizim) nor Jerusalem is the credited place of worship (Jn 4.19-24); Jesus fled again to the mountain alone (Jn 6.15) and was later found on the other side of the lake (Jn 6.25); the bread of life discourse was delivered at the Synagogue of Capernaum (Jn 6.59); Lazarus' tomb was a cave with stone lying in front of it (Jn 11.38); Jesus withdrew to the wilderness area near the village of Ephraim and remained there with his disciples (Jn 11.54); the crowd who had come for the (Passover) feast met Jesus on his way to Jerusalem (Jn 12.12).

7) Particular Jerusalem details are mentioned, including Jesus' going 'up to' Jerusalem's Temple courts for the Passover (Jn 2.13); his going up to Jerusalem for a feast of the Jews to a pool named Bethzatha near the Sheep Gate, which is surrounded by five porticoes, or covered colonnades (Jn 5.1-2); halfway through the Feast of Tabernacles Jesus' going up to the Temple Courts to teach (Jn 7.14), speaking in the treasury area of the Temple (Jn 8.20), and leaving the Temple area (Jn 8.59); the blind man is told to wash in the Pool of Siloam (Jn 9.7); at the Feast of Dedication in Jerusalem Jesus was walking in the Temple area in Solomon's Colonnade (Jn 10.22-3); Jesus and his disciples crossed the brook of Kidron and entered the garden there (Jn 18.1); the other disciple was allowed to enter the courtyard of the High Priest (but not Peter) because he was known to the High Priest (Jn 18.15); Jesus declared he spoke openly in the Synagogue and the Temple, where all the Judeans gathered (Jn 18.20); Jesus was led from Caiaphas to the Praetorium, where Pilate met with them outside (Jn 18.28-9); having gone inside and outside several times, Pilate came out and sat on a juridical seat, in Aramaic called *Gabbatha*, (the ridge of the house) on a place called 'the Stone Pavement', in Greek called *Lithostrōtos* (Jn 19.13); Jesus carried his cross to the Place of the Skull, which in Hebrew was called *Golgotha* (Jn 19.17); the place where Jesus was crucified was near the city (Jn 19.20); near the place where Jesus was crucified was a garden and a new tomb in which no one had been buried (Jn 19.41); Mary Magdalene saw the stone had been removed from the tomb and later announced the resurrection to the disciples (Jn 20.1, 18).

8) While time is developed kairotically in John (the 'hour' of Jesus is or is not come, Jn 2.4; 4.21, 23; 5.25, 28; 7.30; 8.20; 12.23, 27; 13.1; 16.21, 25, 32; 17.1; the 'hour' will have come for the disciples, Jn 11.9; 16.2, 4; and things change 'from that time on' for the mother of Jesus and the Beloved Disciple, Jn 19.27), *hora* and references to time are also used in *explicit, chronological terms*. The 'tenth hour' is when Jesus called his disciples, being the end of the day when finding somewhere to stay for the night would be an issue (Jn 1.39). The 'sixth hour' is the time when Jesus approached the woman at the well, obviating a noon-time event (Jn 4.6). The 'seventh hour' was the time of Jesus' healing word from afar, and it was indeed the same time as the recovery of the royal official's son (Jn 4.52-3). The 'sixth hour' also comes in with reference to the timing of the crucifixion, locating the event in the middle of the day (Jn 19.14). Likewise, 'day' is used seasonally (Jn 8.56; 9.4; 11.9, 53; 12.7; 19.31) and eschatologically (the 'last' day, Jn 6.39, 40, 44,

54; 11.24; 12.48) in John, but it also is used with apparent chronological intention. In general terms, a few days' passing is mentioned (Jn 2.12), and some events follow others on the same day (Jn 5.9; 20.19), but the explicit numeration of days is also employed. On the third day was a marriage (Jn 2.1), after three days Jesus (this temple) will be raised up (Jn 2.19-20), Jesus stayed in Samaria two days (Jn 4.40, 43) and waited two days before travelling to Bethany (Jn 11.6), Lazarus had been dead four days (Jn 11.17), the anointing of Jesus was six days before the Passover (Jn 12.1), and after eight days Jesus again appeared to his disciples (Jn 20.26). Particular years are mentioned (Jn 11.49, 51; 18.13), duration of time is measured in years (46 years it has taken to rebuild the Temple, Jn 2.20; the paralytic had been ill for 38 years, Jn 5.5; Jesus is not yet 50 years of age, Jn 8.57), and winter is mentioned as the time of year for the Feast of Dedication (Jn 10.22). Also, the early part of the day is mentioned (Jn 18.28; 20.1; 21.4) as is the evening (Jn 6.16; 20.19).

9) Graphic and sensory-types of detail also appear in the Johannine narration. Indeed, scholars point out the plausibly symbolic function of much of this material, but the fact that it is presented as empirically inferred detail is striking, nonetheless. Sensorily derived material is a fact in John. John confesses openly that he is not the Christ (Jn 1.20) and reports what he has seen (Jn 1.32-4), Nathanael was under the fig tree (Jn 1.48), six stone purification jars are described as holding two or three *metrētas* (Jn 2.6), Jesus made a whip out of chords (Jn 2.15), Nicodemus comes to Jesus 'by night' (Jn 3.2), the well on the plot of ground Jacob had given to his sons appears familiar (Jn 4.5-6), 200 *denarii* would not buy enough food for the multitude (Jn 6.7), 'much grass' describes the feeding setting with the men numbering 5,000 (Jn 6.10), the loaves are barley (Jn 6.9-13), the sort of fish served and eaten is *opsarion* (a prepared fish, Jn 6.9, 11; 21.9, 10, 13), stones are picked up to kill Jesus (Jn 8.59), spittle and mud are applied to the blind man's eyes (Jn 9.6-15), a bad odour accompanies Lazarus (Jn 11.39), Lazarus is wrapped in strips of linen around his hands and feet and a cloth over his face (Jn 11.44), the house was filled with the fragrance of the pure nard ointment (Jn 12.3), the perfume itself was worth 300 *denarii* (Jn 12.5), the crowd waved palm branches (Jn 12.13), Jesus changes into the clothes of a servant (Jn 13.4-5), when Judas departed it was night (Jn 13.30), lanterns and torches are mentioned in the garden (Jn 18.3), the *right* ear of the servant (whose name is 'Malchus') was severed by a disciple (Peter, Jn 18.10), it was cold outside the courtyard of the High Priest, and servants and attendants stood around a fire (Jn 18.18), after Peter's third denial the cock crew (Jn 18.27), the soldiers placed a crown of thorns on Jesus' head, and a purple robe was thrown around him (Jn 19.2, 5), Pilate's inscription was written in Hebrew, Latin and Greek (Jn 19.20), four divisions of Jesus' clothes were made and divided up among the soldiers (Jn 19.23), the tunic of Jesus was seamless, woven from top to bottom, which is why lots had to be cast for it (Jn 19.23-4), a sponge on a hyssop stick was dipped in a jar of vinegar and offered to Jesus, and he partook of it (Jn 19.29-30), water and blood came forth from

the side of Jesus (attested by 'the eyewitness', Jn 19.34-5), the type and weight of the spices are mentioned (about 100 *litras* of a mixture of myrrhs and aloes, Jn 19.39), it was still dark when Mary came to the tomb on the first day of the week, and she saw the stone had been removed from the tomb (Jn 20.1), when the other disciple and Peter arrived and looked into the tomb they saw strips of linen lying there with the head cloth folded and placed separately away from the rest (Jn 20.5-7), the disciples had gathered behind closed doors (Jn 20.19, 26), the flesh wounds of Jesus are seen and touched by Thomas (Jn 20.25-7), the right side of the boat is the one to throw the nets down on (Jn 21.6), Peter put on his coat on (because he was naked) before jumping in the water (Jn 21.7), the charcoal fire had fish on it and bread (Jn 21.9), and despite the number of the fish being 153 the nets were not broken (Jn 21.11).

10) Names of persons are mentioned in John in ways that imply familiarity. Andrew (Jn 1.40, 44; 6.8; 12.22) is described as the person whose brother Peter was, Thomas (Jn 11.16; 14.5; 20.24, 26, 27, 28, 29; 21.2) is referred to by the nickname *Didymos* (Jn 11.16; 20.24; 21.2), the sons of Zebedee are mentioned only once (Jn 21.2), *Cēphas* is the Aramaic name given to Simon Peter (Jn 1.42), and Peter (Jn 1.40, 44; 6.8, 68; 13.6, 9, 24, 36, 37; 18.10, 11, 15, 16, 17, 18, 25, 26, 27; 20.2, 3, 4, 6; 21.2, 3, 7, 11, 15, 17, 20, 21) is described as the son of Jonas (Jn 1.42; 21.15, 16, 17), Judas is described in consistently treacherous terms (Jn 6.71; 12.4; 13.2, 26, 29; 18.2, 3, 5), although another Judas (not *Iscariot*, Jn 6.71; 12.4; 13.2, 26; 14.22) is also mentioned (Jn 14.22), Nathanael is described as an Israelite in whom there is nothing false (Jn 1.45, 46, 47, 48, 49; 21.2), Philip is mentioned more prominently in John than in all the other gospels combined (Jn 1.43, 44, 45, 46, 48; 6.5, 7; 12.21, 22; 14.8, 9), two unnamed disciples are mentioned (Jn 1.35, 37; 21.2), one unnamed (the other, another) disciple is mentioned (Jn 18.15, 16; 20.3, 4, 8), and the enigmatic Beloved Disciple is given a special place of honour in the Johannine narrative (Jn 13.23; 19.26, 27; 20.2; 21.24). Among these references relationships are heightened, and personal knowledge is conveyed in ways that sometimes further the narrative, and in ways that sometimes do not.

In addition to Jesus' disciples who accompanied him in his ministry, Annas (Jn 18.13, 24) is mentioned as the father-in-law to Caiaphas, the High Priest (Jn 11.49; 18.13, 14, 24, 28), Joseph of Arimathea (Jn 19.38) is presented as the generous benefactor of the tomb, Barabbas is described as a robber (Jn 18.40), Joseph is referred to as the acknowledged father of Jesus (Jn 1.45; 6.42), the mother of Jesus is mentioned, but not by name (Jn 2.3; 19.25), Lazarus is mentioned as a close friend whom Jesus loved (Jn 11.1, 2, 5, 11, 14, 43; 12.1, 2, 9, 10, 17), as are his sisters Mary (Jn 11.1, 2, 19, 20, 28, 31, 32, 45; 12.3) and Martha (Jn 11.1, 2, 19, 20, 21, 24, 30, 39; 12.2), Mary of Magdala encounters the risen Lord (Jn 19.25; 20.1, 18) and brings her witness to the others, Malchus was the name of the servant whose ear was severed (Jn 18.10), Nicodemus comes to Jesus by night (Jn 3.1, 4, 9; 7.50;

19.39), the woman of Samaria becomes an effective evangelist to her people (Jn 4.7, 9, 11, 15, 17, 19, 21, 25, 27, 28, 39, 42), and Pilate is described dramatically as the impotent potentate at the trial scene (Jn 18.29, 31, 33, 35, 37, 38; 19.1, 4, 6, 8, 10, 12, 13, 15, 19, 21, 22, 31, 38). In these ways other actants are brought into the narrative, adding colour and tension to its fabric. Some of this material is even accorded red or pink status by the Jesus Seminar in acknowledgement of its likely historicity.[49]

Obviously, it is possible that all of these details were simply fabricated in mimetic form as art imitates reality, and some scholars will argue such.[50] Indeed, many of the details may be included for rhetorical reasons or as a means of heightening the lucidity of a passage as other contemporary literature may have done. It must be acknowledged, however, that the closest parallels to John, the Synoptic Gospels, show the reverse of mimetic proliferation of detail. Mark and John have far more non-symbolic illustrative detail than the Matthew and Luke, and where Matthew and Luke take over a Markan passage, they tend to eliminate names and places and to leave out details in summaraic form. If John operated similar to its closed literary parallels, the abundance of detail is more likely attributable to the oral stages of the tradition, as was probably the case for Mark. In fact, the best explanation of the detail common only to John and Mark is that buzz words and images were shared between the oral stages of the two traditions, perhaps in interfluential ways. Because influence in only one direction, to the exclusion of the other, is impossible to establish between two autonomous traditions, 'interfluence' is the best way to describe these relationships. The relative absence of this sort of detail from Luke and Matthew suggests what is left out when engaging a written form of Mark's tradition. Luke's access to the Johannine material also appears to have collected several Johannine details during its oral renderings: notably the right ear being cut off and Satan entering Judas. Of course, none of the above detail may have originated in events, but these and other inclusions of apparently primitive material give one pause before asserting that John was late-and-only-late. The obvious fallacy here is the assumption that John's finalized lateness discounts *all* of John's apparent earliness. Something between these two poles is far more plausible.

---

49. The detail about Annas' being the father-in-law of that year's high priest, Caiaphas (Jn 18.13) is one of the only Johannine passages listed in red, and the taking of Jesus from the place of Caiaphas to the governor's residence (Jn 18.28) is listed in pink (having plausible likelihood – a 3 on a scale of 1-4) in the voting of the Jesus Seminar (Funk *et al*, 1998, pp. 429, 431).

50. Erich Auerbach (1953) argues that mimetic imitation is used broadly in making a narrative more readable and believable. R.L. Sturch (1978) applies such an inference to John, seeking to overturn the works of Westcott and Dodd in their connecting of apparent eyewitness detail with the eyewitness claims of the redactor by identifying their mimetic associations. While some details 'resist elimination', he claims to have shown that alternative explanations mean that demonstrating the 'Evangelist was an eyewitness of nearly all that he reported...cannot in fact be achieved' (p. 324). Again, the fallacy presents itself operationally: because *all* of J is not H, *none* of J is H. This overstates the case in the obverse direction.

4) *Criteria for Determining Historicity*

The task of determining historicity in investigating the historical Jesus has evolved several criteria for making these judgements. The criterion of dissimilarity distinguishes later predictable portrayals from more primitive ones. The criterion of multiple attestation singles out units that appear more than once to describe an event or saying in the ministry of Jesus. The criterion of coherence distinguishes a presentation that seems to cohere with what Jesus is thought to have been like over and against other portrayals. The criterion of naturalism distinguishes the mundane from the more fantastic renderings, crediting the former with greater plausibility. Other criteria are used, but these four continue to be applied across gospel studies, and it is their employment that has laid the foundation for the majority of modernist Jesus studies.[51]

a) *Strengths:* Indeed, later developments reflect the emerging history of Jesus traditions rather than offering a window into the historical Jesus. Examples from Synoptic studies include the identification of ecclesial interests emerging in the Matthean tradition over and against less developed Mark and Luke's presentation of Jesus as a just man. Indeed, John's adapting of Jesus to fit the tastes of Hellenistic audiences and the needs of late-first-century believers probably reflect more closely the emergent history of the Johannine situation than the originative history of the material, so this criterion is of some benefit in the combining of Jesus and Johannine studies. The second criterion also works well in that it produces a set of test cases for conducting comparative gospel analysis. The passages most conducive to inter-gospel analysis include the ministry of John the Baptist, the Temple cleansing, events surrounding John 6 (the feeding, sea crossing, the discussion of the feeding and the confession of Peter), the anointing of Jesus, the Passion narratives and the appearance narratives. This being the case, however, over half of John is not only distinctive but unique among the Gospels, which raises questions as to its proximity to the historical Jesus. The third criterion is one of the most significant in these matters because the impression of Jesus who speaks in short, pithy sayings, who imparts wisdom as a sage, who prefers secrecy to publicity, and who calls for the Way of the Cross is very different from the exalted and self-confessing Messiah we find in John. The fourth criterion pushes the miraculous renderings of Jesus in the gospels to sources other than historical ones, and this is expected in the Modern era. Cause and effect relationships provide better windows into historicity, and a divine Jesus striding over the

---

51. In addition to these criteria *'embarrassment'* is included by John P. Meier (1991, pp. 167–95), as are secondary criteria, including *traces of Aramaic, Palestinian environment, vividness of narration, tendencies of the developing synoptic tradition* and *historical presumption.* Stanley E. Porter (2000) highlights Gerd Theissen's 'plausibility' as a criterion and puts forward *Aramaic and Greek as languages of Jesus, Greek language in its context, Greek textual variance* and *discourse features.*

earth in John appears to be rooted more in mythology than in history. Therefore, these criteria are valuable in distinguishing the Christ of faith from the Jesus of history, and their results are especially telling for assessing the relation of John's narration to the Jesus of history, producing a largely negative set of results.

b) *Weaknesses*: Problems with each of these methods abound, and they are especially problematic when taken together. The criterion of dissimilarity, if pushed hard, for instance, assumes that Jesus did nothing that his followers assimilated into their values and practices. It also infers that Jesus did nothing conventional, or if he did, it cannot count as part of the database distinguishing him from other prophets and rabbis in his day. While this method may indeed clarify what aspects of historicity are least likely to have been invented by later Christians, making a portrait out of the 'odd' memories is sure to produce a distorted presentation. So, even if the criterion of dissimilarity does produce clarity on some matters of historical plausibility its very emphasis upon distinctiveness produces a skewed image.[52]

The second criterion, multiple attestation, also is helpful for investigating the Jesus of history, especially when the presentations are not identical. Where they are identical, redaction may be inferred, and this diminishes the likelihood of more than one attestation being present. It may reflect a derivative relationship between gospel traditions. The Gospel of John, despite its distinctiveness, overlaps with other Gospels in significant ways, and it may therefore be assumed that Jesus probably did connect with the Baptist, create a Temple disturbance, preside at some sort of feeding and sea rescue, receive an anointing, undergo the Passion events, and was experienced in some way by his followers after his death. Indeed, these connections between John and the Synoptics provide the best test cases for analysis, and these have been the classic passages receiving analytical attention. What cannot be said, however, is that a singular or minority report is necessarily less credible. It may also be the case that particular details and distinctive presentations reflect an authentic historical memory, so this criterion can only be used to affirm, not to discount. For instance, if John were familiar with Mark, perhaps with the evangelist having heard a public reading of the material, or at least parts of it, distinctive material in John may be included with intentionality because such was not present in Mark. Again, this criterion may be used to affirm, but it cannot be used to deny a passage's historicity.

The third criterion, coherence is important for the distinguishing of the sort of Jesus we believe to have ministered in Palestine from more fanciful renderings in early Christianity. A lucid example of a non-cohering Jesus is the

---

presentation of boy-Jesus in the Infancy Gospel of Thomas, who makes pigeons out of clay that fly away after he claps his hands, who kills his friends with a curse when they anger him (only to bring them back to life again to make a happy ending), and who is instructed by Zacchaeus (a perfect child-size teacher) despite having written the languages himself. Despite some parallels with Luke's childhood narratives, this book falls way short of anything historical, largely because its rendering of Jesus does not cohere with more solid impressions. The vulnerability of this criterion, however, lies with its circularity. The impression of Jesus to which other presentations do or do not conform is itself based upon those same sources when applied to canonical Gospel analysis. This being the case, when the picture of the 'historical' Jesus is determined on the basis of information in the Synoptics – excluding John – and then this grid is applied over the Fourth Gospel to determine its authenticity, it is no wonder that John loses. What if the reverse were performed? What if a picture of the historical Jesus were determined upon the basis of John – the one purportedly eyewitness account – and material in the Synoptics were sifted through a Johannine grid and voted upon by scholars applying their criteria for determining historicity? The results would be entirely different from those starting with the Synoptics only. Perhaps the problem lies with excluding *any* primitive tradition when forming one's impression of a coherence standard – including John. When tradition-critical inclusion/exclusion methodologies build upon the Synoptics and second-century Gnostic texts to the exclusion of John, and then are used to find John wanting, this circular operation cannot but be regarded as dubious and critically flawed.

Nonetheless, in addition to the many aphoristic Jesus sayings in John mentioned above, many of the other 'coherent impressions of Jesus' rooted in Mark can also be found in John, though in slightly different forms. The 'Messianic Secret' in Mark, however, should not be regarded as Jesus' diminishing his messianic mission;[53] it is more precisely a reference to Jesus' eschewing popularistic and sensationalisitic appraisals of his ministry. Likewise, John presents Jesus as rejecting these features in his fleeing the crowd's design to rush him off for a Messianic coronation (Jn 6.14-15), his rebuking those requesting Messianic signs (Jn 2.18-19; 4.48; 6.26, 28-30; 20.29), his refusal to disclose himself openly because of a reluctance to embellish human testimony (Jn 2.23-5) and in these ways, the Johannine Jesus also eschews popularistic and sensationalistic notoriety parallel to the Messianic Secret of Mark. Likewise, in his declaration that his 'hour' was not yet come (Jn 2.4), but later in declaring the actualization of the *hora* of Jesus (Jn 12.23; 13.1; 17.1), the Johannine narrator works in a way parallel to the culmination of the Messianic Secret in Mark: tell no one until after the

---

53. This was Albert Schweitzer's review of Wrede's work: 'Because Wrede does not deal with the teaching of Jesus, he has no occasion to take account of the secret of the kingdom of God.' (Schweitzer, 2001, p. 312)

resurrection (Mk 9.9) when the meaning of his mission would be apparent. Therefore, the Messianic Secret has interesting parallels in Mark and John, and the mistake is to delimit a Markan trait to a narrow category. A second Markan motif is found pervasively in John, and that is a theology of the cross.[54] Indeed, the Johannine Jesus also invites his followers to join him in his suffering and death, and in Jesus' Johannine aphorisms (Jn 12.24-6), in his final discourses (Jn 15.15-16.33), and in his culminating section in the bread of life discourse (Jn 6.51-70), Jesus calls his followers to embrace the Way of the Cross. To ingest the flesh and blood of Jesus is to partner with him martyrologically, as the bread he offers is his flesh, given for the life of the world on the cross.[55] The point here is that if the distinctively Johannine rendering is accounted for, John is not as far away from the coherent view of Jesus; and, John may even contribute in its distinctive sort of way to the multiple attestation of Jesus' teachings about the Messianic Secret and the Way of the Cross. It cannot be said that these are totally absent from John.

The fourth criterion, naturalism, is one of the primary bases for questioning John's historicity to begin with. John's supranatural presentation of Jesus bears with it considerable problems for historicity. The Johannine Prologue presents Jesus in pre-existent terms, but it obviously does not qualify as part of the Johannine narrative. Jesus is presented as 'knowing' what is in people's hearts (Jn 1.48; 2.24-5; 4.3, 16-19; 5.6, 42; 6.15, 64) and is able to escape attempts to arrest and kill him (Jn 7.30; 8.59; 10.39). He also declares things in advance in order that their fulfilment might attest to his having been sent from God (Jn 13.18-19; 16.2-4; 18.8-9, 31-2), and his disciples experience his predictions' having come true (Jn 2.19-22; 3.14; 4.50-3; 6.51, 64-5; 7.33-4, 38-9; 8.21, 28; 10.11, 15-8; 11.4, 23; 12.24, 32-3; 13.33, 38; 14.2-3, 18-20, 23; 15.13; 16.16, 20, 28, 32; 18.9, 32), especially regarding his glorification. Jesus' signs, of course, are extremely problematic for a naturalistic modernist, although recent historical Jesus questers have been willing to allow for at least some healing and exorcist work to have been done by Jesus in keeping with contemporary figures. Certainly, the signs of Jesus were used apologetically as means of convincing members of the Johannine audience that Jesus was indeed the Jewish Messiah, and the embellishment of such narratives is likely. The problem with ascribing all of John to the canons of ahistoricity because of its wondrous elements is that John also has a great deal of incarnational and fleshly-Jesus material in it.[56] Out of his side flow physical blood and water

---

54. See J. T. Forestell (1974) for a full development of this theme.

55. See an intensive treatment of John 6 in Anderson (1996, pp. 48–250). Parallel to the 'sacramental' imagery of Jesus' reference to the drinking of his cup and sharing in his baptism in Mark 10.35-45, John 6.51-8 likewise calls the hearer/reader to the martyrological willingness to suffer and die with Jesus if demanded by life to do so, and this is *why* the disciples were scandalized and why some abandoned him. They did not misunderstand Jesus; they understood full well his hard saying as a reference to the cost of discipleship and the Way of the Cross (1996, pp. 110–36, 207–20).

56. See Udo Schnelle (1992) and Marianne Meye Thompson (1988).

(Jn 19.34), Thomas is allowed to touch with his finger the flesh wounds of Jesus (Jn 20.27), and his disciples must ingest his flesh-and-bloodness (Jn 6.51-8) if they hope to participate in the life he avails. Jesus also weeps (Jn 11.35), his heart is deeply troubled (Jn 11.33; 12.27; 13.21), he groans (Jn 11.33, 38), on the cross he thirsts (Jn 19.28), and he loves his own (Jn 11.3, 5, 36; 13.1, 23, 34; 14.21; 15.9, 10, 12; 19.26; 20.2; 21.7, 20) with *pathos,* enough to be called the 'pathetic' Jesus.[57] Indeed, John's elevated presentation of Jesus has been one of the most provocative aspects of Christian material, leading the Church into centuries of debate over metaphysical aspects of Christology, but every bit as present is John's presentation of the incarnational Jesus.[58] Just as the Church Fathers and Mothers had to keep these polar aspects of the Johannine dialectic in tension, so must modern critical scholars if they are to remain fair to John. Holding John's elevated material at bay is understandable for the modern critic, but if the elevated Christological elements in John are considered apart from the humiliated elements, and the entire historicity of the Fourth Gospel is rejected on the basis of such a distortion, such moves commit the fallacy of a sweeping generalization and are less than worthy as 'critical' scholarship. It could also be that the apparently miraculous in John does not always require a supernatural categorization, but to neglect the entirety of John's incarnational thrust is to push John beyond itself. Such is flawed as an exegetical and as a historiographic move.

Part of the problem in applying the above methods to determining degrees of historicity within John is that the standards over and against which John is measured do not include Johannine content to begin with in setting the template. John is especially excluded from setting dissimilarity and coherence standards, and when these grids are plied back over the Johannine text it is little wonder that they produce a dearth of historical material. Where the great promise of critical scholarship has been its objective neutrality, the historical treatment of John comes across as less than that. When John's material is deemed different from the Synoptics it is excluded; where it is similar it is relegated to a derivative relationship to a non-Johannine source (either Mark or a hypothetical source that looked like Mark), elevated Christological themes are credited to mythological origins, and mundane references are attributed to mimetic imitations of reality. Therefore, not only the results of the scholarly 'consensus' regarding John's irrelevance to the Jesus quest deserve fresh critical analysis, but so do the *procedures* by which these 'results' have been established.

---

57. For further detail, see Anderson (2000b).

58. The fact of John's Christological tensions is the most interesting feature of Johannine theology, and they possess basically four epistemological origins: the agency Christology rooted in Deuteronomy 18, the dialectical thinking of the evangelist, the evolving needs of the Johannine situation, and the evangelist's employment of rhetorical devices as a means of engaging the reader in an imaginary dialogue with Jesus. See Anderson (1996, pp. 252–65 and 1999b).

If specific criteria for performing analyses of John's historicity were to be devised, in addition to the above, some of them might include the following. a) Examine passages most similar between John and the Synoptics in order to get a full sense of particular similarities and differences. These passages would include the treatment of John the Baptist, the Temple cleansing, events surrounding John 6 (feeding, sea-crossing, discussion of the feeding and Peter's confession) the anointing of Jesus, the Passion narratives and the appearance narratives, among others. b) Consider the material omitted and used by Matthew and Luke (in their redactions of Mark) and see if that sort of analysis suggests anything about John. Upon analysis, two primary kinds of material in Mark tend to be omitted: non-symbolic illustrative detail, and theological asides. As the presence of these sorts of material is more prolific in Mark and John, this may lend insight into the oral rather than written character of the Markan and Johannine traditions. c) Make allowance for the Johannine paraphrasing of earlier tradition and integrate such material with potential parallels emerging from Synoptic studies. Conceptual parallels should be considered and explored in addition to extended identical verbal ones only. d) Allow knowledge of John's development to impact one's understanding of Synoptic developments. Perhaps Mark's compilation was not entirely ordered by chronological information, but some of it appears to have involved grouping all the Jerusalem events and most of the judgement sayings at the end. Perhaps Luke and Q used the oral Johannine tradition as one of their sources. Perhaps the Matthean and Johannine traditions were in dialogue with each other about governance and how Christ would lead the church. The benefits of intertextual gospel analysis extend in more than one direction. e) Reconsider the pneumatic teaching of the Johannine Jesus in the light of charismatic appraisals of the historical Jesus. Despite distinctive presentations, not all early-Christian spirituality was Gnostic. More congruities may exist there than we might have supposed. These are a few of the means for exploring historicity we might construct if we were doing historical Jesus studies with John in the mix.

5) *The History-of-Religions Background of John*
If John's narration is not rooted in the life and ministry of Jesus an alternative explanation must be put forward as to where the material came from, and the mythological religious background of the evangelist is the best option available. With the miracle-working stories of the likes of Apollonius of Tyana in the region several decades after Jesus' ministry, and with the reports of Simon Magnus in Acts, it is easy to conceive of the Johannine narration's embellishment along these aretological lines. Likewise, many signs and wonders from the Hebrew Scriptures have echoes in John, and just as Homer described great narratives of sea rescues and wondrous adventures, so does the Fourth Evangelist.[59] Bultmann's view, of course, was that a *Theios Anēr* (a miracle-

---

59. See above descriptions of the Moses and Elijah typologies embodied by the Johannine Jesus.

working God/Man) mythic construct prevalent in the contemporary social milieu would have affected the telling of the Jesus story, that the evangelist found himself both furthering such mythic constructs, and that he also found himself needing to deconstruct such aretologies existentially. Likewise, revelation discourses found in contemporary Jewish and Gnostic literature would have impacted the ways the teachings of the Johannine Jesus were crafted and rendered. If the origin of John's material were mythological, these reported events need not have happened in history for them to have been narrated meaningfully in John's first-century Jewish and Hellenistic setting.

a) *Strengths*: Several attractive features to this view include the fact that stories of miracle-workers and divine men abounded in the first-century Mediterranean world.[60] The wisdom myth of early Judaism is presented as the pre-existent and creative agency of God;[61] Philostratus described how Apollonius of Tyana performed many miracles and even described how Apollo of Delphi could turn water into wine if he wanted to;[62] when the son of Rabban Gameliel was ill, Hanina ben Dosa prayed for him from afar and he was made well that very hour;[63] the well in Asclepius' temple had healing powers to it when the waters were stirred;[64] at the consummation of time the treasuries of heaven will open and manna will descend from heaven;[65] the histories of Seutonius and Tacitus report the emperor Vespasian's applying spittle to a blind man's eyes and the resultant recovery;[66] and Homer describes a thundering response from heaven as the prayer of Odysseus was apparently well received by Zeus.[67] In these and other ways the investigation of John's history-of-religions background is essential for understanding the origin and formation of the Johannine narrative.

b) *Weaknesses*: While Jewish and Hellenistic hero stories and mythic constructs clearly would have impacted gospel narrations of Jesus' ministry, this is not the same as claiming that they comprised the sole origin of the Johannine

---

60. The *Hellenistic Commentary to the New Testament*, edited by M. Eugene Boring *et al.*, (1995) presents 132 Hellenistic parallels to the material in the Gospel of John. Most of these are later, but they nonetheless suggest the sorts of Jewish and Hellenistic mythic views that would have been embraced by the Fourth Evangelist and his audiences.

61. *Ibid*, p. 238. See Jn 1.1-5, Proverbs 3.19; 8.22-30, and Bultmann's reconstruction of this myth (pp. 22–3).

62. *Ibid*, p. 249. See Jn 2.1-11 and Philostratus, *Life of Apollonius of Tyana* 6.10.

63. *Ibid*, p. 266. See Jn 4.46-54 and *Berakoth* 34B.

64. *Ibid*. See Jn 5.1-15 and Aelius Arestides, 'Regarding the Well in the Temple of Asclepius', *Speech* 39:14-15.

65. *Ibid*, p. 271. See Jn 6.1-31 and *2 Bar.* 28.2.

66. *Ibid*, pp. 238–308. See Jn 9.6, Seutonius, *Lives of Caesar* 7, and Tacitus, *Histories*, 4:89.

67. *Ibid*, p. 292. See Jn 12.29 and Homer, *The Odyssey* 20:97-104.

narrative. This is the first and cardinal weakness of assuming that the presentation of Jesus in the mould of contemporary mythic constructs has thoroughly displaced the historical origin of the entire Johannine narrative. A narrative's developmental history cannot disprove its originative history. A second weakness is the fact that evidence for non-Johannine sources has not been convincing enough to merit credence in the sort of source-critical inferences made by Bultmann and others as to where the Johannine material may have come from.[68] That being the case, aretological and Gnostic material coming into the Johannine tradition from afar is diminished in its plausibility. A third weakness with imputing Hellenistic mythic constructs onto the Johannine tradition is that John's Jewish background is already quite clear. As mentioned above, the Johannine Jesus clearly is presented as fulfilling the Jewish typologies of Moses and Elijah, and he is explicitly credited with fulfilling many Messianic associations within the Jewish Scriptures. Even the Logos Christology of the Prologue bears considerable similarities with Genesis 1, and if the Dead Sea Scrolls had been discovered 20 years earlier, Bultmann would not have been able to have written the commentary that he did. Dualism was Jewish as well as Hellenistic, and John's Jesus is portrayed clearly as a Jewish Messiah repackaged for later Jewish and Hellenistic audiences.[69] A fourth weakness is that despite the many similarities to contemporary mythologies, John's narration is time and again closer to the Synoptic renderings of Jesus, though it cannot be said that John is close enough to have depended upon them. This being the case, the bi-optic theory of John and Mark – representing two individuated and yet somewhat interfluential gospel traditions – offers the best explanation of their primary historical origins. History-of-religions information illuminates the background and world-views of John and its audiences, but it cannot suffice as the sole, or even the primary, historical origin of the Johannine narrative.

6) *Emerging Portraits of Jesus*
One of the contributions emerging from recent Jesus studies is the sketching of several 'portraits' of Jesus, each of them rooted in first-century historical images of religious and philosophical leaders. Marcus Borg's digest of images of Jesus in contemporary scholarship has been very helpful for understanding these constructs (1994). Borg lists four major portraits of Jesus representing some of the most creative work of contemporary Jesus scholars. First, envisioning Jesus as a non-eschatological prophet allows us to see him against a backdrop of Jewish prophets who were not about apocalyptic futurism but about justice and social reform in the present. Second, envisioning Jesus as a wisdom-imparting

---

68. Robert Kysar's changing of his mind regarding evidence for sources underlying John (p. 40) in *The Review of Biblical Literature* 1 (1999, pp. 38–42) represents a significant shift, I believe.

69. Maurice Casey (1991). See, however, the impressive analysis of the history-of-religions background of the Johannine Prologue by Karl-Josef Kuschel (1992, pp. 363–95).

sage fits with the Q tradition and his short, pithy sayings about the character of the Kingdom of God. Third, envisioning Jesus as an institution-challenging cynic fits his tendency to challenge the conventionality of his Jewish and Roman setting, and it coheres with his dining with 'sinners' and healing on the Sabbath as provocative actions. Fourth, envisioning Jesus as a holy man reconnects his healings and spiritual ministries with the sorts of things that an indigenous healer and exorcist might do. A fifth portrait, not covered by Borg but substantive nonetheless, involves envisioning Jesus as an apocalyptic messenger.[70] Each of these portraits provides a heuristic lens through which to understand more clearly the ministry and message of the Jesus of history.

a) *Strengths*: Because each of these portraits is rooted in socio-religious models contemporary with the historical Jesus, it does not take much imagination to reconfigure one's understanding of Jesus within one or more of these moulds. This is why John's presentation of Jesus who speaks primarily of his relation to the Father, who speaks about himself and the authenticity of his mission, and who performs miraculous signs while at the same time de-emphasizing their importance might seem at odds with any or all of these portraits. That being the case, the Jesus of the religious anthropologist becomes more attractive historically than the spiritualized Jesus of the Fourth Gospel for many a Jesus scholar.

b) *Weaknesses*: However, a closer look at the Johannine text makes such disjunctive judgements hard to understand. Despite John's pervasive non-dependence upon the Synoptic traditions, the case can be made that each of these portraits does find a home in John's presentation of Jesus, in some ways more clearly than his presentation in any one of the Synoptic Gospels. Consider, for instance, the presentation in John of Jesus as a non-eschatological prophet. The primary history-of-religions image embodied by the Johannine Jesus is the prophet-like-Moses typology rooted in Deut. 18.15-22.[71] Rather than a Gnostic revealer-myth, the Father–Son relationship in John is ordered by Jesus' sense of having been sent by the Father claiming to speak only what he has seen and heard from the Father (Deut. 18.15). Therefore, God's words will be his words and vice versa (Deut. 18.18), people will be held accountable by God in reference to their response to Jesus as God's agent (Deut. 18.19), and the way the authentic prophet is distinguishable from the false prophet is that the true prophet's words come true (Deut. 18.22). The Johannine Jesus fulfils the Mosaic typology in multiple ways,[72] and it is even arguable that

---

70. See especially Bart D. Ehrman's *Jesus: Apocalyptic Prophet of the New Millennium*, Oxford / New York: Oxford University Press (1999) for an excellent overview of this portrait.

71. See Anderson (1999a).

72. Jan-A Bühner (1977); T.F. Glasson (1963); and Adele Reinhartz (1989) support this typology being found in John.

John's Mosaic-prophet typology may have been closer to the historical Jesus' self-understanding than the Synoptic king-like-David royal typology. The Johannine Jesus claims to be sent from the Father, not speaking on his own behalf, but claiming to represent the Father fully, in keeping with the agency typology of Deut. 18.15-22. In these ways, he fits the prophetic model entirely.

The Johannine Jesus can also be conceived within the portraiture of a wisdom-imparting sage. In the Fourth Gospel, Jesus not only brings divine wisdom; he *is* the Word and Wisdom of God (Prov. 8.22-30) to the world and imparts saving knowledge to all who believe. John's Wisdom Christology has not gone unnoticed by scholars, nor has its sapiential thrust. Jesus not only brings light to penetrate the darkness of worldly thought; he *is* the Light of the world (Jn 1.4, 5, 8, 9; 3.19; 8.12; 9.5; 12.46). Those who come to him are drawn by the Father and are taught by God (Jn 6.44-50; cf. Isa. 54.13; Deut. 8.3),[73] and Jesus has amassed great learning without having received formal training (Jn 7.15). Even Greeks come from afar to drink from the wisdom of Jesus (Jn 12.20-1). The theme of personified wisdom is more centrally featured in John than it is in Q, and indeed, the case can be made that the 'bolt out of the Johannine blue' in Matthew and Luke actually reflects the Q tradition's dependence on the primitive Johannine tradition.[74] The point is that the Johannine wisdom motif is used to describe the mission and message of Jesus in ways that are striking and also independent from the Synoptic traditions.

John also presents Jesus readily as an institution-challenging cynic in that Jesus cleanses the Temple at the beginning of his ministry, heals on the Sabbath, confronts religious authorities in Jerusalem prolifically, and is willing to challenge the Roman governor in the name of God's transcendent truth and reign. The Johannine Jesus challenges all that is of human origin, being the manifestation of the divine initiative, and the revelation of God scandalizes political, religious and worldly authority. It can also be claimed that the juxtaposition of the Beloved Disciple and Peter in John functioned to challenge rising institutionalization within the late first-century church, and it did so in the name of Jesus' original intentionality. At least seven parallels in John can be identified with some relation to the keys of the Kingdom passage in Matthew 16.17-19, and yet, they are all different. Does this imply that they may have been corrective parallels, clearing the ground within the Christian movement for the pneumatic work of the *Parakletos*?[75] Indeed, the

73. Raymond E. Brown (2003) includes a special section on 'Wisdom Motifs' (pp. 259–65). In this section Brown argues that personified wisdom associations with Jesus are even stronger than in any of the other canonical gospels. See also Michael E. Willett-Newhart (1992), Sharon H. Ringe (1999) and Ben Witherington III (1995) for the wisdom motif in John.

74. Certainly this is more plausible than inferring a characteristically Johannine theme came from one small unit in Q – the theme is pervasively Johannine (see Anderson, 2002b, pp. 48–50).

75. See Table #20 in Anderson (1996, p. 240); likewise, see Anderson (1997, pp. 50–7).

presentation of Jesus challenging conventionalities and all that is of human origin in the name of the transcendent God is as clear in John as it is anywhere in the New Testament.

Likewise, Jesus certainly comes across with spiritual power as a *holy man* in John. While he does not perform exorcisms, the Johannine Jesus is encountered by people epiphanically. Like Nathanael and the Samaritan woman, actants in the Johannine narrative experience themselves as being known by God in their encounters with Jesus, and even a royal official believes Jesus might be able to do his household some good. Jesus' signs demonstrate that he is come from God, and his teachings are experienced as authoritative by those who are open to the truth. Upon encountering the presence of the divine in Jesus, those who meet him experience themselves as being known by God. Indeed, in telling the Johannine story the Greek device of *anagorisis* (a recognition marker)[76] is used, but this does not mean that the reports themselves were entirely fictive in their origins. They may have been, but proving so has yet to be established. Given the Johannine belief that the work of 'another' *Parakletos* is continuous with the ministry of Jesus, it is not too far off the mark to consider that Jesus is remembered as evoking human-divine encounter, much like any holy or spirit-imbued person would have done. In that sense, Jesus as a holy man cannot be said to be incompatible with the Johannine presentation of Jesus. This portrait also fits John well.

A final portrait also works with John's presentation of Jesus, and as an apocalyptic messenger, the Johannine Jesus comes to the world dividing the children of God from those whose spiritual origins and investments are other.[77] All who come to the light receive the newness of life and are given the authority to become the children of God (Jn 1.12). The time is come, and now is, that even the dead will hear the voice of the Son and will live (Jn 5.25), and those who believe will be raised up at the end of the age (Jn 6.39, 40, 44, 54). The Johannine Son of Man indeed comes as an eschatological agent, and the paradoxical exaltation of Jesus on the cross brings about the glory of God. The prince of this world is overthrown by Jesus in John (Jn 12.31), and eschatological judgement is effected by the mission and glorification of the Son of Man, who ascends and descends in ways Danielic (Dan. 7.13; Jn 1.51; 6.62). In these and other ways, despite John's mystical passages and emphases upon loving one another, the apocalyptic motif comes through clearly, and the entire ministry of Jesus is presented eschatologically in John. What certainly cannot be said is that the portraiture of

---

76. See the development of this feature in R. Alan Culpepper (1998, pp. 71–83).

77. John's dualism is somewhat parallel to the dualism of the *War Scroll* of Qumran. The strife between the Children of Light and the Children of Darkness connects with John's dualism of decision, and the response to Jesus as the saving/revealing agent of God is itself an eschatological event in John. See Raymond E. Brown (2003, pp. 139–42), and see John Ashton (1991, pp. 205–37).

Jesus as an apocalyptic prophet is fundamentally at odds with the Johannine narration. It too is found in John, but in an autonomous and distinctive set of ways.

A consideration of the 'portraits' of Jesus emerging from the latest Jesus scholarship demonstrates that each of these, rather than being at irreconcilable odds with the Johannine presentation of Jesus, finds impressive echoes and actualization in John despite John's autonomous rendering of Jesus and his ministry. One might even make the case that any of these portraits might be sketched more clearly from Johannine material than from any of the other Gospels, and this is a puzzling prospect if John's irrelevance to historical Jesus studies is to be taken as an established fact. The fact is, though, that such is not a fact, but a hypothesis, and it is a hypothesis that has many exceptions and problems to it. One also wonders what might happen if new grids were developed for conducting Jesus research employing such second-century works as the Acts of Pilate, the Apocryphon of James, the Dialogue of the Saviour, the Gospel of Truth and the Gospel of Judas – in addition to the Gospel of Thomas – in seeking to establish a new set of criteria for investigating the Jesus of history in ways more consonant with the Johannine witness. How do we know, for instance, that the charismatic and Spirit-emphasizing Jesus of history is not replicated in the pneumatic Jesus of the Fourth Gospel?[78] One could argue a sustained case that John contributes key elements, not only of the historical outline of Jesus' ministry, but also of the spiritual character of his work. As a plank in the platform of the de-Johannification of Jesus, the presentation of recent Jesus portraits *versus* John appears to demonstrate the opposite when examined critically.

In summary, of the planks in the platform of the de-Johannification of Jesus, all of them are constructed in response to real problems needing to be addressed, and all of them have certain strengths. However, when each of them is considered critically to see how solid it might be, each of them betrays considerable weaknesses and multiple exceptions to the norms that are claimed. While John is close to Mark, none of John's similarities are identical. In that sense, the bi-optic view of John and Mark is confirmed as two traditional sources plausibly going back to the ministry of Jesus. Diachronic theories have failed to demonstrate alien material as foundational sources for John, and a two-edition theory of composition is the most likely. John's lateness does not discount the possibility of primitivity, and in fact there is a great deal of detail in John that is best accounted for on the basis of having

---

78. Consider, for instance, Martin Hengel's monograph (1981) in the light of John's pneumatic presentation of Jesus, for instance; or, consider insights into the Spirit-based ministry of historical Jesus from the perspective of Gary Burge's monograph (1987) as potential ways forward. If Jesus challenged institutions and society in the name of spirituality and unmediated access to the divine, John as a resource has not yet begun to be tapped for historical-Jesus studies.

been earlier rather than later. Criteria for determining historicity are often circular, and being largely constructed out of Synoptic material, thus say very little about John when used to discredit John's historicity. A history-of-religions analysis of John shows that John is closer to the Synoptics than pagan or Jewish aretologies and mythologies, so arguing derivation from such sources rather than influence is specious. Finally, the portraits of Jesus emerging from Synoptic studies actually *affirm* John's authenticity rather than discredit it, as each of them may be fulfilled by the Johannine presentation of Jesus with independent lucidity. Despite the rigour with which John has been marginalized from Jesus studies, the above analysis suggests that because none of these planks possesses compelling integrity, the larger platform itself cannot be said to be able to support much weight. Like the de-historicization of John, the de-Johannification of Jesus is an equally feeble foundation on which anything of critical worth may be established.

Findings

As neither the de-historicization of John nor the de-Johannification of Jesus is constructed of solid material, neither can be said to be able to support much weight for constructing gospel or Jesus studies. Indeed, each of the planks in both platforms is constructed in response to real problems, but not a single one of them is compelling in laying a foundation for either platform. In many cases fallacies of logic are evident, and in most cases only parts of the data are considered. Distortions of Johannine and Synoptic material might appear to make a plank more sturdy, but when analysed critically, the facts and procedures themselves raise questions with the analyses and their conclusions. In fact, some of the planks in each platform possess greater weaknesses than strengths, and a critical appraisal of the subject must question sweeping generalizations that are made on such presumptions.

So, in response to our earlier question, is the de-historicization of John and the de-Johannification of Jesus an open-and-shut case, a 'consensus' among critical scholars (which fails to include most of the leading Johannine scholars over the last two centuries) to be embraced as a solid set of platforms on which to construct future investigations? One might be happy if it were so. Jesus studies could just continue along without Johannine interference, and Johannine studies could just continue without raising historical-critical questions. Unfortunately, neither platform, nor any of the planks composing it, is solid. In the light of the above analysis, the 'critically established consensus' is *neither*; more work has yet to be done.

Table 2.6

A Brief Comparison/Contrast between John and the Synoptics

A. *Differences*:

Synoptics   John

1. *The Beginnings of the Respective Gospels*:

Matthew and Luke include birth narratives	John begins with the Prologue
Matthew and Luke profess the virgin birth	John declares the Logos to be preexistent
John the Baptist introduces Jesus	John the Baptist magnifies Jesus

2. *Style and Language*:

Special vocabulary: 'repent', 'demon', 'tax collectors', 'adultery', 'inherit', 'forgiveness'	*Special vocabulary*: 'only begotten', '*Logos*', 'fulness', 'true' 'world', 'Father', 'Son'
Special themes: righteousness, purity, sin, first-last ordering, following Jesus	*Special themes*: knowing, seeing, believing, love, light, life, being sent by God, truth
Parables describe the Kingdom of God	I-Am sayings describe Jesus as the King
Adversaries are Pharisees and Sadducees	Adversaries are 'the Jews' and Judeans
Sayings are short and pithy	Discourses are long and extended
Dialogues are short and simple	Dialogues with Jesus are many and complex

3. *Chronology and Order of events*:

One year of Jesus' ministry	Three Passovers imply 2 or 3 years of ministry
Jesus goes *once* to Jerusalem and is then killed	Jesus goes to and from Jerusalem many times
Last Supper on Friday (as a Passover meal)	Last Supper on Thursday (day of Preparation)
Temple is cleansed at the end of Jesus' ministry	Temple is cleansed at the beginning
Jesus is arrested due to the Temple incident	Jesus is arrested due to the sign of Lazarus
First miracles were in or near Capernaum	First miracles were in Cana of Galilee
Peter's confession follows the feeding of the 4,000	Peter's confession follows the feeding of the 5,000
Jesus' ministry begins after the Baptist's arrest	Jesus ministers concurrently with the Baptist

4. *Inclusions of Events/Portrayals of Jesus*:

Missing from John	*Only in John*
John the Baptist's immersing of Jesus	The Wedding at Cana – the first sign
The temptation in the wilderness	The challenging of Jesus to provide more bread
Peter's confession: Jesus is 'the Christ'	John the Baptist's witness: 'the Lamb of God'
The Transfiguration	The raising of Lazarus
Jesus prays for himself at Gethsemane	Jesus prays for his followers
The institution of the Eucharist at the last supper	Jesus' washing of his disciples' feet
The cry of dereliction	The piercing of Jesus' side
The calling of the Twelve	The calling of the four
The predicted martyrdom of the sons of Zebedee	The predicted martyrdom of Peter

Synoptics	John

5. *Deviations* (differences in portrayal):

Synoptics	John
The Baptist fulfils Elijah and Moses typologies	The Baptist denies being Moses or Elijah
Jesus goes out often to pray before critical times	Jesus knows full well what will happen
Jesus commands Messianic secrecy ('Tell no one…')	Jesus advocates Messianic disclosure ('I am…')
Plot development is linear	Plot development is cyclical-progressive
Jesus' sayings are self-contained	Jesus' sayings expand upon the signs
Jesus' head is anointed (Mt. and Mk)	Jesus' feet are anointed (and Lk.)
The cock crows twice (Mk)	The cock crows once (and Mt. and Lk.)

6. *The Miracles of Jesus*:

Synoptics	John
Exorcisms are the most common miracle	Exorcisms are totally absent
Jesus healed many lepers	Jesus healed no lepers
The Kingdom advances by binding the strong man	The Kingdom advances by the furthering of truth
Miracles are works of power	Miracles are vehicles of revelation
Miracles are often the result of faith	Miracles are intended to lead people to faith
The dearth of miracles betrays lack of human faith	The dearth of miracles avails the glory of God
Little tension – miracles establish the Kingdom	Much tension – signs are elevated and diminished

7. *Significant Theological Differences abound*:

Synoptics	John
Jesus instructs his disciples to baptize (Mt.)	It is emphasized that Jesus never baptized
Peter (and company) receive 'keys' (Mt.)	Peter affirms Jesus' singular authority
Disciples are the light of the world (Mt.)	Jesus himself is the light of the world
Jesus' return is promised before disciples' death	Jesus did not promise such a return
Elijah and Moses are present at the Transfiguration	Jesus fulfils Moses and Elijah typologies
Jesus' divinity is a factor of the Virgin Birth	Jesus' divinity is a factor of being the *Logos*
The feeding's value is 'they ate and were satisfied'	Flawed valuation is 'they ate and were satisfied'

B. *However, Despite Many Differences, there are Significant Similarities*:

- Basic structure of the Passion narrative: Jesus' entry, supper, garden praying, separation from the disciples, his arrest, trials (Jewish and Roman), execution, burial, resurrection and appearances
- A basic similarity of chronology (beginning, middle, ending)
- Various similarities (John 6) feeding, sea crossing, discourse, confessions of Peter
- Various sayings are quite similar: love of others, love of God, life comes from dying, etc.
- Comparable metaphors of sheep/shepherd, seed – death/life, light of the world, etc.

Part III
Interfluential, Formative and Dialectical –
A Theory of John's Relation to the Synoptics

'In addition to the material drawn from this independent tradition, John has a few elements that
seem to suggest a more direct cross-influence from
the Synoptic tradition.'

Raymond E. Brown, *An Introduction to the Gospel of John*
(ed. by Francis J. Moloney; New York: Doubleday,
2003, p. 104)

While John's tradition is pervasively autonomous and independent of the Synoptics, the Johannine tradition shows evidence of engagement with various aspects of the Synoptic Gospels and traditions. Multiple non-identical similarities with Mark suggest an 'interfluential' set of relationships between the pre-Markan and the early Johannine tradition. At least three dozen times Luke departs from Mark and sides with John, suggesting that Luke has drawn from the Johannine tradition, probably within John's oral stages of development. Even Q shows evidence of Johannine influence, and this fact demands investigation. Matthean and Johannine traditions appear to have engaged similar issues related to their local Jewish communities, and they also evidence an intramural set of discussions regarding the emergence of structure and matters of egalitarian and Spirit-based aspects of leadership. Within this theory of John's relation to the Synoptics, John's tradition is assumed to have been both early and late. While John's tradition appears to be finalized latest among the Gospels, it is neither derivative from alien (non-Johannine) sources nor any of the Synoptic traditions. Rather, the Fourth Gospel represents an independent reflection upon the ministry of Jesus produced in at least two editions, and these factors will be drawn together in suggesting an overall theory of Johannine-Synoptic relations.

John's relation to the Synoptic Gospels has been a fascinating area of study over the last century or more, and yet many studies fall prey to errors that affect adversely the quality of one's analysis. One fallacy involves the notion that John's relation to Matthew, Mark and Luke would have been uniform rather than tradition-specific. Whatever their degree and character, contacts between John and each of the gospel traditions probably had its own particular history, and these factors probably extended to differing traditional forms as well as content-related issues. A second fallacy is the notion that the lateness of John's finalization implies necessarily John's dependence upon Synoptic traditions as the primary option for consideration. John's tradition was early as well as late, and it may be more suitable to view the Johannine tradition as having had an effect on other traditions instead of viewing Synoptic influence upon John as the only possibility. A third fallacy involves the uncritical assumption that the tradition histories and editorial processes operative between the traditions and workings of the first three evangelists are necessarily indicative of those of the Fourth. John's tradition appears *not* to have been transmitted or gathered in disparate formal categories or units as does the pre-Markan material, and evidence that the Fourth Evangelist employed alien (non-Johannine) written sources, as did the First and Third Evangelists, is virtually nonexistent.

An adequate theory of John's relation to the Synoptics must bear these potential pitfalls in mind, seeking to move ahead on the basis of the most plausible inferences to be drawn from the best evidence available. The Fourth Evangelist was probably aware of written Mark and may even have done some patterning of his written account after Mark's gospel genre. It is less likely that the Fourth Evangelist knew Luke or Matthew in their written forms, and yet traces of Johannine material can also be found in Acts. This is an interesting and provocative fact. The Johannine and Matthean traditions appear to have shared a common set of goals in reaching local Jewish communities with the gospel of Jesus as the Jewish Messiah, but their communities apparently had also endured hardship within the process. With the rise of further problems with Gentile Christians and issues related to church maintenance and organization, these traditions appear to have been engaged in dialectical sets of explorations regarding apologetics, ecclesiology and Christocracy – the effectual means by which the risen Lord continues to lead the church. In these and other ways, John's relation to the Synoptic traditions appears to have been interfluential, formative and dialectical.

The present discussion is necessitated, among other things, by the pervasive failure of the last century's leading critical approaches to the tradition-history of the Fourth Gospel. As a critical scholar, one is entirely pleased to accept and assimilate any theory of John's composition that is sound and plausible. However, the soundness of an argument depends on the veracity of the premises and the validity of its reasoning. In addition, the plausibility of an overall view must be considered as it relates to other constellations of issues. On these matters, the best of the twentieth century's investigations into the history and development of the Johannine tradition produce a dismal set of prospects when trying to find something solid on which to build. One can understand why the last three decades of Johannine studies have seen the near abandonment of historical/critical investigations altogether by some scholars, opting instead for analyses of the literary features and artistry of the Johannine text. Indeed, investigations of John's rhetorical design and capacity to elicit particular responses from the reader are worthy of consideration, and they are genuinely helpful to interpreters regardless of what can be known or inferred of John's authorship, composition or tradition-history.

On the other hand, the genre of John, while it was indeed a rhetorically oriented composition, is not that of an imaginative fiction. While narrative features are definitely intrinsic to the composition of John, these narratives presuppose actual events, claiming at times to be reflections upon them – wrongly or rightly – and even these narrations must be considered in the light of other traditions internal and external to the Jesus movement. These findings, while argued in greater detail elsewhere, now become the starting place for further investigations of the epistemological origins of the Johannine tradition. While this tradition appears to have been finalized the latest among the gospels, it is by no means devoid of its own claims to autonomy, and even primacy. In fact, the Johannine tradition comes across as the most complete and self-assured of the four canonical traditions, and yet it probably enjoyed at least contact with the other gospel traditions along the way. Ascertaining those relationships will be the primary task to which the rest of the present investigation is dedicated.

A. *John's Relation to Mark: Interfluential, Augmentive, and Corrective*

Because Johannine source-critical hypotheses by and large lack sufficient evidence to convince (although the venture itself is not misguided), and because John was completed around the turn of the first century CE, many scholars have moved back toward a view of Synoptic dependence, against the previously accepted judgement of P. Gardner-Smith that John's was a pervasively independent tradition. While many of these studies have rightly identified similarities – and therefore possible connections – between John and the Synoptics, the assumption that John simply knew one or more of the Synoptics in written form and 'did his own thing' with earlier material is often wielded in unrestrained and unsubstantiated ways. John is also very different from Mark, and this fact must be accounted for. Connections identified, however, are not redactions demonstrated, and adequate judgements require more considered and examined measures. The Johannine tradition appears to have intersected with each of the Synoptic Gospels, but in different ways, suggested by the frequency and character of contacts with each. In no case are the similarities identical, so as to suggest direct dependence on a written text. In all cases, the contacts appear to have occurred during the oral stages of both Synoptic and Johannine traditions, but these contacts appear also to have developed in different ways and at different times. The following proposals reflect an attempt to weigh and explain the particular evidence adequately.

1) John and Mark: An 'Interfluential Set of Relationships' during the Oral Stages of their Respective Traditions
While Barrett and others have identified clear connections between John's and Mark's vocabulary and ordering of material, huge differences also exist. As demonstrated elsewhere (Anderson 1996, pp. 97–104), there are at least 21 points of similarity between John 6 and Mark 8, and 24 points of similarity between John 6 and Mark 6, but *none* of these are identical contacts. The same sort of phenomena are found between John's and Mark's Passion narratives and at other points of contact – albeit somewhat unevenly – and John's and Mark's outlines of Jesus' ministry show many similarities, but again, no identical ones.[1] This fact is extremely significant as it pertains to the issue of Johannine/Markan relations. It suggests, nay demonstrates, that the Fourth

---

1. See C.K. Barrett (1978, pp. 42–66). Besides the similarities between the events of John 6 and Mark, see, for instance, parallels between Mark and John regarding the ministry of John the Baptist (Jn 1.6-8, 15, 19-34; Mk 1.2-11), the calling of the disciples (Jn 1.35-51; Mk 1.16-20; 3.13-19), the cleansing of the Temple (Jn 2.13-22; Mk 11.15-19, 27-33; 14.57-8; 15.29), the journey into Galilee (Jn 4.1-3, 43-6; Mk 1.14-15), and the dishonoring of the home-town prophet motif (Jn 4.39-45; Mk 6.4-6). In the later periods of Jesus' ministry we have plots to kill Jesus, (Jn 11.45-57; Mk 14.1-2), the anointing of Jesus (Jn 12.1-8; Mk 14.3-9), the entry into Jerusalem (Jn 12.12-19; Mk 11.1-10), the last supper (Jn 13.1-20; Mk 14.17-25) and Jesus' prediction of Peter's betrayal (Jn 13.36-8; Mk 14.26-31), the promise of the Holy Spirit's help during times of trial (Jn 14.15-31; 15.26-7; 16.1-15; Mk 13.11), the garden scene and the arrest of Jesus (Jn 18.1-13; Mk 14.26-52), the

Evangelist did *not* use Mark as a written source, at least not in the ways Matthew and Luke did. Otherwise, there would be at least several identical connections rather than a broad similarity of some words, themes and patterns. Conversely, due to the large numbers of Johannine/Markan similarities, contacts probably did exist between the oral renderings of John's and Mark's traditions, and yet because it is impossible to determine which direction the influence may have gone, the relationship may best be considered one of 'interfluentiality'. It is also unlikely that it only went in one direction between two formative-yet-independent traditions.

It is also a fact that the kinds of material common to John and Mark alone are often conspicuously the same types of material omitted by Matthew and Luke in their redactions of Mark: non-symbolic, illustrative detail (apparently considered superfluous by later redactors of a written narrative source), and *theological asides* (either omitted, perhaps as digressions, or replaced by common-sense conjecture about what Jesus intended or would have done – usually showing marks of the later evangelist's theological inclinations). These two sorts of material are also most prevalent in John and Mark, suggesting proximity to the oral stages of their respective traditions. Luke and Matthew add their own units of material, some of which has these sorts of details and asides, but they by and large do not add details for the sake of embellishment, and when they do add theological points they reflect the commonsense conjecture of the First and Third Evangelists. For instance, Matthew might add something about the fulfilling of all righteousness, and Luke might add something about Jesus' emphasizing prayer or teaching about the Kingdom of God. Neither of these moves need represent particular knowledge of traditional material which Matthew or Luke felt essential to be added. Rather, they offer narrative bridges or punctuating remarks and short commentaries as transitional asides along the way.

Another feature prevalent in Mark and John, but missing from Luke and Matthew, is the 'translation' of Aramaisms into Greek and the 'explanation' of Jewish customs.[2] The answer to the audience-related question here is

---

denials of Peter (Jn 18.15-18, 25-7; Mk 14.66-72), the Jewish trial (Jn 18.19-24; Mk 14.55-65) and the Roman trial (Jn 18.28–19.16; Mk 15.1-15), the crucifixion and death of Jesus (Jn 19.17-37; Mk 15.22-41), the burial of Jesus (Jn 19.38-42; Mk 15.42-7), and the resurrection and appearance narratives (Jn 20.1-21, 24; Mk 16.1-8, 9-20).

2. See, for instance, Mark's 'translation' of Aramaic terms (Mk 3.17; 5.41; 7.11, 34; 15.22) and explanations of Jewish customs (Mk 7.2-4; 15.42). John also does the same sort of thing, but even more so. See the Aramaic/Greek words for 'teacher' (Jn 1.38; 20.16), the Anointed One (Jn 1.41; 4.25), Peter (Jn 1.42), and the translation into Greek of such Hebrew names of places connected to events in the ministry of Jesus as the pool by the Sheep Gate in Jerusalem, which is called in Hebrew *Bethzatha* (Jn 5.2), the pool of *Siloam* (meaning 'sent', Jn 9.7), the Stone Pavement on which Pilate's judgement bench rested is called in Hebrew *Gabbatha* (Jn 19.13), and 'the Place of the Skull' (which in Hebrew is called *Golgotha*, Jn 19.17). Likewise, the Fourth Evangelist 'explains' Jewish customs for non-Jewish audiences (Jn 2.6, 13; 4.9; 5.1; 6.4; 7.2; 11.55; 19.31, 40, 42) suggesting an intentional bridging of the oral narration of events with later audiences of the written text, which would have included Gentiles.

obvious. Mark and John are intended to be understandable to Gentile members of their audiences, which is why they translate Jewish terms and customs. The tradition-related question, however, is a catalysing one: *Why* do Mark and John distinctively preserve Aramaisms and Jewish names of people and places if they were not connected to earlier Aramaic or Hebrew traditions? Were these details simply 'concocted' (using Bretschneider's term), or do they suggest the *primitivity* of Markan and Johannine traditions? Inferring an earlier Aramaic rendering of John need not be performed here to identify an acceptable answer. Interestingly, both the Matthean and Lukan traditions omit these details, and possibly for different reasons. Matthew may have had fewer Gentile members of its audience, whereas Luke may not have felt the traditional need to pass on this sort of material from his utilization of written Mark, although Luke does indeed utilize other material with Aramaic origins. Thus, the possibility is strong that the pre-Markan material and the early Johannine tradition reflect the use of primitive material characteristic of independent oral traditions.

If this were so, insights into some of the contacts between the pre-Markan and early Johannine traditions become apparent. While the presence of apparently non-symbolic, illustrative detail is not in and of itself a sure marker of primitive orality, the particular contacts between Markan and Johannine renderings precisely on these matters of detail (the grass at the feeding, 200 and 300 *denarii*, for instance) suggest the sorts of catchy details preachers would have used and picked up from one another. While it may be finally impossible to know who these preachers were, the presentation of Peter and John preaching throughout Samaria (Acts 8) – especially if there is anything at all to the Papias tradition's connecting of Peter with the production of Mark and John with the testimony of the Beloved Disciple – may legitimate the designation of these early traditions as 'Petrine' and 'Johannine'. These designations will stand, though, *whoever* might have been connected to them as human sources of traditional origin and formation. Early Gospel 'traditions' were *human beings*, and these human beings were firstly preachers. Then again, certainty on these matters finally evades the modern exegete, but the character of the material seems to cohere with the testimonies preserved by Irenaeus and Eusebius and the bulk of second-century opinion.

What is also conspicuous is that as well as peculiar agreements throughout the narratives, these two traditions also differ considerably at nearly every step of the way. Such a phenomenon, however, may imply the traditions' confidence and sense of authority rather than illegitimacy. The Matthean conservative borrowing of written Mark seems less of an approach by an apostolic authority figure (although much of the M and Q traditions probably went back to Jesus) than the bold, trail-blazing path carved out by the Fourth Evangelist. His independent swath reflects the autonomy and confidence of a tradition seeking to present a bold portrait of the Master's ministry, and even more importantly, the original intentionality of Jesus for the emerging needs of the church.

2) *John's Augmentation of Mark*

John also shows evidence of augmenting the contents of Mark, and a comparison/contrast between the first edition of John and Mark suggests something about what such an interest might have been. First, however, the two editions of John must be distinguished. While there may indeed have been many stages in the composition of each of these 'editions', a bare minimum of speculation that accounts for the major aporias[3] in the most plausible way possible is one that infers two basic editions of John. As mentioned above, the first edition probably began with the witness of John the Baptist (Jn 1.6-8, 15, 19-42) and concluded with Jn 20.31. For the final edition the editor then added such passages as the worship material of the Prologue, chapters 6, 15-17 and 21 and the Beloved Disciple and eyewitness passages. What is also likely is that the author of the Johannine Epistles was the editor of the finalized Gospel (impressive stylistic convergences exist between the material in the Gospel's supplementary material and the style of the Epistles). Then 1, 2 and 3 John were probably written between the gathering of the first edition (ca. 80 CE) and the finalization of the Gospel around 100 CE after the death of the Beloved Disciple. This being the case, several things become apparent about the character and inclination of the first edition of John with respect to Mark.

First, John shows considerable similarity to the macro-pattern of Mark, suggesting that the Fourth Evangelist sought to do the sort of thing Mark had done, albeit in a very different way. The beginning of Jesus' ministry is associated with the ministry of John the Baptist, although John's rendering sketches a more realistic presentation of their ministries being contemporary with each other, and to some degree they appear to have been in competition with each other. Jesus returns to the site where John had been baptizing several times, even after the Baptist's arrest, and this seems a more realistic portrayal than a cut-and-dried Markan sequentialism. A few other aspects of John's presentation of the beginning of Jesus' ministry also seem parallel to those in Mark, such as the calling of the disciples, Jesus' coming again into Galilee, and the rejection of the home-town prophet. Toward the end of Jesus' ministry, John and Mark follow a very similar pattern between the entry into Jerusalem, the last supper, the garden scene and arrest of Jesus, and the two trials of Jesus, followed by his death, burial, resurrection and appearances. The middle parts of John and Mark are extremely different, but their beginnings and endings show a broad similarity of pattern.

---

3. Such 'aporias' as the individuality of the Prologue (Jn 1.1-18), the positioning of chapters 4, 5, 6 and 7, the odd transition of John 14.31, and the apparent first ending of John 20.31 are explained by this theory with a minimal amount of speculative reconstruction. As mentioned above, this theory builds most centrally on the two-edition hypothesis of Barnabas Lindars, and it is the most plausible and least speculative among extensive source-dependence and rearrangement hypotheses. See also Appendix I, below.

Second, from this set of similarities some scholars have argued that John copied Mark's larger pattern, if not Mark's gospel narrative; but John is also extremely different, even in terms of these closest similarities. For instance, the actual baptizing of Jesus is not narrated in John, and there are very few close similarities in the presentation of John the Baptist other than his being the voice crying in the wilderness from Isa. 40.3, the Holy Spirit descending as a dove, and John's being unworthy to unstrap the sandals of Jesus. The location of these connections, however, would probably have been the sort of thing preached and remembered from the oral stages of traditions, and given the vastly different presentation of every other aspect of John's ministry, Johannine dependence on written Mark for the material itself seems highly unlikely. These differences are even more pronounced regarding the other aspects of the beginnings of Jesus' ministry.

The Passion material shows a far closer pattern, at least in the outline, but even here, John's tradition departs from Mark's at nearly every turn. The suppers are on different days, neither John nor Peter go to prepare the supper, Jesus does not offer the words of the institution at the last supper, there is no Gethsemane anguish in John, and the Markan apocalypse, the cursing of the fig tree and the final teachings of Jesus in Mark are completely missing in John. Further, Peter's denials in John are far more pronounced, Pilate's miscomprehending dialogue with Jesus and the crowd is far more detailed, and there is no Markan cry of dereliction in John. While the Fourth Evangelist may possibly be inferred here to be following the larger pattern of the Markan Gospel narrative, John's dissimilarities at every turn make a close following of Mark, let alone a Markan-dependence hypothesis, implausible in the extreme.

Nonetheless, several alternative explanations for the similarities and differences are as follows: the first is that an actual sequence of events, roughly similar to the Markan and Johannine Passion narratives, may indeed have occurred, and we may thus have two perspectives on those largely similar sets of events. In that sense, these similar-yet-different connections bolster arguments for the basic authenticity of John and Mark as the two bi-optic Gospels, producing complementary perspectives on the last week of Jesus' ministry. A second possibility is that the early Christian narration of the Passion events may have been fairly well set, even before Mark was written, and the same source from which Mark's material was derived could have played a role in the formation of the Johannine presentation. Conversely, the Johannine narration may have provided the backbone for other traditions, including the pre-Markan. One more fact, however, deserves consideration here. The order of the Passion material could not possibly have assumed any other order. Try placing the resurrection *before* the supper, or the trials *after* the crucifixion, or the appearances *before* the arrest of Jesus, or the arrest *before* the triumphal entry, or even reversing the two trials. None of these transpositions, nor any others, could possibly be made to work! Thus, similarities between the Johannine and Markan Passion narratives do not imply dependence, one way or another, and this is why Bultmann was forced to infer an independent Passion narrative for the Fourth Gospel. The material appears to have been traditional rather than concocted, and while plausibly familiar with Mark, John is not dependent upon written Mark.

A third point here follows, and in several ways, John's first edition appears to augment and complement Mark's Gospel. The first two signs done in Cana of Galilee are probably included to fill out some of the early part of Jesus' ministry felt to be missing from Mark. The first two signs in John thus provide a chronological complement to Mark. It is also possible that the more public ministry of the wedding miracle and the healing of the royal official's son may seem preferable introductions to the miracle-working ministry of Jesus than the more obscure curing of Simon Peter's mother-in-law and the exorcising of a demoniac. Likewise, the signs in John 5, 9 and 11 fill out the Judean part of Jesus' ministry as a geographical complement to Mark's Galilean presentation. Most telling, however, is the fact that *none* of the five signs in the first edition of John are included in Mark! This fact is highly suggestive of the Fourth Evangelist's intention. He apparently wanted to fill out some of the broader material not included in Mark (as Luke and Matthew have done) but did so without duplicating Markan material proper. The five signs also may have been crafted rhetorically in the five-fold pattern of the books of Moses, as Jesus is presented to convince a Jewish audience that he is indeed the prophet like Moses anticipated in Deuteronomy 18. The Fourth Evangelist thus drew on his own tradition as his source, which he himself may largely have been. Then again, a tacit acknowledgement of Mark's material (also explaining why he did not make fuller use of it) may be implied in the ending of the first edition: 'Now Jesus did many other signs in the presence of his disciples, *which are not written in this book*. But these are written in order that...' (Jn 20.30-1). Thus, in a subtle way, Jn 20.30 seems to defend the fact, perhaps against some criticism, of John's intentional non-inclusion of familiar Markan material.

Such a complementary intent would also account for considerable problems regarding major disagreements between Mark and John, especially the Markan material omitted by John, and at this point one must differ with some of the inferences of Gardner-Smith. While he finds it inconceivable that the Fourth Evangelist's knowledge of Mark could have resulted in omitting so much of what is in Mark, he does not allow for the possibility that John might have been written as something of a complement to Mark. Non-dependence is not the same as total independence. The Transfiguration, exorcisms, Jesus' parabolic teachings on the Kingdom of God, the Markan apocalypse, and other significant works and teachings may have been omitted from John precisely because it was felt that they were already included among the 'many other signs Jesus did in the presence of his disciples, which are *not written* in *this* book' (Jn 20.30). Likewise, including controversial debates with Jewish leaders and the Johannine 'I-Am' sayings, and emphasizing Jesus' divine commissioning within the Deuteronomy 18 agency schema appear to have furthered the acutely apologetic interest of the evangelist. This interest of leading the reader to believe in Jesus as the Jewish Messiah (Jn 20.31) may thus explain the desire to include some of the Johannine traditional material that had been crafted within its own dialectical relationships with local Jewish communities. This material reflects distinctively Johannine paraphrasis of the teachings of Jesus, and the crafting of Jesus in the pattern of Elijah and Moses typologies was also an integral part of this apologetic agenda. Therefore, the 'problem' of John's omission of Markan material and inclusion of distinctively Johannine material coincides with the likelihood that the first edition was intended as an augmentation of and complement to Mark.

3) John's Correcting of Mark?

Interestingly, the first edition of John, while following the Markan macro-pattern, also seems intent upon *setting the record straight* regarding Mark's ordering of some of Jesus' ministry and some of Mark's theological nuance.[4] As well as augmenting the early ministry of Jesus and adding other material as a complement to Mark, John's narrative appears at times to provide an alternative presentation of events with knowing intentionality. Does this imply a conscious correcting of Mark's presentation of Jesus, or are the differences due to Johannine 'mistakes' or lack of familiarity with Mark? Contrary to many discussions of the issue, considering John as disagreeing with the presentation of Jesus' ministry in all three canonical gospels misrepresents the issue here. At the time of the production of the first edition of John, Mark was probably the only finalized gospel, and thus the Johannine target need not be construed as broader than Mark's Gospel. Further, the very fact of Matthew's and Luke's expansions of Mark suggests the likelihood that Mark may not have been regarded as the final written word on Jesus' ministry. They sought to improve on Mark, as did the second ending of Mark, and perhaps John did too. If taken in this way, some of John's departures from Mark may indeed be considered in a slightly corrective light as well as in an augmentive light. The narrating, for instance, of the first two signs Jesus performed in Cana of Galilee may have been designed not only to fill out the earlier portrayal of Jesus' ministry, but they may also have served the function of wresting the inaugural ministry of Jesus away from the household of Simon Peter's mother-in-law and the exorcism of the demoniac. For whatever reason, these two miracles may not have seemed to the Fourth Evangelist to have been the best ways to get the gospel narration going, and the numeration devices in Jn 2.11 and 4.54 may have functioned as a corrective to the Markan presentation rather than a numeration device within an alien signs source. Indeed, Eusebius even preserves a tradition declaring that one of John's interests was to present

---

4. These differences with the Markan ordering can be seen clearly in the chart by Peter Hofrichter (1997, p. 188).

a portrayal of the early ministry of Jesus (*Hist. Eccles.* 3.24.7-13), and such an opinion may have some basis in reliable memory.

Another striking difference between Mark and John involves their presentations of the Temple cleansing. Mark places it at the culmination of Jesus' ministry, of course, and most historical-Jesus scholars assume such was the correct chronology. John's presentation at the beginning of Jesus' ministry is thus assumed to have been motivated by 'the theological interests of the evangelist', but such inferences are often fuzzy and unsubstantiated. Several times hence, the disruptive sign in Jerusalem is commented upon as an event that caused other ripples in the Johannine narrative (Jn 4.45), and these imply reflections upon events rather than theologizations. Why, for instance, do the Jerusalem leaders *already* want to kill Jesus after an apparently inane healing of the paralytic? A prior Temple disturbance seems assumed. Conversely, an unlikely move to have been concocted (thus applying the criterion of dissimilarity) is the Johannine rendering of the reason for the Jewish leaders' wanting to kill Jesus as being his raising Lazarus from the dead. It would be perfectly reasonable to have conjectured that the religious leaders wanted to get rid of Jesus because of his having created a demonstration in the Temple, and while Matthew and Luke follow Mark unquestioningly here, this does not imply three testimonies against one. It may simply reflect common-sense conjecture, the very procedure Mark would have followed if he had listed all the Jerusalem events at the end of the narrative, which he clearly did.

On the other hand, Jn 2.20 contains an odd and unmotivated clue to chronology suggesting the historical superiority of the Johannine presentation. Here the Jews claim the Temple has been under construction for 46 years, and, as it was begun around 19 BCE, this would imply a date for that saying of around 27 CE – closer to the beginning of Jesus' ministry than the end. Also, the presentation of Jesus going back and forth from Jerusalem and ministering over the length of three Passovers seems more realistic than the Synoptic view that Jesus attended Jerusalem only once during his ministry, and during that visit, he was killed. Also, some of the motif in Jn 2.13-22 is more unified than its counterparts in Mark 11 and 14. These and other factors, such as Jesus' ministry in Samaria and contemporary engagements with the followers of John the Baptist, cause one to suspect John may have intended to correct some of Mark's presentation of Jesus' ministry, and amazingly such an opinion is echoed by a second-century witness. *None other than John the elder*, according to Papias through Eusebius (*Hist. Eccles.* 3.39.15), is recalled to have asserted that Mark preserved Peter's preaching accurately, but *in the wrong order!* The Elder may thus be representing an authentic Johannine opinion and motivation for producing another gospel narrative as an alternative to Mark's contribution. This possibility may seem unacceptable to scholars holding a harmonizing view of the Gospels, but the textual evidence seems to support such a theory, and so does a striking second-century witness. Thus, the Johannine perspective upon the Markan project may also lend valuable insights into the sort of compilation Mark may have been – a gathering of traditional units into a progressive denouement, with some chronological knowledge present – rather than a strict chronology proper.

As well as matters of chronology, the Johannine project may have wanted to set the record straight on the meaning of miracles (they reveal who Jesus was as the Mosaic agent sent from God), the character of the Kingdom of God (it goes forward by means of the work of the Spirit and is associated with truth), the compassionate and loving trademarks of authentic ministry (versus power orientations), a de-emphasis on the special place of 'the Twelve' (elevating Nathanael, Martha and others, for instance), and the inclusion of women and Samaritans in Jesus' circle of friends. Some of these theological proclivities come into their fullest development in the supplementary material, but they were already at work in the first edition of John. In doing so, John's tradition stakes a claim right alongside the Markan tradition as an authentic interpretation of the ministry and intentionality of Jesus for his followers. It is also not inconceivable that two or more disciples of Jesus, even leading ones, may have seen things differently regarding central aspects of Jesus' ministry. What we appear to have in Mark and John is two bi-optic perspectives on the events and implications of Jesus' gospel ministry. Therefore, John's relation to the Markan tradition appears to have been interfluential in their oral stages, and augmentive, complementary and corrective in their written stages.

B. *John's Influence upon Luke: Formative, 'Orderly' and Theological*

A terrible error among interpreters of gospel traditions is to assume that because John was finalized late, all contacts between John and the other gospel traditions must imply John's dependence upon the Synoptics. This view is nowhere defended as sloppily as it is with regards to the relationship between the Gospels of Luke and John. Many of the great themes and passages most characteristic of Luke are not included in John, whereas at least three dozen times, Luke appears to depart from Mark and to side with the Johannine rendering of an event or teaching. For instance, such great Lukan passages as the parables of the Good Samaritan and the Prodigal Son are missing from John, as are such themes as concern for the poor and the presentation of Jesus as a just man. On the other hand, Luke sides with John against Mark in significant ways, and this fact is best accounted for by assuming Luke had access to the Johannine tradition, and that he used it. Assuming there may have been a common-yet-unknown source is entirely conjectural, and it serves no purpose better than the more solid inference that a source Luke used was the early Johannine tradition.[5]

---

5. The analyses of Lamar Cribbs (1973, 1979) are far more convincing than those of J.A. Bailey (1963), who simply guesses that there must have been a common source for Luke and John. When cast in the light of Luke's multiple departures from Mark and siding with John, the likelihood of Lukan dependence on the Johannine tradition becomes a much stronger case.

1) John's Formative Influence upon Luke

Time and again Luke appears to be siding with John against Mark, and it must be concluded that John's tradition must have been formative in the development of the Lukan Gospel. For one thing, Luke includes a variety of details that are peculiar to John but are not found in Mark. For instance, people question in their hearts regarding John the Baptist (Jn 1.19-25; 3.28 → Lk. 3.15; Acts 11.16) who has a more extensive itinerant ministry (Jn 1.28; 3.23; 10.40 → Lk. 3.3) than in Mk 1.4, double questions are asked regarding Jesus' Messiahship and Sonship (Jn 10.24, 36 → Lk. 22.67, 70), the beholding of Jesus' glory (*doxa*) is added to the Transfiguration scene (Jn 1.14 → Lk. 9.32), Mary and Martha are mentioned as sisters and are presented as having similar roles (Jn 11.1; 12.1-3 → Lk. 10.38-42), a man named Lazarus is presented in both John and Luke and in both cases is associated with death and the testimony of after-death experiences (Jn 11.1-12.17→ Lk. 16.19-31), the crowd acclaims Jesus as 'King' at the triumphal entry (Jn 12.13 → Lk. 19.38), Jesus extols and exemplifies the greatness of servant leadership at the table (Jn 13.1-17 → Lk. 12.37; 22.24-30), the disciples question who would be the betrayer (Jn 13.22-4 → Lk. 22.23), Satan enters Judas at the last supper (Jn 13.27 → Lk. 22.3), Peter's denial is predicted in the upper room (Jn 13.36-8 → Lk. 22.31-4), only John and Luke mention a second Judas – not Iscariot (Jn 14.22 → Lk. 6.16; Acts 1.13), the Holy Spirit will teach believers what they need to know and say (Jn 14.26 → Lk. 12.12), the 'right' ear of the servant was cut off (Jn 18.10 → Lk. 22.50), the court/house of the High Priest was entered by Jesus (Jn 18.15 → Lk. 22.54), Jesus answers Pilate's question (Jn 18.33-8 → Lk. 23.3) whereupon Pilate claims to 'find no crime in' Jesus, the crowd desires to give tribute to Caesar after three assertions of Jesus' innocence and their double demand for his crucifixion (Jn 19.1-16 → Lk. 23.20-33), the tomb is one in which no one had ever been laid (Jn 19.41 → Lk. 23.53), and the day was the day of Preparation (Jn 19.42 → Lk. 23.54), it is said that Peter arrived at the tomb and that he saw the linen cloths lying there (Jn 20.5 → Lk. 24.12), likewise Mary Magdalene becomes a link between the risen Lord and the Apostles (Jn 20.18 → Lk. 24.10), two men/angels are mentioned at the empty tomb (Jn 20.12 → Lk. 24.4), the ascension is mentioned (Jn 20.17 → Lk. 24.51; Acts 1.9-11), Jesus suddenly appears to his disciples standing among them (Jn 20.19 → Lk. 24.36), he invites his followers to touch his wounds (Jn 20.27 → Lk. 24.39-40), bestows peace upon his followers (Jn 20.19, 21 → Lk. 24.36), and eats fish with them after the resurrection (Jn 21.9-13 → Lk. 24.42-3), the Holy Spirit is presented distinctively as 'wind' (Jn 3.8 → Acts 2.2), and the great catch of fish is climactically mentioned (Jn 21.1-14 → Lk. 5.1-11), which in turn becomes associated with the calling of Peter.

How Luke came by this material and not other Johannine material is difficult to assess, but it does appear that Luke has had access to John's oral tradition, and on more than one score. If Luke had had access to written John, the placement of the great catch of fish probably would have been different, although Luke appropriately still includes it as part of the calling (and re-calling) narrative. Likewise, if Luke had access to written John, he might have moved the Temple cleansing to the early part of the narrative, included longer I-Am sayings, presented an alternative Lazarus narrative, and shown Jesus going back and forth from Jerusalem and doing other miracles not included in Mark. Both in matters of inclusion and exclusion, John's material appears to have played a formative role in the development of Luke's Gospel, and that influence seems to have taken place during the oral stages of the Johannine tradition.

2) Does John Provide a Basis for Luke's 'Orderly' Account?
What is meant by Luke's declaration that he seeks to produce an 'orderly' account? Does such a reference imply a penchant for historical detail, or is Luke referring to something broader in its meaning? Again, such an interest is impossible to ascertain, but it does coincide with the fact that several times in his narration of events, Luke appears to change the sequence or to alter the presentation of something in Mark precisely where Luke coincides with John. For instance, Luke only includes one sea-crossing narrative, as does John, and Luke only includes one feeding (the feeding of the 5,000), similar to John (Jn 6.1-15 → Lk. 9.10-17). Luke moves the servanthood discussion to the last supper, where it is in John (Jn 13.1-17 → Lk. 22.24-30), and he also performs a rather striking reordering move in that he relocates the confession of Peter after the feeding of the 5,000 as a contrast to its following the feeding of the 4,000, as it does in Mark. Notice also that Luke begins and ends Jesus' ministry in ways reminiscent of John's rendering: the opening of Jesus' ministry is in the 'hill country near Nazareth' (Jn 2.1-11 → Lk. 4.14-16), and his post-resurrection appearances begin in Jerusalem (Jn 20.19 → Lk. 24.13-49). A certain explanation may elude the theorist, but one fact is clear: in all of these moves, Luke indeed departs from Mark and sides with John.

Luke also appears to *conflate material* between Markan and Johannine pre-sentations, suggesting he saw his work to some degree as bridging these two traditions. For instance, the confession of Peter conflates Mark's 'You are *the Christ*' with John's 'You are the Holy One *of God*', leading to 'You are *the Christ of God*' (Mk 8.29 and Jn 6.69 → Lk. 9.20). Most conspicuously, however, Luke departs from Mark's presentation of the anointing of Jesus' *head*, and presents the event as the anointing of Jesus' *feet* – siding with John (Jn 12.1-8 → Lk. 7.36-50). Movement in the other direction, towards a more elevated and royal anointing, might have been imaginable, but moving to a more modest foot anointing would have been extremely unlikely without a legitimating reason. John's rendering, however, provides a traditional basis for this unlikely move, and it also may account for Luke's conjectural addition of the gratitude motif. In John, the anointing is performed by Mary, the sister of Lazarus, but Luke may have misunderstood the narration due to his aural access to it. Luke may have heard 'Mary' and have thus associated her with another Mary (Mary Magdalene?), which would explain his conjectural addition that the motivation for the anointing was the woman's prolific gratitude in return for the forgiveness of her prolific sinfulness. This may also suggest the oral form of the Johannine tradition to which Luke had access.

Another interesting point made by Lamar Cribbs is that many times where Luke *omits* a Markan narrative or presentation of something, he does so precisely where the Johannine tradition seems to go against such a narration. As an argument from silence, this is a weak form of demonstration, but it coheres with the larger pattern of Luke's rearranging his material to fit the Johannine presentation over and against the Markan. Does all of this cast any light upon Luke's declaration to Theophilus that he is writing an 'orderly account' after having investigated everything, including the consulting of eye-witnesses and servants of the *Logos* (Lk. 1.1-4)? Such an inference indeed is supported by the corollary facts, although certainty will be elusive. Whatever the case, the Johannine tradition appears to have influenced the Lukan at many turns.

3) Did the Johannine Tradition Contribute to Luke's Theology?

Again, this question is finally impossible to answer with certainty, but Luke does show remarkable similarities with several Johannine theological motifs as well as details along the way. For instance, John's favourable treatment of Samaritans comes across clearly in Luke in the parable of the Good Samaritan as well as Jesus' treatment of Samaritans in Luke's narrative. Likewise, the favourable treatment of women in both John and Luke appears to be no accident. Not only are particular women mentioned distinctively in these two gospels, but their apostolic functions are also highlighted, and this connection is impressive. Luke believes women to be included in the new work that God is doing in the world, and Luke probably acquired at least some of this perspective from the Johannine tradition. Another example of theological influence is the common importance placed upon the ministry of the Holy Spirit. Obviously, this theme represents Luke's own theology, but particular connections with the Johannine narrative make it likely that John's tradition may even have contributed to this development within Luke's own theology, apart from the tradition he used from John. These same connections can be seen to contribute to Luke's presentation of the growth of the church in Acts, confirming this hypothesis.

Indeed, one of the most impressive similarities between Luke and John is the way Luke presents the ministry of the post-resurrection Jesus. On the road to Emmaus in Luke we find several Johannine contacts not only suggesting traditional borrowing from John, but motifs reflecting John's theological influence upon Luke's understanding of the ministry of the resurrected Lord. The risen Christ stands among the disciples, speaking peace to them and offering courage. Likewise, the corporate fellowship of believers is enhanced by the sharing of table-fellowship with the Lord – even after the resurrection – in continuity with the historical ministry of Jesus. The evidence of spiritual encounter with Christ is declared as an experiential reality, and the ongoing ministry of the Holy Spirit is held to fulfil the promise of Christ's return. Luke also sides with John in emphasizing the efficacy of prayer, and this is both taught and modelled by Jesus in both Gospels. In these and other ways, Luke appears to be indebted theologically to John's theological presentation of Jesus' ongoing ministry as the risen Lord.

4) Acts 4.19-20 – A First-Century Clue to Johannine Authorship?
A further connection which raises a striking set of implications is the fact that Luke unwittingly provides a clue to Johannine authorship which all sides of New Testament studies have apparently missed until now. Scholars are entirely aware of the view represented by Pierson Parker (1962, p. 35) several decades ago: the 'one assured result of biblical criticism' is that 'John, the Son of Zebedee, had nothing at all to do with the writing of this Gospel'. Indeed, present scholars have pervasively been taught that the earliest known connection between the son of Zebedee and the Fourth Gospel was Irenaeus, who confronted Marcion around 180 CE by citing references to John as the author of the Gospel that now bears his name. Therefore, given John's lateness, spiritual tone and differences from the Synoptic Gospels, most scholars have largely agreed with Parker despite the fact that none of his 21 points are compelling, either individually or collectively. What we have in Acts 4.19-20, however, may be a clue to Johannine authorship that moves the connection a full century earlier than Irenaeus. This finding could be highly significant and deserves scholarly consideration.

In Acts 4.19 Peter *and* John are mentioned as speaking. This, by the way, is the only time John is mentioned as speaking in the book of Acts, and he normally is presented as following in the shadow of Peter. The narration is then followed by two statements, and each of them bears a distinctively associative ring. The first statement, 'Judge for yourselves whether it is right to listen to you rather than God', is echoed by Peter in Acts 5.29 and 11.17, and it sounds like a typically Petrine leveraging of a human/divine dichotomy. On the other hand, the statement that we cannot help speaking about what we have 'seen and heard' (v. 20) is clearly a Johannine logion! A similar statement is declared by the Johannine Elder in 1 John 1.3, 'We proclaim to you what we have seen and heard from the beginning', and in Jn 3.32 Jesus declares what he has 'seen and heard' from the Father. A fitting question to ask is whether such a reference simply betrays Luke's conjectural way of presenting something. Certainly, Luke presents many people who have seen things or heard things, and this could quite possibly represent a Lukan convention. Upon examining the textual results, however, only a few times does Luke present hearing and seeing words together and in this sequence, and the only other time seeing and hearing verbs are used together and in the first person plural, as they are in Acts 4.20, is 1 John 1.3.[6] The first-century connecting of John the apostle with

6. See 'The Papias Tradition, John's Tradition and Luke/Acts' (Anderson, 1996, pp. 274–7).

a Johannine saying here approximates a fact. Luke may have been misguided, or even wrong, but this identification moves the apostolic association of the Johannine tradition with the disciple John a full century before the work of Irenaeus. Given Luke's dependence upon the Johannine oral tradition, and given the formative role John's material apparently played upon Luke's theological developments, this finding could be highly significant!

C. *Contacts between John and Q?*

Could it be that there were also contacts between the Johannine tradition and the Q tradition? This exploration is the most speculative, both in terms of the existence of Q and the question of whether similarities between Matthew, Luke and John imply some sort of contact between hypothetical Q and John. While there are several interesting connections between the Q tradition and John,[7] the most fascinating contact is what has been called 'the bolt out of the Johannine blue' – Mt. 11.25-27 and Lk. 10.21-22. What is fascinating is that this passage, in Matthew and Luke but not in Mark, sounds very Johannine. Explanations assuming that John has employed Q do not suffice here. The best explanation is to infer that the Q tradition included a significant saying that sounds very Johannine. Consider these similarities between Matthew, Luke and John:

Table 3.1

Contacts between Jesus Sayings in John and Q

Mt. 11.25-7. At that time Jesus said, 'I thank you, Father, Lord of heaven and earth, because you have hidden these things from the wise and the intelligent and have revealed them to infants; yes, Father, for such was your gracious will. All things have been handed over to me by my Father; and no one knows the Son except the Father, and no one knows the Father except the Son and anyone to whom the Son chooses to reveal him.'

---

7. See especially Jn 12.25, 'Those who love their life lose it, and those who hate their life in this world will keep it for eternal life', and its parallels in Mt. 10.39: 'Those who find their life will lose it, and those who lose their life for my sake will find it', and Lk. 17.33: 'Those who try to make their life secure will lose it, but those who lose their life will keep it'. See also the following connections between Q and John: a) Mt. 3.11a; Lk. 3.16a; Jn 1.26a; b) Mt. 3.9; Lk. 3.8; Jn 8.39; c) Mt. 9.37-8; Lk. 10.2; Jn 4.35; and d) Mt. 10.17-25; Lk. 12.11-12; Jn 13.16; 16.2; 14.26.

Lk. 10.21-2. At that same hour Jesus rejoiced in the Holy Spirit and said, 'I thank you, Father, Lord of heaven and earth, because you have hidden these things from the wise and the intelligent and have revealed them to infants; yes, Father, for such was your gracious will. All things have been handed over to me by my Father; and no one knows who the Son is except the Father, or who the Father is except the Son and anyone to whom the Son chooses to reveal him.'

Jn 3.35. The Father loves the Son and has placed all things in his hands.

Jn 7.28-9. Then Jesus cried out as he was teaching in the temple, 'You know me, and you know where I am from. I have not come on my own. But the one who sent me is true, and you do not know him. I know him, because I am from him, and he sent me.'

Jn 10.14-15. I am the good shepherd. I know my own and my own know me, just as the Father knows me and I know the Father. And I lay down my life for the sheep.

Jn 13.3-4. Jesus, knowing that the Father had given all things into his hands, and that he had come from God and was going to God, got up from the table, took off his outer robe and tied a towel around himself.

Jn 17.1-3. After Jesus had spoken these words, he looked up to heaven and said, 'Father, the hour has come; glorify your Son so that the Son may glorify you, since you have given him authority over all people, to give eternal life to all whom you have given him. And this is eternal life: that they may know you, the only true God, and Jesus Christ whom you have sent'.

Jn 17.22-5. 'The glory that you have given me I have given them, so that they may be one, as we are one, I in them and you in me, that they may become completely one, so that the world may know that you have sent me and have loved them even as you have loved me. Father, I desire that those also, whom you have given me, may be with me where I am, to see my glory, which you have given me because you loved me before the foundation of the world. Righteous Father, the world does not know you, but I know you; and these know that you have sent me.'

(NRSV)

From these examples it can be seen that the Q tradition shows remarkable similarities with a prevalent Johannine motif. But what are the implications of such a connection? Either Q and John have a common origin in a tradition earlier than Q (perhaps going back to Jesus?), or we have a Johannine motif that has been apprehended and used extremely early, even by Q. The primitivity of the Johannine tradition thus is confirmed by either possibility, although the latter is the most likely. Like the Lukan tradition, the Q tradition has apparently drawn on the Johannine tradition, probably during its oral stages of development. It is not assumed, however, that the bulk of Johannine tradition was available to the Q tradition, as some of it was still in the process of formation. The passages above may suggest Johannine familiarity with some of the content represented in the Q tradition, but more likely is the hypothesis that the Q tradition has drawn from the Johannine rendering of Jesus' ministry. Of course, it is also a possibility that Q and the early Johannine tradition represent independent primitive reflections upon the ministry of Jesus and/or some sort of interfluentiality, parallel to the Johannine and pre-Markan tradition. Because these themes are more pervasively Johannine, however, it is most plausible to infer that Q has incorporated an early Johannine motif.

D. *John's Relation to Matthew: Reinforcing, Dialectical and Corrective*

John's relation to the Matthean tradition appears the most indirect among the canonical Gospels, and it seems to have involved a history of dialogical relationships between at least two sectors of the early church on important institutional and ecclesial matters. In some ways, the Matthean and Johannine sectors of the church were partners in the growing dialogues with local Jewish communities, especially along the lines of evangelizing the Jewish nation to accept its own Messiah: Jesus. These traditions also sought to preserve their own material and to make it accessible for later generations. In doing so, they may even have engaged each other, as well as other Christian traditions, regarding key matters such as discipleship, leadership and the ongoing work of the risen Christ within the community of faith.

1) Matthean and Johannine Sectors of Christianity: Reinforcing Each Other's Missions and Tasks
Several of the contacts or parallels between Matthew and John reveal growing Christian communities which are trying to demonstrate that Jesus was indeed the Jewish Messiah, who is also needed in the world beyond Judaism. Particularly strong are the parallels between their uses of Scripture and showing from the Law and the Prophets ways in which Jesus fulfilled the Scriptures as the Messiah/Christ. They also had considerable pedagogical works they were involved in, and the Matthean and Johannine sectors of the church probably had within their purview the task of discipling Christians, making their communities something like a 'school' or a centre for discipleship and training. Teaching interests and community maintenance concerns can be inferred most extensively in these two Gospels, and such communities may even have reinforced each other in their travelling ministries between fellowships and correspondence otherwise.[8]

8. A particularly interesting connection is the way Matthew and John both expand the passage from Isa. 6.9-10 (Mt. 13.14-15; Jn 12.37-40) as an explanation of why the Jews refuse

A particularly important task that both communities appear to have been sharing involved the managing of outreach to and tensions with the respective local Jewish presence. In the Matthean and Johannine settings alike, one or more Jewish Synagogues must have commanded a significant presence in the community (especially for those seeking to follow a Jewish Messiah), although such was an ambiguous presence. It may be that the *Birkat ha-Minim*, a ban excluding professing Christians from some Synagogues, may have been instrumental in followers of Jesus being excluded from Synagogue life in both settings, but the tensions need not have followed from such a particular development. Nor does the fact of its uneven application imply that things were not difficult for Jewish–Christian relationships in these settings. A possibility just as likely is that these communities probably experienced a mixed reception of openness and hostility from the local Jewish communities, and this ambivalence may even have precipitated the call for an exclusion clause, which the Twelfth Jamnian Benediction was designed to accommodate. Whatever the case, Matthean and Johannine Christians shared a good deal of solidarity with one another. In seeking to evangelize Jewish family, friends and neighbours, they probably received mixed receptions and challenges to the authenticity of Jesus' mission, which led to their continuing emphases upon Jesus as the Jewish Messiah, sent from God after the pattern of the Mosaic prophet of Deut. 18.15-22.

2) Dialectical Relations between Johannine Christianity and Intramural Centralizing Tendencies

As tensions with Jewish sectors of communities grew and then subsided (they appear less acute in the supplementary Johannine material), tensions with Gentile Christians increased. In particular, debates over discipleship and what it meant to come 'out of' the world were acute concerns for the early Christian movement in the later part of the first century CE. These issues were exacerbated by the stepping up of Roman Emperor worship as a broad requirement under the reign of Domitian (81–96 CE). During this era in particular, subjects of the Roman Empire were expected to declare their loyalty openly to Rome by offering public Emperor laud (either declaring 'Caesar is Lord!' or by offering incense to Caesar – an act of worship – or both). This sort of practice had been the custom of Mediterranean residents for centuries, especially in Asia Minor, and it is likely that Gentile believers felt it was far less problematic than Jewish–Christian believers. A further impact of Synagogue exclusion was that those who were not deemed to be part of the Jewish faith would not have been covered by the Roman dispensation for Jews in deference to their peculiar monotheism, and they would then

to believe in their own Messiah. Such a passage was probably used within the worship and/or teaching settings of Matthean and Johannine Christianity. See also the similar Matthean and Johannine presentations of Jesus as one who was 'sent by the Father' as a typical feature of the Jewish agency motif rooted in Deuteronomy 18 (Anderson, 1999a).

have been expected to show loyalty to Rome or to suffer for the consequences of refusing to offer Emperor laud.

These issues led to a variety of further tensions as some Gentile/Christian leaders began preaching that one need not suffer for one's faith, and that it was not a problem to be a member of Roman society outwardly and still be a Christian. At this, the Johannine leadership probably responded, 'We must be willing to follow Jesus to the cross, ourselves, if we expect to be raised with him in the afterlife. Jesus suffered and died for us; can we do any less?', to which the docetizing leaders responded, 'No he did not! He was divine, not human.' In these sorts of ways, Docetism began to gain ground as a movement and as a threat to Christianity from within. It is a mistake, however, to confuse Docetism here with Gnosticism proper. The latter developed more fully in the second century, but it was not full blown in the first-century situation. The great initial appeal of Docetism was simply its implications for an assimilative and less costly view of discipleship. This was the reason it was opposed so vigorously by early Christian communities, especially the Johannine ones, and this explains the emphasis on a suffering and incarnate Jesus so rife in its presentation in the second-edition material and in the Johannine Epistles.

However, not all sectors of the Christian movement responded to these tensions in exhortative ways. Some sought to stave off the threats by means of imposing hierarchical structures of leadership, calling for submission to authoritative church leaders, thereby challenging alternative claims and movements. This can be seen explicitly in the epistles of Ignatius of Antioch, who sought to stave off docetizing defections by calling for adherence to one bishop and one worship service as expressions of one's loyalty to one's Lord and Saviour, Jesus Christ. In doing so, Ignatius built upon the Petrine model of Matthew 16.17-19 and 18.15-20, and he was probably not the only one to have done so. The occasion of the Johannine Elder's writing 3 John to Gaius was that Diotrephes who 'loves to be first' had excluded Johannine Christians and had been willing even to expel members of his own congregation who were willing to take them in (vv. 9–10). Some scholars see the only issue here as having been hospitality, but inhospitality was a symptom of the problem, not the problem itself. The Elder describes writing to the *ecclēsia* (the centralizing church?) about Diotrephes (whence he probably has drawn his positional authority), and he shows signs of also wishing to speak with him directly (Mt. 18.15-17). While this dialogue may not have been between Johannine and Matthean leadership directly, all it takes is one bad example for the Johannine leadership to feel this structural innovation may not have been an improvement after all.

On the matter of leadership, hierarchies and the role of the present Christ in the meeting for worship, the Johannine and Matthean leadership (as well as other Christian groups in the sub-apostolic era) must have invested a good deal of discussion together. At times, however, they may also have disagreed with one another, and such dialogues can be inferred within the dialectical set of relationships between Johannine and Matthean Christianities. For instance, when asking why Diotrephes excluded Johannine Christians to begin with, it may have been due to their egalitarian and Spirit-based ecclesiology – and well he should have been threatened, because such a position would have undermined his very approach to holding his own church together, which was what the hierarchical innovations were designed to effect.

3) The Finalized Gospel of John: A Corrective to Rising Institutionalism in the Late First-Century Church

While the Beloved Disciple was alive and ministering authoritatively, the extending of his witness to the rest of the church may not have seemed as pressing. After his death, however, the compiler of the Fourth Gospel sought to gather and disseminate his witness within the broader Christian movement. In doing so, there was obviously interest in getting his story of Jesus out there where it could do some good, but part of the 'good' it was intended to effect was to outline the original intentionality of Jesus for his church. In John's final-edition material, one can see several impressive developments that confirm such a view. First, as an antidocetic corrective, this later material emphasizes the fleshly humanity of Jesus and the importance of the Way of the Cross for normative discipleship. Second, a great deal of emphasis has been placed in the accessibility and present work of the Holy Spirit as the effective means by which the risen Lord continues to lead the church. Third, the juxtaposition of Peter and the Beloved Disciple, especially clear in this supplementary material, reflects the presentation of the Beloved Disciple as the ideal model for Christian leadership in contrast to that which is represented by the miscomprehending Peter. All of this together suggests an interest in providing an apostolic corrective to rising institutionalism in the late first-century church in the name of Jesus' last will and testament.

Most strikingly, at least seven ways can be identified in which Matthew 16.17-19 is treated in parallel ways in John, but each of these parallels is different. Do these differences suggest a *corrective* interest? Quite possibly. For instance, consider the following:

Table 3.2

Matthew 16.17-19 and Corrective Echoes in John

- Peter's 'correct' confession is considered inspired (Mt. 16.17), but in John 'blessedness' is equated with serving others (13.17) and believing without having seen (20.29). The Johannine Macarisms are not all that striking a contrast to this one in Matthew 16, although the Johannine references to that which is blessed clearly call for a greater spirit of servanthood as far as Peter (and those who follow in his wake) is concerned and they include those who have not seen (beyond the apostolic band) and yet believe. These are both counter-hierarchical themes.

- The 'apostles' and leaders are not only men in John, but they also include women (4.7-42; 20.14-16; 12.1-8). John's presentation of women ministering to and on behalf of Jesus would have gone against the grain of emerging patriarchialism as the church entered the sub-apostolic era. This move (against innovation) suggests John's primitivity and traditional reasons for presenting women in the egalitarian ways it did. In the presentation of women as partners with Jesus in the furthering of God's work, John restores a set of insights – if not traditional memories – reminiscent of what may be assumed about the historical Jesus.

- The confessions of faith in John are reserved for Nathanael (1.49) and Martha (11.27), *not* members of the Twelve. The co-opting of 'the Twelve' in directions hierarchical may have been opposed by the Johannine tradition not because of its non-apostolicity, but precisely *because* of it. It is highly likely that not all members of the apostolic band felt equally enthusiastic about the emerging primacy of Peter, especially if the coinage were used to bolster the authoritarian leadership of some over others. Showing such persons as Nathanael and Martha making confessions, as well as Peter, must have functioned to broaden the base of Christian authority beyond the purview of 'the Twelve', and emerging leaders and others would have felt encouraged in such presentations.

- 'Flesh and blood' cannot recognize that kingly Messiah in Matthew, but in John, the flesh profits nothing (6.63) as discipleship leads to the cross (6.51). The connections here may not be all that close, but it is interesting to note that John's emphasis on assimilating the flesh and blood of Jesus refers to the costly discipleship of being willing to ingest the 'bread' of Jesus' flesh given for the life of the world. The reference is to the 'Way of the Cross' rather than the making of a correct confession, and the practical implications of such a presentation would have been significant.

- The image of the 'church' in Matthew is more 'petrified', while in John it is more fluid ('flock' – ch.10; 'vine and branches' – ch. 15) and exemplified by the Beloved Disciple. Peter is not entrusted with institutional keys in John, but the Beloved Disciple is entrusted with the mother of Jesus, a symbol of familiarity and relationality as bases of authority. In both cases a particular disciple is given an entrustment by Jesus, and these actions and images must have borne with them implications for carrying forward the ongoing work of Jesus. The relationality of the Johannine image, however, strikes against the institutional character of the Matthean image, although familial images within Matthew also abound. John's egalitarian ecclesiology thus appears to be in dialogue with more hierarchical ecclesiologies emerging within the late first-century church.

- Jesus gives Peter authority in Matthew, but in John (6.68-9) Peter gives
  authority to Jesus. Does John thereby present Peter as returning the keys
  of the Kingdom back to Jesus, where they belonged all along? This may
  be overstating it a bit, but the contrast is striking. Peter is portrayed
  throughout John as miscomprehending Jesus' teachings about servant
  leadership (chs 6, 13, 21), and yet the Beloved Disciple always does it right.
  The point of John's rendering, however, is to emphasize the importance
  of Christ, through whom the Holy Spirit continues to lead the church with
  his life-producing words. It is highly significant ideologically that Peter is
  portrayed as affirming the immediacy of the ongoing work of the resurrected Lord. Likewise, while Peter is reinstated in John 21.15-17, it is with
  the proviso that his service be shepherding and nurturing, a contrast to
  the self-serving shepherds of Ezekiel 34.

- Authority (responsibility) to loose and bind is given to *all* followers of
  Jesus in John (20.21-3), not just a few, and Jesus' 'friends' include those
  who know what the Master is doing, and those who do his work (Jn
  15.14-15). John 20.21-3 is the passage most similar to Matthew 16.17-
  19 and 18.15-20, and the threefold content here is highly significant. In
  this passage, the priesthood of all believers is laid out with stark clarity.
  Jesus first pneumatizes his disciples in ways that could not be clearer; he
  breathes on them and says: 'Receive the Holy Spirit!' Next, he apostolizes
  them and emphasizes that as the Father has sent him, he also sends them
  as apostolic envoys in the world. Finally, Jesus *sacerdotalizes* his disciples
  by giving them the responsibility to be forgivers of sins in the world. Here
  we see the expansion of apostolicity rather than its constriction, and such
  a movement would have been at odds with proto-Ignatian autocratic
  modes of governance if they were emerging by this time. Again, while
  similarities with Matthew 18.18-20 are striking here, it is doubtful that
  the Fourth Evangelist had a particular text in mind. Rather, the sort of
  centralizing work of some leaders, carried out by the likes of Diotrephes,
  'who loves his primacy' (3 Jn 9-10) may have catalyzed the Johannine
  corrective in the name of the original intention of Jesus for his Church.

How long the Johannine and Matthean traditions may have been engaged in
such dialogues is impossible to say. They may have been engaged dialogically
for several decades, although the material in the M tradition referenced most
directly in John appears to be the institutionalizing and organizing inclinations
of the post-Markan set of Matthean concerns. It is fair to say that within
Matthean Christianity there appear to have been a fair number of correctives
to the sharper edges of institutionalization, as Matthew is also familial and
is deconstructive – as well as bolstering – of Peter's image.[9] The M tradition

---

9. See Graham Stanton's excellent critique and my response to it in *IBR* 1, 1999, pp. 53–69.

eschews judgementalism and discourages uprooting the tares among the wheat for the good of the community, and while Peter receives the keys of the Kingdom, it is also Peter who is asked to forgive 7 times 70. Thus, the functionality of Matthean organization is typified by its capacity to be gracious and relational as well as structural. All it takes, however, is one strident example – such as Diotrephes and his kin – for hierarchical wieldings of Petrine authority to be experienced adversely within Johannine Christianity and beyond. These allergies to a 'new and improved' approach to organizational church life would have been all that was needed to have elicited a Johannine correction to perceived innovations and departures from the more charismatic and less formal way of Jesus. And, from what we know of the historical Jesus, the Johannine corrective was indeed grounded in authentic historical insight on that matter.

Findings

John's relation to the Synoptic Gospel traditions involved complex sets of relationships, and no monofaceted theory will suffice to account for the multiplicity of evidence and perplexities that present themselves for consideration. While John's Gospel may have been finalized last, its tradition did not originate late, and much of it represents an authentic reflection on the ministry of Jesus and its ongoing implications. But just as the Johannine tradition was not derivative from the Synoptic traditions, this does not mean its pervasive independence was the result of isolation or disengagement. Quite the contrary! The Johannine tradition engaged the pre-Markan tradition in the oral stages of their developments and sought to augment and complement the Markan written Gospel. John's oral tradition was a formative source for Q, and of Luke's two-volume project, and Luke has also left us an unwitting clue to Johannine authorship which has hitherto been completely undiscussed in the literature. John's relationship with the Matthean tradition was a dialectical one, and it posed an alternative answer to the most pressing issue of the church, in the late first-century and always. John's final edition points the way forward in terms of Christocracy: the effective means by which the risen Lord intended and intends to lead the church. In these ways, John's relation to the Synoptic Gospels was independent but not isolated, connected but not derivative, individuated but not truncated. In relation to the other Gospels John's was an engaged autonomy, and an overall theory of Johannine-Synoptic relations must include factors that were interfluential, formative and dialectical.

Table 3.3

A Charting of Johannine-Synoptic Interfluential Relations

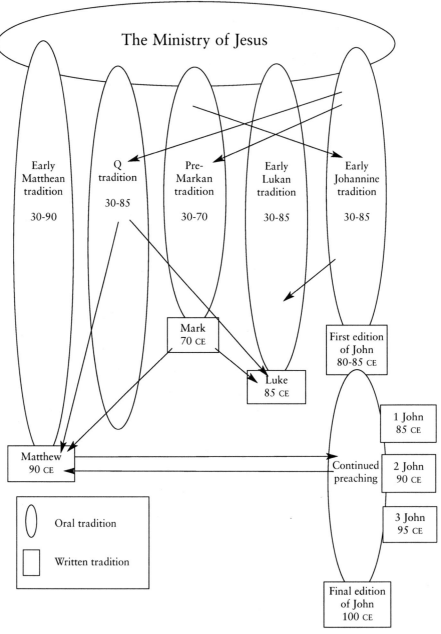

PART IV
JESUS IN BI-OPTIC PERSPECTIVE – CONTRIBUTIONS TO THE JESUS QUEST FROM SYNOPTIC *AND* JOHANNINE SOURCES

'Moreover it is well to remember that where there is a divergence between the Synoptists and St. John, it is not a case of three witnesses against one; for in this respect St. Mark governs the Synoptic tradition; ... The divergence then is between the Second Gospel and the Fourth.'

William Temple, *Readings in St. John's Gospel*
(First Series: Chs. I-XII; London, Macmillan and Co. 1939, p. xii)

Given that John and Mark reflect bi-optic perspectives on the ministry and teachings of Jesus, a more nuanced approach to the issues of John, Jesus and history involves a laying out of particular contributions made by each of these traditions to the quest for the Jesus of history. Despite the fact that the present work challenges the modern tendency to favour the Synoptics over John in the historical quest for Jesus, this does not mean that the Synoptics are devoid of historical content. Rather, both John and the Synoptics make their own contributions to the historical quest for Jesus, and a more integrated approach to these issues suggests how this might be so.

The first consideration is the many ways in which John and the Synoptics indeed overlap with each other in presenting the mission of Jesus. Despite extensive differences, multiple attestation between John and the Synoptics lends a considerable set of impressions as to the character of Jesus' works, and teachings and events in his ministry. The second consideration involves some of the primary ways in which the Synoptics contribute to a realistic impression of Jesus' ministry, and the third does the same with John. Space will not allow a full development of these impressions, but at least a skeletal outline of *Jesus in bi-optic perspective* deserves to be sketched involving both Synoptic and Johannine traditions.

A. Dual Attestation – John and the Synoptics

While John and the Synoptics are characterized by distinctive presentations of Jesus and his ministry, impressive similarities nonetheless exist. Despite the fact that none of the contacts between them are fully identical, minimizing the likelihood of dependence in one direction or another, one cannot say that there are no similarities. In fact, John is more like the Synoptics than Hebrew Scripture, Gnostic and contemporary religious mythic parallels, including other ancient literature such as the Hermetic corpus and stories of such figures as Apollonius of Tyana. The most plausible conjecture from this set of facts is that the Johannine tradition represents an independent memory and narration of the ministry of Jesus, which developed in its own distinctive and autonomous way. This being the case, the many ways in which John and the Synoptics converge deserves consideration as a backbone of dual-attestation impressions worth considering in the quest for the Jesus of history at the outset.

While many more parallels between John and one or more of the Synoptics could be presented, the following 31 accounts are common to all four Gospels. In terms of multiple attestation alone, this is an impressive set of accounts, and while not all of the details or presentations are entirely close, they nonetheless might serve as a skeletal framework upon which to construct an impression of Jesus and his ministry based upon similar accounts in all four Gospels. Consider the following:

Table 4.1

Accounts Common to All Four Gospels

Account	Matthew	Mark	Luke	John
The ministry of John the Baptist	3.1-6	1.2-6	3.1-6	1.19-23
The voice crying in the wilderness	3.11-12	1.7-8	3.15-18	1.24-8
John's baptism of Jesus	3.13-17	1.9-11	3.21-2	1.29-34
Jesus enters Galilee	4.12	1.14a	4.14a	4.1-3
Jesus begins his Galilee ministry	4.13-17	1.14b-15	4.14b	4.43-6a
Jesus feeds the 5,000	14.13-21	6.32-44	9.10b-17	6.1-15
The sea crossing	14.22-33	6.45-52	(8.22-5)	6.16-21
Peter's confession	16.13-20	8.27-30	9.18-21	6.67-71
The anointing at Bethany	26.6-13	14.3-9	7.36-50	12.1-8
The triumphal entry	21.1-9	11.1-10	19.28-40	12.12-19
The Temple incident	21.12-13	11.15-17	19.45-6	2.13-17
Religious leaders plan Jesus' death	26.1-5	14.1-2	22.1-2	11.47-53
Jesus predicts his betrayal	26.21-5	14.18-21	22.21-3	13.21-30
The last supper	26.26-9	14.22-5	22.15-20	13.1-35
Jesus predicts Peter's denial	26.30-5	14.26-31	22.31-4	13.36-8
Jesus enters the garden	26.36-46	14.32-42	22.39-46	18.1
The arrest of Jesus	26.47-56	14.43-52	22.47-53	18.2-12
Jesus' Jewish trial	26.57-68	14.53-65	22.54-71	18.13-24
Peter's denial	26.69-75	14.66-72	22.56-62	18.25-7
Jesus delivered to Pilate	27.1-2	15.1	23.1	18.28
Jesus' Roman trial	27.11-14	15.2-5	23.2-5	18.29-38
Jesus versus Barabbas	27.15-23	15.6-14	23.17-23	18.39-40
Pilate delivers Jesus to be crucified	27.24-6	15.15	23.24-5	19.16
The road to Golgotha	27.31b-2	15.20b-1	23.26-32	19.17a
The crucifixion	27.33-7	15.22-6	23.33-4	19.17b-27
Derision on the cross	27.38-43	15.27-32a	23.35-8	19.18-19
The death of Jesus	27.45-54	15.33-9	23.44-8	19.28-30
Witnesses at the cross	27.55-6	15.40-1	23.49	19.25-7
The burial of Jesus	27.57-61	15.42-7	23.50-6	19.38-42
Women at the tomb	28.1-8	16.1-8	24.1-12	20.1-13
Jesus appears to women	28.9-10	16.9-11	24.10-11	20.14-18

From the above list of parallels in all four Gospels, the following impressions emerge: a) the beginning of Jesus' ministry appears to be connected with that of John and his baptism by John in the Jordan River; b) the bulk of Jesus' ministry was in Galilee, where he served as a healer and teacher; c) Jesus faced growing resistance from Jewish leaders, revolving around his healing on the Sabbath, claiming divine authorization for his works and words, and clearing the Temple; d) Jesus was anointed by a woman at Bethany, prefiguring his death and burial; e) Jesus' ministry culminated with his entry into Jerusalem shortly before a particular Passover, and he shared a last supper with his disciples before going out into a garden with them; f) Jesus was arrested in the garden and tried by Jewish and Roman tribunals; g) Jesus was sentenced to death by Pilate and was crucified and buried; h) post-resurrection appearances to his followers were reported in all four Gospels.

Some of the sequences among these elements are a bit different, but all four Gospels portray similar beginnings, middles and endings of Jesus' ministry, and once things get to the final events in Jerusalem, the sequence of basic events is common: a) Jesus' triumphal entry into Jerusalem, b) a last supper with his disciples, c) his departure to the garden, d) betrayal by Judas, e) his arrest, f) his Jewish trial and g) Roman trial, h) his denial by Peter and the crowing of the rooster, i) his being sentenced to death by Pilate, j) including Pilate's unsuccessful attempt to exchange Barabbas for Jesus, k) the crucifixion of Jesus including a posted sign that he was the 'King of the Jews', l) Jesus' death; m) his burial, and n) his appearances to various followers. From this commonality of ordering in the Passion narratives, scholars have at times inferred that dependence on a common tradition must be the explanation. While such is not impossible, it is also a fact that the basic order of these elements cannot conceivably be presented in any other way. The reason this point is significant is that it challenges traditional dependence as the only and best explanation for the fact of Passion-narrative similarities. Alternative explanations are required. Given the fact that John's tradition adds new material not contained in the Synoptics, and given the fact that John does not follow Mark all that closely here, it is more plausible to infer that we have a duality of traditions between John and the Synoptics, with both trajectories contributing to a basic impression of Jesus' ministry.[1]

In addition to his works and deeds, the teachings of Jesus also show some impressive similarities between John and the Synoptics, despite their differences. They show a Jesus who a) calls disciples to be with him, functioning as an itinerant teacher leading his band of followers; b) teaches his close followers and others about the Kingdom of God, often in contrast to conventional ways of being and doing; c) challenges Jewish authorities regarding an authentic understanding of the Scriptures and the Law of Moses; d) uses agrarian and commonplace imagery to convey his message; e) emphasizes the paradox of servanthood and leadership – those who would lead must be willing to serve others; f) emphasizes love for God and for one another centrally; g) fulfils Scripture in a variety of ways; and h) calls for his followers to be willing to suffer and die for their convictions if necessary. While many more parallels can be inferred between John and Matthew and Luke, note the following ways that speech and discourse are presented in parallel ways in John and Mark – even if slightly paraphrased or distinctive.

---

1. The fact of John's independent Passion material forced Bultmann to infer an independent Passion source underlying John. If the evangelist had no Jesus tradition of his own, some other traditional source for John's distinctive presentation must here be inferred.

Table 4.2

Memorable Sayings Common to John and Mark

- Jesus declares, 'Rise, take up your pallet', to a paralytic (Mk 2.11 – Jn 5.8).
- Jesus declares, 'A prophet is not without honour except in his home town/ own country' (Mk 6.4 – Jn 4.44).
- Jesus is called 'the Holy One of God' by another (Mk 1.24 – Jn 6.69).
- John comes baptizing 'with water' and is not worthy to untie the sandals of Jesus (Mk 1.7-8 – Jn 1.26-7).
- Disciples comment on the cost of feeding the multitude as amounting to 200 *denarii* or more (Mk 6.37 – Jn 6.7).
- Jesus commands the crowds to be seated in the grass (Mk 6.39 – Jn 6.10).
- Jesus makes several absolute '*egō eimi*' statements with similar associations – on the lake, in association with Yahweh and the burning bush, and before Pilate (Mk 6.50; 12.26; 14.62 – Jn 6.20; 8.58; 18.37).
- After Peter's confession, Jesus declares 'Get thee behind me, Satan' / 'One of you is a devil' (Mk 8.29-33 – Jn 6.68-70).
- Ascending and descending are associated with the apocalyptic Son of Man (Mk 14.61-2 – Jn 1.51).
- Jesus invites his disciples: 'Follow me!' (Mk 2.14 – Jn 21.19).
- A saying about John the Baptist being the bridegroom is mentioned (Mk 2.19-20 – Jn 3.29-30).
- Jesus is called 'the Son of God' by another (Mk 3.11; 15.39 – Jn 1.34, 49; 11.27).
- Religious leaders come to Jesus requesting a sign (Mk 8.11 – Jn 6.30).
- Jesus rebukes people's desire for a sign (Mk 8.12 – Jn 4.48).
- Jesus refers to a dead person as being 'asleep' (Mk 5.39 – Jn 11.11).
- To receive Jesus is to receive the One who sent him (Mk 9.37 – Jn 12.44-45; 13.20).
- The destroyed 'temple' Jesus will restore in three days (Mk 13.2; 14.58; 15.29 – Jn 2.19).
- Requirements for entering the Kingdom of God are described (Mk 10.15 – Jn 3.5).
- Seeking to save one's life is to lose it, while releasing one's life will save it (Mk 8.35 – Jn 12.25).
- Jesus is criticized by Jewish leaders for breaking the Sabbath and for healing on the Sabbath (Mk 2.23-8; 3.1-6 – Jn 5.16, 18; 7.23; 9.16).
- Jesus declares his soul is troubled, prays to his 'Father', and labours over drinking the 'cup' before him (Mk 10.38; 14.34-6 – Jn 12.27; 18.11).
- The poor you have with you always, but not so Jesus (Mk 14.7 – Jn 12.8).
- 'Hosanna, blessed is he who comes in the name of the Lord!' is declared by the crowd upon Jesus' entry into Jerusalem (Mk 11.9 – Jn 12.13).
- At the anointing of Jesus by the woman, disciples comment on the

extravagant expense of the perfume as costing 300 *denarii* (Mk 14.5 – Jn 12.5).

- Jesus invites his disciples to follow his example as a servant of others (Mk 9.35; 10.43-5 – Jn 13.16).
- Jesus discusses the resurrection (Mk 12.18-27 – Jn 5.29; 11.24-5).
- Jesus declares that one of his disciples would betray him (Mk 14.18 – Jn 13.21).
- The one with whom Jesus dips in the dish is the betrayer (Mk 14.20 – Jn 13.26).
- The disciples question whom Jesus is speaking about, and Peter declares that he will not deny Jesus (Mk 14.19-29 – Jn 13.22-37).
- The threefold denial of Jesus by Peter is predicted before the cock crows (Mk 14.30 – Jn 13. 38).
- Jesus says, 'Rise, let us depart' (Mk 14.42 – Jn 14.31).
- Whatever is requested by Jesus' disciples will be granted (Mk 11.23-4 – Jn 14.13-14; 15.7; 16.23-4).
- Those who do the will of God / what Jesus commands are members of Jesus' family / his friends (Mk 3.35 – Jn 15.14).
- Jesus teaches on the vineyard and the vine/branches, including references to the son of the father being killed (Mk 12.1-12 – Jn 15.1-13).
- Jesus declares that his disciples would be hated by the world (Mk 13.13 – Jn 15.18).
- Jesus' followers will receive divine guidance as to what they should say during the time of trial (Mk 13.9-11 – Jn 14.26; 15.18-21; 16.1-2).
- The time will come when the sheep / Jesus' followers will be scattered (Mk 14.27 – Jn 16.32).
- Peter denies Jesus thrice (Mk 14.66-72 – Jn 18.15-18, 25-7).
- Jesus declares at his trial that he has taught openly in the Temple and elsewhere (Mk 14.49 – Jn 18.20).
- The crowd calls out, 'Crucify him!' (Mk 15.13-14 – Jn 19.15).
- Jesus is asked by Pilate if he were the 'King of the Jews' (Mk 15.2 – Jn 18.33).
- Roman soldiers strike Jesus and mockingly declare, 'Hail, King of the Jews!' (Mk 15.18-20 – Jn 19.2-3).
- After his positive response (Mk 15.2 – Jn 18.37), Pilate posts a sign on the cross declaring as much in different languages (Mk 15.26 – Jn 19.19).
- The timing of the *Parousia*, before / not necessarily before the last of eyewitnesses had died is declared / clarified (Mk 9.1 – Jn 21.20-3).

From these modest examples of contacts between sayings in John and Mark,[2] it must be acknowledged that many parallels exist between traditions underlying John and the Synoptics, even among the sayings. Most of these associated sayings occur as attributed to Jesus, but many involve questions and comments by disciples, religious leaders, the crowd, the Romans and others. The fact that none of these contacts are identical makes it implausible to infer that John is dependent on Mark, or that Mark is dependent on the Johannine tradition. Three basic possibilities therefore exist: a) the links go back to Jesus or earlier tradition(s); b) some interfluentiality may have existed between the oral stages of the pre-Markan and early Johannine tradition – perhaps even as a feature of secondary orality; and c) either evangelist may have been aware of the other tradition and may have been commenting on or responding to it. Interfluentiality is supported by involve the apparent reference in Jn 4.44 to what Jesus had said in Mk 6.4, and the apparent reference in Mk 14.58 and 15.58 to Jesus' prediction in Jn 2.19 about rebuilding the Temple in three days implies Markan familiarity with either John's tradition or what may have preceded it.

While analyses of Johannine contacts with the Matthean and Lukan traditions may prove interesting, they might not imply all that much about the Jesus of history for two reasons. First, the contacts between the Johannine and Matthean traditions appear to have been later in their development, probably representing the 70s–80s of the late first-century Christian situation. They especially appear in the supplementary material added to the first edition of John (esp. chs 6, 15-17 and 21; although some connections in chs 14 and 20 may be found), and in the Matthean tradition within the material finalized after the completion of Mark. For this reason, the distinctive Johannine-Matthean contacts suggest more about the history of developing issues within early Christianity than the historical quest for Jesus. This is why they have been omitted from this part of the exercise.

Reasons for omitting the Lukan-Johannine contacts at this point are other. Given that Luke departs from Mark and sides with John, the Johannine–Lukan contacts are factors of Luke's dependence on John rather than indicators of independent Jesus traditions. For this reason, Lukan employments of the Johannine tradition may be interesting as an indicator of what *Luke* might have been doing, but they add very little to the historical quest for Jesus other than to accentuate the fact that at least one first-century historian considered the Johannine testimony worthy of use and consideration.

---

2. Indeed, many more could also be presented; for instance, C.H. Dodd (1963) develops five categories of contacts between Johannine and Synoptic sayings (pp. 315–420). Among discourse and dialogue sayings Dodd finds 12 parallels between John and the Synoptics; 30 parallels among sayings common to John and the Synoptics; 13 parallels among parabolic forms; 6 parallels among the sequence of sayings; and 17 parallels among the predictions of Jesus. Clearly, many other contacts exist, and alternative lists are mentioned in the previous two chapters above.

What might be helpful, though, in ascertaining something of the earlier tradition underlying Matthew and Luke in connection with the early Johannine tradition, is to consider the contacts between John and the inferred Q tradition. Of course, such a source is itself hypothetical, and attempts to reconstruct Q are necessarily speculative (indeed, the minor agreements between Matthew and Luke imply an alternative hypothesis – say, Luke's employment of Matthew rather than a separate Q source), but the contacts between Matthew/Luke and John may also reflect some of the earliest Christian traditions, so the following connections are indeed worthy of consideration.

Table 4.3

Possible Contacts Between the Johannine and Q Traditions

- The 'bolt out of the Johannine blue' in the Synoptics implies Q's access to Johannine tradition, in such Johannine motifs as: all things have been 'handed over to the Son' by the Father; 'no one knows the Son except the Father'; and 'no one knows the Father except the Son' and those to whom the Son chooses to reveal him (Jn 3.35; 7.28-9; 10.14-15; 13.3-4; 17.1-3, 22-5 – Mt. 11.25-7; Lk. 10.21-2).
- Jesus is tempted regarding bread and power in the wilderness, and Scripture is cited against Scripture (Jn 6.25-70 – Mt. 4.1-11; Lk. 4.1-13).
- Jewish leaders who claim Abraham as their father as a defence of their legitimacy (Jn 8.33, 39 – Mt. 3.9; Lk. 3.8) are confronted.
- John or Jesus is accused of having a demon (Jn 7.20; 8.48, 52; 10.20 – Mt. 11.18; Lk. 7.33).
- Unworthy stocks and branches are severed and burned in the fire (Jn 15.1-8 – Mt. 3.10; Lk. 3.9) as a factor of judgement.
- Jesus declares that he who loves his life will lose it, and whoever hates his life will find it (Jn 12.25 – Mt. 10.39; Lk. 17.33 – a second set of mentions in addition to Mk 8.35).
- The ripeness of the harvest is mentioned by Jesus in emphasizing the urgency of mission to his followers (Jn 4.35 – Mt. 9.37-8; Lk. 10.2).
- Jesus' healing of the Capernaum official's son from afar / of the Capernaum centurion's servant from afar suggests a traditional connection (Jn 4.46-54 – Mt. 8.5-13; Lk. 7.1-10).
- The 'gate' is mentioned as the way to salvation (Jn 10.1-10 – Mt. 7.13-14; Lk. 13.23-4).
- The foundation of discipleship is hearing the words of Jesus and obeying them (Jn 13.17 – Mt. 7.24-7; Lk. 6.47-9).
- Sheep and shepherd imagery is used of Jesus and believers (Jn 10.11-18 – Mt. 18.10-14; Lk. 15.3-7).
- Advice on asking and receiving in prayer is laid out (Jn 14.13-14; 15.7;

16.24 – Mt. 7.7-11; Lk. 11.9-13 – a second mention in addition to Mk 11.23-4).
- A servant/disciple is not above his master/teacher (Jn 13.16 – Mt. 10.24; Lk. 6.40).

From these three sets of contacts between John and all three other gospels, memorable sayings in John and Mark in particular, and contacts between John and the Q tradition, an impressive set of inferences may be drawn regarding the Jesus of history employing John as a key player among the gospel traditions. While some of the contacts are close, many of them are merely associative, involving also major differences. For instance, while Peter refers to Jesus as 'the Holy One of God' in Jn 6.69, it is the demoniac in Mk 1.24 who refers to Jesus by that title. And, the Capernaum official's son in Jn 4.46-54 seems to be quite a different person from the Capernaum centurion's servant in Lk. 7.1-10. The point is to lay out the similarities and contacts between John and these other traditions in order to make inferences on the basis of *multiple attestation* as to what the ministry of the historical Jesus might have been like. From these connections, the following impressions emerge.

1) Jesus' Association with John the Baptist and the Beginning of his Public Ministry
Including the Johannine presentation of John the Baptist in the mix, several additional impressions help clarify Jesus' relation to John, and even the work of the Baptist. In particular, 'Bethabara beyond the Jordan' (as Orogen and some early manuscripts read) has been investigated recently as the trans-Jordan site of the Baptist's ministry, and archaeologists have found impressive pilgrimage sites along with a wadi flowing into what must have been a large pool, marking the site at which the Jesus movement began. In that sense, the Fourth Gospel contributes to the historicity of Jesus' relationship with John, and one gets the sense that not only did the public ministry of Jesus begin there (Jn 1.19-42), but Jesus apparently visited there at other times during his ministry (Jn 3.22-30; 10.40-2). Based upon the Johannine rendering, people also came to Jesus at that site and elsewhere (Jn 3.26; 4.1-3) on the basis of their favourable association of Jesus' and John's ministries. It also clarifies the Elijah connection, in that Bethabara was the site where Elijah ministered, and this clarifies why the Jewish leaders would have come from Jerusalem to inquire as to whether or not John was Elijah, the Prophet, or the Christ (Jn 1.19-27) – a clear set of messianic associations according to Mal. 3.1-5 and 4.1-5.

A second insight into the character of John's ministry is also contributed by the Johannine rendering, in that the question about 'purifying' raised by the Jewish questioner (Jn 3.25-36) contributes to a fuller understanding of what John's ministry (and therefore Jesus' ministry) was all about. Note that the question about purification suggests a tension between the work that John was doing and conventional means of Jewish purification rites. At Qumran, and also in Jerusalem as one enters the Temple area, there are Jewish purification baths (*Mikva'ot*) having one set of stairs going down and several sets of stairs coming back up, divided by a rail. The purification pool at Qumran, for instance, is a large cistern with four staircases coming up out of the water, with each gradation probably reserved for the particular sort (and degree) of purification one had undergone. Why might this have been the case? Probably because impurity was transferred by touch, and one coming up out of the water would not want to be contaminated by someone going down into the water. This being the case, John's baptism in the free-flowing Jordan, or in such places as Bethabara across the Jordan, or Aenon near Salim (Jn 3.22-5), made an intentional contrast to formal means of ritual purification.

With reference to the Markan insight that John came baptizing for repentance and the remission of sins (Mk 1.4-5), this presentation poses an ethical contrast to purification rites which made no difference in the person's life. Thus, people were called to repent of such sins as collaborating with Romans and refusing to stand for justice, and this social-ethical critique was part of the appeal of John's ministry. From the Johannine contribution, another contrast is also intriguing. The emphasis is not to constrict baptismal practices, but to proliferate their availability beyond religious settings, moving them to common ones. The point of John's baptism in the free-flowing waters of the Jordan is to declare the prolific availability of the free-flowing Spirit – accessible to all who come openly and authentically to God. Jesus' submitting to John's baptism therefore becomes a statement of solidarity with the challenging of delimiting, ritual means of purification, and doing so in the name of God's love for humanity. Therefore, Jesus' association with John implies a concern for authenticity in one's relation to God and moral integrity in one's relation to society. (see Anderson, 2004a)

2) Jesus' Calling of Disciples as a Corporate Venture
One of the things we see about Jesus in all four Gospels is that he did not minister alone; rather, he called people to be with him as partners in ministry. This apparently included women as well as men. John contributes to this presentation in several ways. First, if several of the first disciples called by Jesus were originally followers of John the Baptist, this would provide a further explanation for the fact that the Jesus movement bore so many close connections to the work of the Baptist. It also clarifies some of the reasons why John the Baptist emphasizes that he is not the Messiah, but that Jesus is. As there were many followers of John the Baptist among Jews in Palestine and elsewhere in the first century CE, John's special emphasis on Jesus' being the Messiah, and not he, would have pointed later followers to Jesus as well.

A second feature of Jesus' working with his disciples relates to the different presentations of how they came to be followers of Jesus. In Mk 1.16-20, the first Synoptic calling narrative process, Jesus is passing along the Sea of Galilee and calling Simon and Andrew to leave their nets and follow him. He then called James the son of Zebedee and his brother John, who left their nets, their father and the hired servants and followed Jesus. Jesus here takes the initiative, and his followers respond faithfully to being called as his disciples. The calling narrative in John 1.35-51, however, is presented in a much more informal and unfolding way. Instead of Jesus' calling his followers as the active agent, John the Baptist declares in the presence of two of his disciples, 'Behold the Lamb of God!' After hearing this, Andrew found his brother Simon Peter and said to him, 'We have found the Messiah!' Andrew brought Peter to Jesus, and Jesus gave him the name *Cēphas*, which is the Aramaic word for rock. Jesus travelled on to Galilee the next day, and there he found the Philip who was from the village of Andrew and Peter – Bethsaida. Philip then found Nathaniel, and he also became a follower of Jesus, though not one of the Twelve.

The second calling narrative in the Synoptics involves the calling of Levi, who was a tax collector (Mk 2.3-17). When criticized for his dining with sinners and tax collectors, Jesus replied that he came to call not the righteous but sinners to be his followers. Like a fisherman, a tax gatherer would have been an unlikely choice of disciple for the Messiah, and the selection of followers from the common walks of life is an apparent intention of the redemptive work of Jesus. The third calling narrative in Mark (3.13-19) presents Jesus as ascending the mountain (Luke adds that he was praying all night, Lk. 6.12), calling his followers, appointing the Twelve to be with him and sending them out to preach and to cast out demons. Whereas Peter is given a nickname *Cēphas* in Jn 1.42, the sons of Zebedee are surnamed *Boanergēs* in Mk 3.17, and in Lk. 9.56 they are willing to call down fire from heaven upon the unreceptive Samaritans. Their martyrdom is predicted by Jesus in Mk 10.38-41, and in Jn 21.18-20 Jesus predicts the martyrdom of Peter. The realism of the presentation of the disciples is also typified by the fact that the sons of Zebedee are presented in the Synoptics as wanting to be first in the Kingdom (Mk 10.35-7), and Peter is presented as miscomprehending pastoral leadership in John (Jn 13.1-17; 21.15-17). In both cases, however, Jesus emphasizes the priority of serving one another as the true basis of leadership.

In bi-optic perspective, some combination of Jesus' intentionality and the initiative of others appears to be a more realistic way to envision the relation between Jesus and his disciples. In Jn 1.38 the disciples call Jesus *Rabbi*, and in the Synoptics Jesus not only teaches them about the Kingdom, but he also sends out as many as 70 disciples in teams of two, seeking to further the Kingdom by the ministries of healing and deliverance (Mt. 10.5-16; Mk 6.6-13; Lk. 9.1-6; 10.1-20). Jesus' role as an itinerant teacher is confirmed by the Synoptic presentation of Jesus as one who tells his disciples that the Son of Man has no place to lay his head (Mt. 8.18-22; Lk. 9.57-62). Therefore, his followers must be willing to abandon family and friends in joining a new community on the move. An interesting detail in John is that even some of Jesus' disciples abandon him and walk with him no longer (Jn 6.66). The Twelve, in John, are mentioned for the first time in v. 67, where Jesus turns to the 'remnant' and asks if they too will flee or if they will be faithful.

In all four Gospels the disciples of Jesus are presented as not understanding his words and deeds, but they also are presented as coming to fuller understandings in post-resurrection consciousness. This must have involved a radically different set of cognitive reflections on what they thought they had understood earlier. It is also likely that the ministry gifts, limitations and rhetorical interests of the human purveyors of gospel traditions would have crafted the Jesus story not only according to the needs of the church (as Papias claims the Petrine preaching underlying Mark did), but also as it reflected the investments of the human sources of emerging gospel traditions. In that sense, the constructive work of Jesus' followers, and their followers, and those who had heard or had some contact with their reflections, played a significant set of roles in the development of traditional memory and its conveyance.

3) *A Revolt in the Desert?*[3]

An interesting fact is that the feeding of the 5,000 (and perhaps the sea crossing, if one allows Lk. 8.22-5 as an account of this tradition) is the only miracle common to all four Gospels. While critical scholars have engaged this issue in terms of naturalism versus supernaturalism debates, the most important historical consideration involves the cluster of events surrounding the feeding and the social impact this must have made on the Galilean populace regarding their understandings of Jesus and his mission. Whether the feeding involved the miraculous multiplication of loaves and fishes, or whether it may have involved something even more astounding – the contagious generosity of people sharing their resources with one another – the social and political impact of such an event must be considered. On one hand, note the cluster of happenings that are dispersed in the Synoptics and unified in John 6: a) crowds come together in following Jesus, seeking to engage his ministry in a first-hand way; b) seeing that the crowd (5,000 and 4,000) was hungry, Jesus gathers food that people had brought, blesses it, multiplies it, has his disciples distribute it, and then instructs them to gather up the leftovers into baskets (12 and 7); c) some sort of sea crossing and sea rescue is reported; d) discussions of the feeding and the meaning of the loaves follow, with commentaries upon the teachings of Jewish religious leaders versus the teachings of Jesus being part of the discussion; e) a confession by Peter is made, leading to a statement by Jesus emphasizing the Way of the Cross and the priority of embracing the example of the suffering Son of Man.

Whether any or all of these reported events indeed happened in history, in all probability at least something seems to have happened. At the very least, Jesus was perceived as a prophetic messianic figure, someone fulfilling the

---

3. Hugh Montefiore's essay (1962) develops this idea graphically.

typologies of Moses or Elijah, who also fed the Israelites in the wilderness. Given the likelihood of embellishment, wondrous elements of the story are likely to have grown rather than diminished. In bi-optic perspective, however, social and political aspects of the events are thrown into sharp relief. First, notice that only the men are counted, and Mark presents their seating in 'companies' of 50 or 100 as a marker of revolutionary association. Second, John notes that the Passover was near, which more likely involved a nationalistic and militaristic association than a religious or a cultic one. Third, John's presentation of the reaction of the crowd, wishing to rush Jesus off for a royal coronation, makes it clear that the crowds might have hoped that Jesus would be leading a revolutionary march to Jerusalem. Fourth, even Jesus' disciples are presented as being personally invested in his (and their) triumph, an aspiration Jesus bluntly rejects. Fifth, the emphasis of Jesus that the way of the Son of Man must be the Way of the Cross, involving his own suffering and death and perhaps that of his followers, leads to the scandalization of his disciples and his abandonment by some of his followers. Whatever sort of event it might have been in the wilderness, it probably was interpreted as a messianic uprising destined to march toward Jerusalem and to liberate the nation from its Roman oppressors. This would also explain the dramatic reception of Jesus at his triumphal entry and the apprehension of the Romans as Jesus entered the city.

A comment deserves here to be made regarding the coherence and integrity of the Johannine presentation of these events. Whereas they are dispersed and variant in the Synoptics, they are unified and coherent in John, and this fact deserves a critical comment or two. First, while John presents one feeding and sea crossing (Jn 6.1-15, 16-21), two are presented in the Markan traditions. Mark includes the feeding of the 4,000 (Mt. 15.32-9; Mk 8.1-10) and the feeding of the 5,000 (Mt. 14.13-21; Mk 6.32-44; Lk. 9.10-17). Note that Luke departs from Mark and follows John in including just one feeding – that of the 5,000. Did Jesus perform the event twice, or do we have alternative traditional memories included by Mark? Whatever the case, 17 common elements between the two stories in Mark may be found, and the telling difference is the number of baskets – 7 and 12. If the twelve represents the way Jewish Christianity would have conceived of a full complement of apostolic leadership, that would explain the first feeding account; if the seven represents the way Hellenistic Christianity understood the full complement of diakonic leadership (Acts 6.1-7), that might explain the emergence of the alternative rendering as the story was circulated among the Gentile churches, or even among the seven churches in Asia Minor (Rev. 2-3). Given the fact that the Mk 8.14-26 discussion of the meaning of both feedings seems to have become embedded within the earlier tradition, one can understand why Mark as a collector would have been inclined to include both accounts. This might also explain the comment from Papias that Mark sought to be faithful to what he had received, seeking not to leave anything out (*Hist. Eccles.* 3.39). Mark's second feeding is thus 'explained'.

Second, while only Mark 6 and Matthew 14 present the feeding and sea-crossing together, and while only Mark 8 and Matthew 15-16 present the feeding of the 4,000 with the confession of Peter, John's is the only account which includes all three elements – a feeding, a sea crossing, and the confession of Peter – in the same unit. Luke departs from Mark and sides with John in favouring one feeding, and more tellingly, moving Peter's confession to follow the other feeding – the feeding of the 5,000, coinciding with John. Third, the graphic realism of the Johannine presentation suggests traditional primitivity as well as later development. The 'much grass' on which the people are sitting (parallel to 'green grass' in Mark); the boats coming across the lake from Tiberias and then cutting back across the lake to Capernaum; 25 or 30 *stadia* as an accurate measure of the middle of the lake that is about 7 miles across; the mention of the Synagogue in Capernaum; the costing of 200 *denarii* to feed the multitude (as in Mark); the impulse to rush Jesus off and make him a prophet-king like Moses; the mention of Jesus' parents by the crowd when questions of origins emerge – all of these bespeak the dramatic and historical realism of the distinctively Johannine rendering of the events.

Finally, Peter's confession in John appears closer to the 'historical Peter' than the more confessional Synoptic accounts. Indeed, Peter may have called Jesus 'the Christ' (Mk 8.29 – more plausible than Matthew's fuller 'the Christ, the Son of the living God', Mt. 16.16), but on the basis of dissimilarity, pure historicity is difficult to maintain. The title certainly becomes meaningful for Christians and at the very least would represent later confessional commitments if not an originative one. 'Holy One of God', however, does not fare well as an emerging confession, although Peter makes a similar statement in Acts 3.14, claiming Israel had rejected the 'Holy and Righteous One'. What *is* telling, though, is that the demoniac in Mk 1.24 declares Jesus to be the 'Holy One of God' (followed by Lk. 4.34). If Peter's preaching may indeed have been a primary source of Mark's tradition, 'Holy One of God' might be arguably closer to the 'historical Peter' than the more confessional Markan presentation. It appears also that Luke has harmonized the Markan and Johannine accounts, rendering Peter's confession as believing that Jesus is *'the Christ...of God'* (Lk. 9.20). In these and other ways, the Johannine rendering of these events is more coherent, empirically rooted and historically plausible than the Synoptic accounts. Luke's siding with John against Mark also confirms the existence of that opinion as early as the late first century CE.[146]

4) Jesus as a Healer; Healing on the Sabbath
In all four Gospels Jesus is presented as healing people on the Sabbath, which then led to debates over keeping the Sabbath and other aspects of Sabbath-regulation laws. This makes one wonder if challenging Sabbath-regulation

---

4. For a fuller treatment of these issues surrounding John 6 and their literary, historical and theological implications, see Anderson (1996, pp. 70–251).

laws was a central interest of Jesus' healing ministry. Put otherwise, many people went untouched directly by Jesus' ministry, even when it was most actively engaged. In addition to a therapeutic interest in bringing health to humans, perhaps Jesus was also concerned to bring well-being and wholeness to humanity – the very thing the Sabbath was intended to effect. In this and other ways, Jesus intends to produce a sense of *cognitive dissonance* by the clashing of experiences with perceptions (Anderson, 2004a). In dining with 'sinners', in cleansing the Temple, in extending baptismal purification beyond its delimiting cultic settings, in teaching about the way of the Kingdom, and in healing on the Sabbath, Jesus was apparently seeking to transform the understandings of his audiences – calling them back to the heart of the Law and the Prophets, and also calling them forward to the unfolding of the divine will and presence for the redemption of humanity.

This being the case, the reactions of the religious authorities are understandable. They were threatened by Jesus' teachings and actions, interpreting them as subversive of religious systems and structures, and indeed, they were. Therefore, debates followed these Sabbath healings along two noted lines. First, clarifications were explored as to the intention and purpose of the Sabbath, and Jesus emphasized that humanity was not made for the Sabbath, but that the Sabbath was made for the good of humanity. Healing, redemption and wholeness were the reasons to observe the Sabbath, and these concerns also reflect the divine will for humanity. Second, aspects of Jesus' authority come into play here – especially in John. When challenged as to the basis for his 'breaking' Sabbath regulations, Jesus attested to his having been sent by the Father. Especially in John 5 and 7-10, Jesus' claims to have been speaking as a factor of divine agency (Deut. 18.15-22) became a further matter of contention. Such discussions of authority and legitimation probably had an originative root in the actual ministry of Jesus and his ambivalent reception, and yet, Jesus' divine agency and identity also became matters of debate in the later Matthean and Johannine traditions as questions of Jesus' Messiahship inherited a fresh set of contentious discussions. As a factor of challenging Sabbath regulations, however, at least some of this probably went back to the actual ministry of Jesus. How else would a provocative northern prophet have been received by the religious leaders in Jerusalem and elsewhere?

5) Jesus' Sense of Prophetic Agency from the Father and Religious Resistance
While many Christological titles used for Jesus are found in the Gospels, the earliest ones probably related to Jewish Messianic typologies such as a King like David, or a prophet like Moses. It must also be said that the Isaiah tradition is likely to be confusing on this point in particular. Within Isaiah, the 'Anointed One' (*Messias* in Hebrew; *Christos* in Greek) is directly associated with King Cyrus of Persia, who delivered the Jews from Babylonian exile and helped them with the restoration and return to the homeland in the last third of the sixth century BCE. While Isaiah contrasts the messianic figure of Cyrus with the 'Suffering Servant' of Yahweh (the faithful servant would not break

a bruised reed or snuff out a smouldering candle, but would be a non-violent leader), these typologies became easily conflated before and during the ministry of Jesus. Nonetheless, Jesus appears to have thought of himself most centrally as a prophet like Moses, who would not speak or do anything of his own initiative, but only what he was commanded by God.

Rooted in Deut. 18.15-22, several elements of this prophetic-agency typology can be identified in all four Gospels, but they are especially clear in John: a) God will raise up a prophet like Moses from amidst the people of Israel, and they must listen to him; b) he will not speak anything on his own behalf but will only say what he is commissioned by God to say; c) people must listen to him as though listening to God, and God will hold them accountable; d) in answer to the question regarding how the authentic prophet is to be distinguished from a false one, the true prophet's words always come true; e) therefore, if a prophet's words come true he is to be heeded; if a prophet's words do not come true, that is a false prophet, and he is to be killed or disregarded. One can understand how King-like-David typologies might have emerged, especially in association with Bethlehem traditions and the Zechariah motifs, but Jesus' self-understanding probably bore a closer resemblance to the prophet-like-Moses (*schaliach* – sending) typology than any other, and John contributes to this presentation every bit as much as – if not more than – the other Gospels. It is within this typology that most of the Father-Son imagery in the Gospels – especially in John – should be understood.

Parallel to this agency typology is the Son of Man motif – undoubtedly the most likely self-designation of Jesus, occurring in all four Gospels. Like the Mosaic prophet typology, the Son of Man motif is also absent from all the Christological hymnic passages in the writings of Paul and elsewhere. Other than in the witness of Stephen in Acts 7 (where both of these titles occur) the only place the Son of Man occurs in the New Testament is in the self-referential words of Jesus in the gospels, so it is unlikely to have represented later Christian worship embellishment. It most probably goes back to Jesus. Yet, *why* did Jesus choose such a phrase with which to refer to himself? Was it a reference to the humble and obedient Son of Man in Ezekiel – a child of the dust of the earth, or was it a reference to the apocalyptic Son of Man in Daniel – a divine agent coming from the heavens with eschatological finality? Perhaps Jesus chose such a title precisely because of its bi-polar ambiguity! Then again, Jesus may have used it with reference to his lowly faithfulness to his divine commission, and his followers may have added the more embellished apocalyptic associations after the resurrection – in anticipation of his second coming. Whatever the case, Jesus' self-references as the Son of Man and as the faithful Prophet both bespeak his sense of divine agency and desire to be faithful to that commission. On this John and the Synoptics agree.

6) *Jesus' Cleansing of the Temple*
All four Gospels tell the story of Jesus' cleansing the Temple, and it is presented as a pivotal event in all four, despite being at the culmination of

Jesus' ministry in the Synoptics and at the beginning of Jesus' ministry in John. This event fulfils nearly all the criteria for determining historicity – it is multiply attested, it fulfils both dissimilarity and embarrassment criteria, it does not go against the grain of naturalism, and it coheres with the sort of prophetic work Jesus is thought to have performed – and the fact that it is presented differently in John bolsters its historical plausibility. Common elements among the various traditions include: a) Jesus' entering the Temple and driving out the sellers, money changers and animals and overturning their tables; b) Jesus' declaring a scriptural word about the authentic use of the Father's house versus its corrupted uses; c) resulting questions about Jesus' authority; and d) thematic connections between the destruction of the Temple and the death and resurrection of Jesus – connected explicitly only in John.

Whether this event was an inaugural or a culminative sign, it certainly is pivotal in Johannine and Synoptic traditions alike. Here the northern prophet, when confronted with the mercantile character of the sacrificial system, saw it as a sacrilege and sought to expunge its flaws. In all four Gospels, this event pits Jesus against the central cultic and national institution of Judaism, which leads directly to his opposition and demise at the hands of religious leaders, though carried out by the Romans. Jesus is presented as advocating the authentic worship of God – opening the heart of Judaism to those with open hearts of prayer and worship. In post-resurrection consciousness, the theological meaning of the event appears to have shifted for the Johannine and Markan traditions to an association with the 'Temple' being destroyed and rebuilt in three days as a reference to the resurrection. The Johannine tradition renders explicit what is implicit in the subsequent recognition motif – his disciples later came to understand that Jesus was speaking of his body, and after the resurrection, they understood the fuller meaning of the ambiguous word (Jn 2.19-22). This is an example of history and theology intertwined from the beginning of the tradition until its canonical finalization.

7) *The Culmination of Jesus' Ministry – his Arrest, Trials and Death in Jerusalem*

Mark has often been called a Passion narrative with a long introduction, and the same can be said of the other Gospels, as well. Indeed, the events following the entry into Jerusalem are even 30 per cent longer in Matthew and John, but so are their overall Gospels. Given that the heart of the *Kerygma* of the apostles involved centrally the death and resurrection of Jesus, one can understand how the Passion narratives came together quite early in the respective gospel traditions. Common elements between the Johannine and Synoptic Passion narratives are not necessarily a factor of inter-tradition dependence. They could represent a common set of historical events, developed independently in the Markan and Johannine traditions, but they could also reflect common elements in early Christian preaching. Either way, the Passion narratives reflect *early* gospel traditions.

Nonetheless, the following common elements are found in all four canonical traditions and either individually or on the whole should be regarded as having a high degree of plausibility: the triumphal entry; the Temple incident; religious leaders plan Jesus' death; Jesus predicts his betrayal; the last supper; Jesus predicts Peter's denial; Peter declares he will not deny Jesus; Jesus and his disciples enter the garden; Judas' betrayal of Jesus; the arrest of Jesus; Jesus' Jewish trial; Peter's denial; Jesus' deliverance to Pilate; Jesus' Roman trial; Jesus versus Barabbas; Pilate delivers Jesus to be crucified; the road to Golgotha; the crucifixion; derision on the cross; the death of Jesus; witnesses at the cross; the burial of Jesus; and women at the tomb. Therefore, even more than the beginning of Jesus' ministry, its culmination coheres in an extensive and corroborative set of ways. Indeed, many of the details are theologically charged, but given the multiplicity of attestation and distinctiveness of parallel presentations, theological reflections on historical events are a more likely explanation than the inference of historicization of theological interests. Some of the latter may have been the case, but the political realism of the arrest, trials and death of Jesus in Jerusalem lend these events a high degree of historical plausibility. They are confirmed in bi-optic presentation.

8) Attestations to Appearances and the Beginning of the Jesus Movement
While recent Jesus scholars have been nearly unanimous in affirming the basic historicity of the Passion narrative, fewer have been willing to affirm the historical veracity of the resurrection. The Jesus Seminar, for instance, consigned these reports to the canons of faith rather than historicity and refused to vote on the post-resurrection sayings and deeds of Jesus. It is also a fact that these reports are far more diverse than the pre-resurrection narratives, and given their highly supernaturalistic character and theological significance, modern historical-Jesus investigations have raised far greater challenges to the post-resurrection narratives than they have to the pre-resurrection ones. Nonetheless, an impressive number of appearance reports may be found among all four of the canonical Gospels, although the dearth of such reports in the first ending of Mark was rectified in the later addition of the second (Mk 16.9-20).

While the details themselves vary considerably, note the following impressive similarities among the accounts. First, women came to the tomb early on the first day of the week in order to anoint the body of Jesus with spices. While the particular names are various (although Mary Magdalene appears in all of them), their intentions to embalm Jesus bears witness to their belief that he had indeed died – an unlikely conjecture if the resurrection were assumed from the beginning rather than discovered. Second, these women reported having encountered the risen Lord and were told to go and tell the other disciples what they had seen. Again, this may have been embellished, but the fact that *women* are presented as the agents of the post-resurrection evangel attests to the unlikelihood of their concoction. Third, Jesus' appearances to his followers include a striking variety of presentations, ranging from an ethereal presence to an emphasis upon his physical flesh-wounds. Jesus eats with his followers and appears to them in Jerusalem and in Galilee, and as a factor of their experiences they become bold witnesses, willing to suffer martyrdom and death as a factor of their conviction. However it might have been experienced, physically or numinously, appearances to his followers are reported after the death of Jesus in all four Gospels, and if not historicity, these accounts at the very least document an attestation of conviction and belief.

In summary, from the multiple attestations of Jesus' ministry in all four canonical gospel traditions, an impressive array of historical information comes across for the reader. No fewer than 31 units of material are included in all four traditions, including John within the mix despite its tradition's often being presented in considerably different ways. Likewise, John has at least 44 memorable sayings in common with Mark and as many as 13 possible contacts with the Q tradition, demonstrating the fact that while John's material is distinctive, it can by no means be considered unique. John's dialogical autonomy is here confirmed in analysing John's distinctiveness as well as similarities with other traditions. Most interesting in considering the eight major features of Jesus' ministry found in all four Gospels is the fact that in each case John contributes something valuable and unique to the mix – contributing to a fuller sense of texture and realism regarding the subject. Put otherwise, if John's tradition were not available, not only would the theological presentation of Jesus' ministry be impoverished, but so would the historical enterprise aspiring to understand more of the Jesus of history as well as the Christ of faith. Then again, if one's critical inference is that there is nothing historical in John, one must also deny the historicity of all the above features or modify one's claims. On the basis of dual attestation between John and the Synoptics, the modernist platforms of John's non-historicity and a non-Johannine Jesus fall flat on the basis of evidence.

B. *Synoptic Contributions to the Quest for the Jesus of History*

While most of the above eight points could have been constructed without the benefit of the Johannine tradition, John definitely adds to the texture of these events, and varied similarity strengthens the degree of historical plausibility even further. Given a general sense of coherence, the more variety that is added to a particular tradition's rendering, the more arguable is its basic degree of historicity. As with the case of John, John's tradition is different enough that it does not appear to depend on any of the Gospels – including Mark – so therefore the events and sayings treated in all four Gospels have a greater degree of plausibility. John's differences from the Synoptic renderings of similar events thus corroborate the presentation as an alternative perspective on a common set of events. However, they are distinguished from the following eight points, which are either not treated in John or are presented differently in John. Nonetheless, distinctively Synoptic contributions to the quest for the Jesus of history deserve consideration, as they are certainly intrinsic to the quest. Some aspects of these elements will have been mentioned in the groupings above and below, and particular historical contributions in each case will be highlighted, at least briefly.

1) *Jesus' Teachings about the Kingdom of God in Parables and in Short, Pithy Sayings*

One of the distinctive features about Jesus and his ministry is the way he taught about the Kingdom of God in parables. In contrast to most Jewish leaders and rabbis of his day, the Jesus of the Synoptics built upon real-life situations, familiar relationships and agrarian metaphors to describe the spiritual and authentic character of the ways and workings of God. Central to his teachings were several principles. First, the sovereign reign of God transcends human ventures, institutions and organizations. It is a dynamic reality rather than a static one, and humanity is invited to lift its eyes beyond loyalties to nation, religion and kinship and to join in partnership with God in the furthering of the divine will on earth as it is in heaven. Second, the way of the Kingdom is one of transvaluation. The first become last, and the last become first. Wishing to save one's life is to lose it; only in releasing one's life does one paradoxically find it. Third, for this reason, entry into the Kingdom involves child-like faith – recovering a sense of basic trust in the love and life of God and receiving by faith the divine embrace of grace.

The parables and other teachings of Jesus in the Synoptics are designed to convey the way of the Kingdom in ways that are creative and compelling. It advances by love and by light, not by force or by violence, and Jesus' command to love one's enemies is indeed revolutionary. On these matters the presentation of Jesus' teaching in the Synoptics deserves historical precedence over the presentation of Jesus' teaching in John. Jesus does address the way of the Kingdom in two passages in John (Jn 3.3-8; 18.36-8), but both passages are contrastive rather than illustrative. In contrast to endeavours which are of creaturely origin, entering the Kingdom of God hinges upon being born from above. And, in contrast to the power of political and military force, the character of authority and the essence of Jesus' kingdom is one of truth. Jesus does speak in somewhat parabolic forms in John, including the gate and the shepherd of the sheep (Jn 10.1-18) and the vine and the branches (Jn 15.1-8), but the parabolic form of the teachings of the Synoptic Jesus probably represents a closer portrait of the Jesus of history than do the more theologized sayings of Jesus in John.

2) *The Messianic Secret and the Hiddenness of the Kingdom*

One of the striking characteristics of Mark is the presentation of the Messianic Secret. After Jesus heals people he instructs them to tell no one but to go straight to the religious authorities that the healings might be confirmed with modesty and authenticity (Mk 1.44; 5.43; 7.36; 8.26). He does the same with exorcized demoniacs (Mk 1.34; 3.12). Perhaps most striking is the fact that after Peter's confession that Jesus is the Christ (Mk 8.29-30), Jesus instructs Peter to tell no one that he is the Messiah, something that appears to be the main point of the question. Things get a bit clearer at the Transfiguration, as Jesus adds timing to the equation. His disciples are to tell no one about these striking events until *after* the Son of Man has risen from the dead (Mk 9.9). While the Messianic Secret is more muted in Matthew and Luke, it comes across as a central motif of the Gospel of Mark. As Mark is the earliest Gospel, and as this feature fits the criterion of embarrassment, this motif probably represents the Jesus of history more adequately than do the messianic disclosure statements of the Johannine Gospel.

This leads to the question of *why* Jesus emphasized messianic secrecy. It probably had to do with wanting to distinguish himself from more popular-istic and nationalistic messianic figures that were prevalent in Palestine according to Josephus. In contrast to Judas the Galilean, Jesus emphasized giving unto Caesar what is Caesar's, yet giving to God what is God's. In contrast to the revolutionary use of force by such figures as the Samaritan, Theudas and the Egyptian, Jesus advocated turning the other cheek and returning good for evil. It may also have been that Jesus sought to resist sensa-tionalistic and popularistic appeal, aiming instead for authenticity and truth. That being the case, the Johannine Jesus *does* demonstrate parallels with the Markan Jesus. He challenges those who are seeking for a sign, and he flees the crowd's designs on his future after the feeding of the multitude as they seek to rush him off for hasty coronation as a prophet-king like Moses (Jn 6.14-15). Nonetheless, the self-referential language of the Johannine Jesus seems more the creation of the Fourth Evangelist rather than the presentation of the Jesus of history. On the issue of messianic secrecy, Mark's rendering takes historical precedence.

3) *Jesus' Healing and Exorcizing Ministries*
While John only has two healing miracles in addition to the resurrection of Lazarus, the more extensive presentation of Jesus as a healer in the Synoptics seems to be the more representative from a historical standpoint. Aside from problems of naturalism versus supernaturalism, Jesus probably would have been associated with other healers of his day, although he appears to have been regarded with a fair degree of exceptionality. The authority of his healing work becomes both a basis for his popular appeal and a central factor in his being a threat to the religious leadership. These features are both present in John as well, but the presentation of his healing work in the Synoptics betrays a more extensive pattern that seems more likely as a representation of someone who was engaged in this work seriously.

A feature also deserving of note in the Synoptic tradition is the relation between faith and miracles. While some of this connection may have gone back to Jesus, it certainly plays a role in the Markan and Matthean emphases on the role of faith in the actualization of wonders. Conversely, from a

Cognitive-Critical perspective, the relative dearth of miracles is explained in the Synoptic traditions as a factor not of divine failure, but of the failure of human faith. Given the lack of faith in Jesus' own hometown, Nazareth, even he was unable to do any miracles there (Mk 6.4-6). By contrast, the Johannine treatment of the relative dearth of miracles came to revolve around the revelational significance of what was seen, and the theological meaning of what was reported without having been seen (Jn 20.29). Whether either of these interpretive schemas went back to the Jesus of history is finally impossible to know. At the very least, we do have two individuated and distinctive approaches to the relation between signs and faith, and in that sense both the Synoptic and Johannine traditions are factors of theological developments as much as historical events (Anderson, 2004b).

In addition to his healings, the most common miracle performed by Jesus in the Synoptics involves his exorcisms. John, on the other hand, has no exorcisms, and here the Synoptic accounts must be given the nod of historicity. Jesus would not have been the only healer-exorcist in his day, and many of his healing miracles are accompanied by his casting out of demons from the individual being healed. Indeed, some of the healings performed by Jesus in the Synoptics bear a close resemblance to psychosomatic disorders or epilepsy, and deliverance from inward sources of oppression may indeed have been experienced therapeutically. Jesus also is presented as declaring the forgiveness of people's sins in conjunction with a healing, and imagining the paralysis of guilt and its somatic effects makes it not impossible to infer a connective link between the two conditions. Some of the stories of demoniacs in the Synoptics appear to have developed in folkloric ways, but the combination of the healing, exorcizing and forgiving work of Jesus in the Synoptics seems more historically plausible than the Johannine rendering.

This being the case, however, the problem of John's omission of Jesus' forgiving and exorcizing work is problematic. Did the Fourth Evangelist *not* know of exorcisms, or did he leave them out intentionally? Whatever the case, two facts are noteworthy from a Cognitive-Critical perspective. First, whether this person had anything to do with the Johannine tradition or not, John the apostle is presented in Acts as not doing any miracles. Peter and Paul do, but John does not. Might this have played a role in the denigration of signs within the Johannine tradition? Second, at least one disciple is presented in the Synoptics as being uncomfortable with the exorcizing work of others, enough to ask Jesus if he should instruct those who were carrying forth such ministries to desist. That disciple is named as John the son of Zebedee. Might *all* followers of Jesus have been equally comfortable with his exorcizing work? Some, reportedly, were not. Alternatively, might all audiences, including Gentile ones, have been equally comfortable with hearing about exorcisms? Given the fact of narrative selectivity (Jn 20.30; 21.25), such omissions are perfectly understandable as factors of alternative agendas and audiences. The Synoptics, though, make the more historical contribution on this matter of interest.

4) Jesus' Sending out his Disciples to Further the Work of the Kingdom
While the Gospel of John does not present Jesus as sending out his disciples
in ministry teams, the presentation of Jesus as doing so in the Synoptics
appears valid historically. Not only did Jesus perform healing and exorcizing
work, but he also sent his followers out to do the same, and this feature lends
important insights into the goals and strategies of Jesus. He not only came to
be the one ministering to the needs of others on behalf of God's love; he came
to reproduce such service as a means of multiplying the transforming love of
God for the healing and redemption of the world. Further, he sent them out
in twos and in groups so that they could be of mutual support to one another,
bolstering the strength of the movement. This also must have extended the
scope and influence of Jesus' ministry, bringing about an impressive impact
on Galilee, Samaria and Judea, continuing even after the departure of Jesus.

Given the fact that Peter and John and other followers of Jesus are presented
as travelling in ministry in the book of Acts, the itinerant ministries of leaders
in the later Jesus movement attest to Jesus' having involved his followers in
ministry alongside him. Peter and John are reported as travelling in ministry
together in Samaria (Acts 8.14-25), and such leaders as Stephen, Peter, Paul
and Philip are presented as continuing in the trajectory of Jesus, even if
coming later into the movement, by doing the works that he had done:
preaching, witnessing, healing the sick, raising the dead and exorcizing
demons. One can imagine that the ministries of such leaders would also have
impacted their memory and presentation of the historical ministry of Jesus,
as the stories one tells say as much about the narrator as they do about one's
subject.

Note, however, that while John is presented as travelling with Peter in
Acts, he apparently does no miracles or wonders, and the only time he speaks
is in conjunction with Peter in Acts 4.19-20. Whether Peter and John, or people
like them, had anything to do with the traditions underlying the bi-optic
Gospels, Mark and John, as Papias and Irenaeus argued, one fact is certain:
the content and presentation of Jesus' ministry in the Second and the Fourth
Gospels coheres remarkably with the apparent giftedness – and lack, thereof
– of these two apostles as reported in Acts. Therefore, in Cognitive-Critical
perspective, the distinctive presentations of Jesus' ministry in the Synoptics and
John may have as much to do with the human sources of those traditions,
including their perspectives and experiences, as it does with the content itself.
Even among his followers Jesus is reported as being understood variously in
all four traditions, and these differences must have included early impressions
as well as later reflections (Anderson, 2004b).

5) Jesus' Dining with 'Sinners' and Provocations toward Renewal
A striking feature in the Synoptic tradition is the fact that Jesus is presented
as dining with sinners, tax collectors and other societal outcasts. Given the
criterion of embarrassment, this is not the sort of feature that is likely to have
been concocted or added to a developing tradition. Rather, it probably has its

basic origin in the historical ministry of Jesus. The question, though, has to do with *why* Jesus extended table-fellowship to unlikely guests. Behind this action is the Jewish belief that sharing table-fellowship reconciles people to one another before God. Offerings for communion between neighbours were a common form of sacrifice in Hebrew Scripture, and the breaking of bread together was understood to be a reconciling action between all parties involved. This is why the psalmist was able to say of the divine shepherd, 'Thou preparest a table before me in the presence of mine enemies' (Ps. 23.5). He was not commenting primarily on eating, but on forgiveness and reconciliation. Likewise, Jews in Jesus' day were forbidden to eat with Gentiles, and even to enter their houses. Therefore, when Jesus extended table-fellowship to those who were ritually, morally or religiously impure, he was breaking the rules of societal propriety, and he was doing so in the name of God.

Yet why did he do it? Was it an extension of inclusive love, or was it intended to create cognitive dissonance as a means of transforming people's understandings of what God requires? The answer might include aspects of both. As a prophetic agent of God's love for the world, Jesus would have looked upon the dejected and harassed with compassion; at least he is presented that way within the Synoptic traditions. Therefore, his inclusion of the downtrodden into the loving embrace of God coheres with the character of his mission. Inclusive love, however, was not his only goal. He also apparently sought to extend the reach of loving inclusiveness, challenging the structures of society, especially religious ones that alienate and dehumanize the other. In demonstrating God's love, acceptance and forgiveness in public table-fellowship – even before the welcomed guests had repented – Jesus was making a profoundly theological statement. God's gift of grace is extended freely to all, and all are invited to receive that gift in faith.

6) Jesus' Cleansing of the Temple as an Intentional Challenge to the Restricting of Access to God
A particular detail in the Gospel of Mark (Mk 11.11) shows Jesus entering the Temple area after he had first come into Jerusalem. He apparently looked around at the situation and then departed because it was late, deciding to return the next day. It was then that he cleared the Temple, driving out the merchants, overturning the tables, and disrupting the selling of sacrificial animals (Mk 11.15-17). From these details the apparent motivation and intention of Jesus is clarified. Rather than seeing the Temple incident as a fit of rage or an uncontrolled outburst, Jesus' actions show signs of resolve and intentionality. Embedded within the account of the cursing and withering of the fig tree (Mk 11.12-14, 20-6), the action bears with it associations related to a prophetic sign. In the tradition of the Hebrew prophets, this prophetic enactment declares judgement upon a religious institution and enterprise, then pointing the way forward toward the redemptive way of God.

This being the case, two central implications arise. First, in the light of Jesus' challenging of other religious institutions, this dramatic action condemns a system functioning to establish religious purity and acceptability on the basis of ritual and transactional means. What had originally been intended as a means of ensuring that sacrificial animals were in good condition and fittingly offered had become an elaborate set of stipulations resulting in the conditionality of divine love, acceptance and forgiveness. Jesus' action here declares that God's grace is not conditioned by outward ways of doing it right. Rather, God looks on the heart, and those who come to God authentically received God fully. This concern is punctuated by the words Jesus declared regarding God's house being 'a house of prayer for all the nations' instead of a 'den of thieves' (Isa. 56.7; Jer. 7.11; Mk 11.17). It also explains the understandable reaction of the chief priests and scribes, who reportedly sought to find a means to destroy Jesus, not because he had disrupted their business, but because they feared the sympathy he had engendered among the crowd regarding the challenging of the Temple enterprise. To make the Temple a house of prayer for all the nations is to challenge the religious equity of transactional access to God's saving presence and grace. They were threatened by Jesus *because* they understood him correctly (Anderson, 200a and 2004a).

A second implication relates to the unintended consequences of exclusionary systems of management. Because ritual purity required particular means of attainment sacrificially, involving the exchanging of Roman currency for Jewish money and the purchasing of a 'clean' and appropriate sacrificial animal, both at a markup, this meant that most poor people would not have been able to afford the sacrificial means by which to attain ritual purity. Therefore, Jesus' prophetic action in the Temple must be understood also in its socio-economic perspective. Luke's presentation of Jesus' concern for the poor is especially relevant on this point. Jesus came challenging a system that functioned to exclude the poor and downtrodden from the very thing they needed most, and which a loving Father is most eager to provide. Therefore, Jesus' cleansing the Temple in the Synoptics not only declares that God's saving grace is not conditioned by outward ritual means of attainment; he also declared the openness and accessibility of God's presence and love, available to humanity in all strata of society.

7) Jesus' Teaching on the Heart of the Law – the Love of God and Humanity
One of the most impressive aspects of Jesus' teachings in the Synoptics is the fact that he is presented as getting to the heart of the Law rather than its legalistic perimeters. As an approach to fulfilling the Law in the Sermon on the Mount ('You have heard it said, but I say unto you...'), Jesus gets at the centre – hatred rather than killing; lust rather than adultery; integrity rather than swearing about honesty (Mt. 5.21-37). Likewise, when asked to name which commandment was the greatest (the sort of trick-question designed to produce nine wrong answers for every correct one; Mt. 22.34-40; Mk 12.28-34; Lk. 10.25-8) Jesus avoided a legal answer and went to the heart of the matter. As the first four of the Ten Commandments relate to the human-divine relationship (Exod. 20.3-11), and the last six relate to human-human

relationships (Exod. 20.12-17), Jesus did well to summarize them all in his response. He also did well to avoid an impossible question successfully within the given parameters by citing two Torah passages outside the Decalogue: the love of God (Deut. 6.5) and the love of neighbour (Lev. 19.18).

Jesus also is presented as calling for the love of enemies and the returning of forgiveness and prayer for those from whom one has suffered maltreatment. While a significant aspect of turning the other cheek, giving one's cloak as well as one's coat, and going a second mile when commanded to go one, and giving to the one who begs (Mt. 5.38-48; Lk. 6.29-36) is that Jesus advocates finding a creative alternative to imposed dichotomies, he also calls for people to love others authentically. Indeed, only a loving response to force can be genuinely disarming, and Jesus advocates the need to love especially when it is undeserved by the other. From these sorts of moves, some of the most interesting aspects of Jesus' teachings involve not simply *what* he taught, but *how* he taught. Rather than focusing on the legalistic perimeter of the Law, he went to the centre. That centre involves the enduring love of God, and this is what Jesus invites humanity to receive and to share with others.

On this matter, John's presentation is rather different. The Johannine Jesus says nothing of loving one's enemies or neighbours, but he poses a new commandment, which is for his followers to love one another (Jn 13.34-5). John also presents the love of God in clear ways, but the emphasis is upon God's love for humanity rather than humanity's love for God (Jn 3.16). On this note, the Synoptic seems the most historically plausible, as the Johannine rendering reflects developments within the Johannine situation. Hence, the exhortation to love one another is 'an old commandment' which has been heard 'from the beginning' (2 Jn 4-6). And, it is not that we have loved God, but that God has first loved us (1 Jn 4.7-21), that becomes the basis for hope. Indeed, as Johannine Christians faced the needs of getting along amid the pressures of maintaining a religious community, Jesus' teachings on the love of God and others evolved appropriately, as needed within the Johannine situation. In that sense, the Johannine adaptation of Jesus' moral teaching *appropriates* its content rather than distorting it.

8) *Jesus' Apocalyptic Mission*

In teaching about the Kingdom of God, Jesus taught that God's active and dynamic reign was a present reality, to be engaged in faith and faithfulness. As such, Jesus must be considered among the apocalyptists of Judaism in that he cultivated visions of the end of time as well as declaring what the faithful should be about in the meantime. In the prayer he taught his disciples (Mt. 6.7-15; Lk. 11.1-4), Jesus instructs them to pray that God's Kingdom would come and that it would be actualized on earth as it is in heaven. In that sense, Jesus invites his followers to join him in partnership in the furthering of the divine will and the way of the Kingdom by their obedience and participation with his mission. In contrast to human force and the resorting to violence, Jesus calls for a profound trust in God and the furthering of God's work in the world.

Jesus also is presented as delivering an apocalyptic discourse in Mk 13.3-37 and its corollaries (Mt. 24.3-51; Lk. 21.7-36). Building on a prediction of the destruction of the Temple (Mt. 24.1-2; Mk 13.1-2; Lk. 21.5-6), Jesus launches into a litany of apocalyptic themes – signs of the end, predicted persecution, the abomination which causes desolation, warnings about false Christs and prophets, the eschatological advent of the Son of Man, the parable of the fig tree, and calling for people to take heed and to watch for the coming of Christ. This discourse expands on the prediction of Jesus in Mk 9.1 that those present would not taste death until they see the Son of Man coming in all of his glory, and such an anticipation became something of a crisis when believers started to die before the *Parousia* had been actualized (1 Thess. 4.13-17). While these discourses probably have some basis in the apocalyptic character of Jesus' mission and message, they also show signs of adaptation to the pressing needs of the early church, so not all of their history is primitive.

While John contains a few apocalyptic references (Jn 5.21-9; 6.44, 62), the apocalyptic work of Jesus in the Synoptics deserves historical preference. On the other hand, Jesus' prediction of the *Parousia* (Mk 9.1) might not have represented the intention of the Jesus of history if Jn 21.20-3 is to be taken seriously. When faced with the delay of the *Parousia*, one of the first major disillusionments of early Christianity, believers either interpreted the statement otherwise or kept waiting for the Lord's coming. Luke, for instance, presents Pentecost as something of a second coming, although he still holds open the hope that Christ would return as he ascended. John, however, presents a distinctive alternative, declaring that Jesus never intended such a meaning as inferred from Mk 9.1 to be taken. Given the apparent death of the Beloved Disciple, the Johannine narrator clarifies that Jesus never said that he would not die; he only said to Peter, 'What is it to you if he lives until I come again?' It appears that John is claiming that the statement made in Mk 9.1 is not rooted in history but in a historical misunderstanding. While much of the apocalyptic character of Mark appears plausible, John's content on this point might get the nod of historical plausibility.

From the above passages and themes it is obvious that the quest for the Jesus of history is greatly furthered by the Synoptic witness to his ministry. Even in the themes and passages that are not found in John, many of these resources cast valuable light on the historical ministry of Jesus and its historical situation. If we only had the Gospel of John, the above windows into the intentions and character of Jesus' ministry would be missing, and that would be a genuine loss for Jesus studies. His teaching in parables on the way of the Kingdom, the Messianic Secret, his exorcizing work and sending his disciples out on ministry tours, his appeal to the heart of the Law and the double priority, his dining with 'sinners' and tax gatherers, and his apocalyptic vision – all of these contribute significantly to a historical understanding of Jesus and his ministry. Therefore, even if John's historicity is strengthened, this does *not* discount the historical self-standing contributions of the Synoptic traditions. At least they must be regarded together in bi-optic consideration. Whether that bi-optic presentation reflects a foundational difference of perspective, evolving distinctives based on traditional development, or even some dialogical conversations between the traditions requires further analysis. Such will hinge, though, upon a similar consideration of particularly Johannine contributions to the quest for the Jesus of history.

C. *Johannine Contributions to the Quest for the Jesus of History*

While John indeed *is* theological, this does not mean that aspects of the Johannine tradition do not also cast light on historical considerations regarding the Jesus of history. Some of the Johannine windows into the ministry and teachings of Jesus augment a Synoptic presentation; they provide a fuller texture of understanding for later interpreters. Some of the Johannine tradition might not root in originative history, but in developing history, and at many turns the Synoptic presentation of Jesus is still to be preferred over the Johannine. Thus, the modernist impulse to question John's historicity and relevance for Jesus studies is not entirely without its merits. At several turns, however, the Johannine presentation of Jesus is historically preferable over the Synoptics, and the following features are examples of such a possibility. At times, they fill in where the Synoptics are silent, providing a greater sense of historical realism regarding the ministry of Jesus. At other times, though, they appear to be in dialogue with Mark – correcting and providing an alternative perspective, either as a witting or an unwitting dialectical testimony to events and emphases in the ministry of Jesus. This feature has gone largely undeveloped in Johannine and Jesus studies, partially because it has not been accompanied by a clear and plausible theory of John's literary relationships with parallel traditions; given such a model, however, the following features and their implications may be significant in more ways than one.

1) *Jesus' Simultaneous Ministry alongside John the Baptist and the Prolific Availability of Purifying Power*
Striking in the Johannine narrative is the distinctive role of John the Baptist. His role is so prevalent within the Johannine tradition that he even makes it into the worship material included in the Johannine Prologue (Jn 1.6-8, 15), albeit in a contrastive sort of way. He was *not* that Light, but he came as a witness to that Light, and this was his testimony regarding Jesus' precedence.[5] Among the various witnesses in the Fourth Gospel, John stands out as the preeminent witness, and from the beginning he declares Jesus to be the

---

5. One might even infer that the Baptist's testimony as to Jesus' precedence in terms of position and importance in the Johannine narrative (Jn 1.30) has been developed into a cosmological and pre-existent confession (Jn 1.15 → 1.1-5) in the worship hymn underlying the Prologue. This is argued more fully in the author's essay (2006b).

Son of God, the Agent of the Father, and the Lamb of God that takes away
the sin of the world. This being the case, much of John's testimony furthers
the theological and apologetic interests of the evangelist, and it reflects the
developing history of the Johannine situation more directly than the originative
history of the tradition. Here's how.

Beginning with the apologetic interests of the evangelist and the developing history of the tradition, the role of John the Baptist functions to declare
to emerging audiences that he is *not* the Messiah, but that Jesus *is*. According
to John 1, the first four followers of Jesus were originally followers of John
the Baptist, and they must have been insiders to the Baptist movement. After
becoming followers of Jesus, however, their contacts with the Baptist
movement did not terminate; rather, they continued, seeking to point others
toward Jesus. The whole reason John came baptizing was to point to Jesus
(Jn 1.31), declares the baptistic hero, and therefore, any true follower of his
must consider his pointing the way to Jesus. An apologetic interest in turning
Baptist adherents to Jesus was one of the primary missional concerns within
the first phase of the Johannine situation (30–70 CE), and at least two aspects
of its development are apparent. First, within Palestine, Baptist adherents are
pointed to Jesus as the Messiah by the testimony of their hero. Even in the
Synoptics, the heroic status of John is apparent, suggested at least by Jesus'
disjunctive question to the chief priests and the scribes about whether John's
ministry was from heaven or from below (Mt. 21.23-7; Mk 11.27-33; Lk.
20.1-8). They were unable to answer in either direction because if they
acknowledged his spiritual authority, this would have been an indictment
against their rejecting his message (Mt. 11.17-19; Lk. 7.24-35); if they
denigrated his authority, the crowds would have turned against them because
it was widely believed that he was a genuine prophet.[6] It was this sort of
widespread appreciation of John in general, and some special adherence in
particular, that the Johannine presentation of the Baptist's Christocentric
witness is designed to affect.

A second scope of influence would have extended beyond Palestine to the
appropriation of the Baptist's authority within the ministries of others – even
within the Jesus movement. Given the moral authority and social impact of
his declaring the prolific availability of spiritual purification, typified by
informal baptisms as a public witness to one's repentance, others continued
his baptismal ministry as an extension of its impact. Some of Jesus' followers
did so (although the narrator clarifies that Jesus himself did not, Jn 4.2), and
apparently so did Paul, Cephas and Apollos (apparently partisan baptism had
become a matter of division in 1 Cor. 1.10-17). An interesting situation
emerges, though, in Acts 18.24-19.10. Apollos of Alexandria came to Ephesus,
speaking boldly in the Synagogue, and while he spoke effectively of 'the way
of the Lord', he knew only the baptism of John. After Paul visited Ephesus,

---

6. Even Josephus regards John the Baptist as a genuine prophet, contrasting him to such
pretenders as Judas the Galilean, the Samaritan, Theudas and the Egyptian (*Ant* 18.116-19).

he found some of Apollos' followers, but while they knew the baptism of John, they did not know there was a Holy Spirit. Paul therefore corrected the difference between the baptism of John unto repentance versus the baptism of Jesus into the Holy Spirit (Acts 19.2-7), and after being baptized again in the name of Jesus, Paul laid his hands on them, and they were filled with the Holy Spirit. This clarifies the fact that every time the baptisms of John and Jesus are mentioned together in the New Testament, the combination functions to highlight the priority of the latter over and against the former. This is empha-sized also in Jn 1.19-42 and 3.22-4.2, and it is punctuated by Jesus' words to Nicodemus in Jn 3.3-8. One must be born of water *and the Spirit* (Jn 3.5); water baptism cannot alone suffice!

In addition to shedding valuable light on the developing tradition and its apolo-getic outreach toward its audiences, the Johannine presentation of the relationship between Jesus and John the Baptist sheds valuable light on the historical ministries of Jesus and John. First, Jesus is presented as ministering alongside John, for some time, rather than simply getting things going after the demise of John. The disciples of John are presented as feeling threatened by the fact that perhaps even more people are following Jesus than their leader (Jn 3.26), though John here provides the exemplary response of an authentic leader: 'He must increase, and I must decrease' (Jn 3.30). A similar theme is found in a Q passage, where the imprisoned John sends a delegation of his followers to Jesus asking, 'Are you the Messiah, or should we wait for another?' (Mt. 11.2-6; Lk. 7.18-23). Here as in Jn 10.40-42, the contrastive emphasis is upon Jesus' having performed signs: healing the sick, granting sight to the blind, empowering the lame to walk, raising the dead and preaching good news to the poor. The important point here is that especially in John Jesus is presented as ministering alongside John the Baptist simultaneously. This presentation appears to be made with historical intentionality. It is explained by the fact that the narrator clarifies when the discussion in Jn 3.22-30 is to have taken place – *before* John the Baptist had been thrown into prison (Jn 3.24), which appears to have been an explicit corrective to Mk 1.14. The beginning of Jesus' ministry did not simply begin sequentially *after* the ministry of John. They ministered together for some period of time, and questions back-and-forth between them and their followers bear the semblance of historical realism. It is also a fact that Mk 1.14 anticipates the imprisonment and death of John the Baptist, which is not narrated until Mk 6.17-29, so the Johannine presentation is not entirely against the Markan. In John, however, the point of their simultaneous ministries is not simply asserted; it is depicted. This feature of the Johannine presentation is historically preferable over that of the Synoptics.

A second feature of John's distinctive presentation of John the Baptist relates to the question of Elijah and Moses. An odd fact is that both presentations of Elijah and Moses in Mark appear to be corrected in John. First, whereas John is clearly associated in Mark with the ministries of Elijah and 'the prophet' Moses (Mk 6.14-15; 8.28), he is presented as denying such associations in Jn 1.19-25. Interestingly, Peter distances Jesus as the Messiah from Elijah and 'the prophet' in Mark, while the Baptist distances himself from Elijah and 'the prophet' in John, pointing to Jesus as the Messiah, who fulfils both of these roles. Here historical and theological interests within the Johannine presentation of John the Baptist coincide. The Johannine tradition intentionally counters the traditional association of John with Elijah and Moses precisely because of the theological convictions of the evangelist. Jesus is indeed presented as fulfilling the sign-working typology of Elijah in John, and he also fulfils the Prophet-like-Moses typology of the divine agent from God rooted in Deut. 18.15-22. This may also explain a second distinctive feature: why the Johannine narrative omits the Transfiguration scene. Rather than seeing this omission as 'proving' the non-authorship of John, it may reflect a theological inclination to show that the comings of Moses and Elijah were indeed fulfilled in the realistic ministry of Jesus rather than on some mountain-top epiphany. The historical implications of these theological investments are highly significant! What cannot be said is that differences between John and Mark imply John's patent ahistoricity in deference to the superior view in Mark. Something more complex and nuanced may underlie these contrastive presentations of the relation between Jesus and John the Baptist. At the very least, in deconstructing alternative associations, the Johannine Gospel presents a theological portrayal of Jesus as the Messiah that has profound implications for investigating the Jesus of history and the Christ of faith. On this point at least, historical presentation is clarified through the lens of theological conviction.

A final contribution of the Johannine presentation of the relation between John the Baptist and Jesus relates to the topographical allusions regarding John's ministry, confirmed by archaeological and geographical realism. As mentioned above, far from disconfirming the historical veracity of the Johannine narrative, Jn 1.28 actually bolsters a sense of historical realism, which sheds light on the ministries of John the Baptist and Jesus alike. Whereas 'Bethany beyond the Jordan' has come to function for some scholars as a geographical mistake, 'proving' the evangelist could not have been an eyewitness, or even a Palestinian, the thinking here is shallow and wrong. Wrongly assuming that the Bethany near Jerusalem has been mistakenly located some 20 miles away, across the Jordan River, is the first mistake. There could have been more than one Bethany, so the name itself may be insignificant as a solid determiner of historical error. A second fact is that early manuscripts also bear the names, *Bethabara* and *Betharaba*, and given the fact of scribal familiarity with Bethany as the home of Lazarus, Mary and Martha, it would have been an easy transposition. What is confirmed by present archaeological investigations is the fact that a major traditional baptismal site has been discovered about a mile east of the Jordan River, across from Jericho, and everything about this site confirms the accuracy of the Johannine rendering of 1.28 and 10.40-2.[7] This Judean and wilderness

---

7. Indeed, even Origen attests to *Bethabara* as the name of the baptismal site of Jn 1.28, based upon local tradition and a visit to the area in his commentary on John (*Comm.* 6.40), so the connection is quite primitive.

connection would also explain why Jewish leaders came from Jerusalem to interview John the Baptist in Jn 1.19-25, and why he might plausibly be associated with the Qumran community just a few miles away. This was also the geographical region with which Elijah's ministry is associated, so this may be a further aspect of the Baptist-Elijah connection. Given the fact that John's baptismal work was apparently practised in Samaria (Aenon near Salim, Jn 3.23) and perhaps even in the Jordan River north of the Sea of Galilee,[8] the geographically extensive character of the Baptist's ministry becomes apparent because of the Fourth Gospel. While theological implications of these features are many, it must be said that the Johannine presentation of the relation between John the Baptist and Jesus casts valuable light not only on the Jesus of history, but also upon the quest for the historical Baptist.

2) *Jesus' Cleansing of the Temple as an Inaugural Prophetic Sign*

One of the strongest reasons for questioning John's historicity and chronology is the fact that John presents the cleansing of the Temple at the beginning of Jesus' ministry rather than at the end. The default inference is that John's early placement of this event was a factor of theological interest rather than chronological knowledge, but upon closer analysis, such a conjecture is problematic. First, it cannot be claimed that *nothing* is said later in John's narrative as a reflection upon an earlier Temple incident. Already in John 5.18, the Jewish leaders in Jerusalem are presented as making plans to kill Jesus. Why would they have wanted to take such drastic measures if he were simply guilty of healing a paralysed man on the Sabbath? Implicit within the narrative is the understanding that Jesus had caused problems in Jerusalem before, and the Temple leadership was growing determined to put an end to Jesus' disruptive behaviour. Conversely, the Galileans had come to welcome Jesus because they had witnessed the signs he had performed, including the demonstration in Jerusalem at the feast (Jn 2.23; 4.43-5). These narrative echoes make it impossible to claim that the earliness of the Johannine Temple incident served a singularly theological function. Its early sequence is central to the advance of the narrative's progress, and its purported theological significance within an inferred Paschal system of Pauline atonement theology is forced and extremely thin. The Johannine presentation may be wrong, but it cannot be said that it has no chronological or intentional place in the progress of the narrative. The nearness of the Passover in Jn 2.13 plays a locative and contextual role in the unfolding of events, rather than a primarily theological one.

A second problem with assigning the Johannine Temple cleansing to the canons of theology rather than history is that it builds all too facilely on the assumption that 3-against-1 proves the Synoptics right and John wrong.

---

8. Given that another traditional baptismal site of John the Baptist is located near Bethsaida, the home of Philip, Andrew and Peter (Jn 1.44-5; 12.21), one wonders if this might this have been a factor in their becoming followers of John the Baptist to begin with.

Given the likelihood of Markan priority, if Mark got it wrong, Matthew and Luke would have also. Of course, Jesus could have performed the incident more than once, but from a critical standpoint this indeed appears to have been the same event forcing a judgement between the Synoptic and Johannine presentations. Harmonizing here will not do. More will be said about this later, but given the fact that Mark locates all the Jerusalem events at the end of Jesus' ministry raises a serious question about the historical plausibility of at least this aspect of Mark's chronology. Indeed, Mark was also motivated by theological and narrative interests rather than solely historical ones, and given the individuated character of the constituent elements in the Markan narrative, most of the ordering probably fell to the narrator rather than the tradition itself.

This being the case, Mark appears to have constructed the progression of the story to culminate appropriately in Jerusalem, but this may have led the evangelist to locate all the Jerusalem events and their associated material with Jesus' last days in Jerusalem as a narrative construction. Indeed, Jesus sets his sights on Judea in the march to Jerusalem in Mk 10.1, and after travelling to the Transjordan and through Jericho, Jesus and his followers arrive in Jerusalem in Mark 11. After cleansing the Temple in Mk 11.15-17, Jesus teaches lessons from the withered fig tree (Mk 11.20), defends his authority (Mk 11.27-33), tells the parable of the wicked tenants (Mk 12.1-12), addresses questions about paying taxes (Mk 12.13-17), engages Sadducees regarding the resurrection (Mk 12.18-27), teaches about the first and second command-ments (Mk 12.28-34), explains his Davidic Messiahship (Mk 12.35-7), denounces the scribes (Mk 12.38-39), and extols the widow's contribution to the Temple's collection box (Mk 12.41-4). After coming out of the Temple, Jesus launches into his apocalyptic discourse on the destruction of the Temple (Mk 13.1-8), the prediction of persecution (Mk 13.9-13), the desolating sacrilege (Mk 13.14-24), the coming of the Son of Man (Mk 13.24-7), another lesson from the fig tree (Mk 13.28-31), and the exhortation to watchfulness (Mk 13.32-7). These collections of sayings are followed, then, by the plotting of the chief priests and the scribes, who were looking for a way to arrest Jesus and put him to death (Mk 14.1-2). The point here is that Mark appears to have intentionally connected the Temple incident with at least 15 judgement sayings, followed by the plotting of the Jerusalem leaders to kill Jesus. What cannot be said about this arrangement is that reflects a solely chronological account based on baldly historical information at the expense of the Johannine rendering. Rather, Mark's account appears to have been crafted so as to organize all the Jerusalem events into a sensible narrative, wherein Jesus' march to Jerusalem, the Temple incident, his teachings on judgement and finality, and the events leading to his death cohere from a narrative standpoint. Even conjecturally, the crafting of the plot to kill Jesus arising after such a disruptive demonstration in the Temple is perfectly under-standable, but at this point, the Johannine presentation of the plot to kill Jesus (and Lazarus) as a factor of his growing popularity after the resurrection of

Lazarus is a less likely inference, and thus less likely to have been concocted. Therefore, the reasons for *not* considering John's presentation of an early Temple cleansing as rooted in historical or chronological intentionality are flimsy indeed.

A further set of points deserves to be made regarding the historical realism of the Johannine Temple incident before moving on. First, the incident bears a sense of realism, given the detail of the types of animals being driven out (including sheep and oxen), bolstered by Jesus' having made and used a whip of cords (Jn 2.14-16). These details serve no symbolic function; they simply convey the narrated events graphically. Second, in response to the request for a sign by the Jewish leaders, Jesus declares a prediction about destroying the Temple and building it back up again in three days (Jn 2.18-22). This prediction is actually attested in Mk 14.58, where at the Jewish trial of Jesus, anonymous members of the crowd declare that they had heard him say that he would destroy this temple and raise it up in three days – using it as an accusation against Jesus, claiming he was speaking ill of the Temple. Likewise, Jesus is also derided by the crowd while on the cross, and they challenge him saying that he had declared he would destroy the Temple and raise it up in three days – why not save himself from the cross (Mk 15.29)?[9] Now these comments could have referred to Jesus' words in Mk 13.1-2 about the predicted destruction of the Temple, but that event appears to have only been in the company of Jesus' disciples, and the added motif of raising it up in three days is missing. Therefore, two Markan passages appear to corroborate knowledge of a Jesus saying that is found only in John, and this fact has impressive implications for the primitivity and perhaps even historicity of the Johannine rendering.

Third, an unwitting chronological detail in Jn 2.20 bears impressive implications for considerations of John's historicity. After Jesus declared that he would raise the Temple up in three days, the Jewish authorities challenge him saying it had taken 46 years to build the Temple so far; how could he claim to raise it up in three days? As many scholars have noted, this detail marks this event as having happened in 26 or 27 CE, given the fact that Herod had begun his construction project on the Temple in 19 BCE. Assuming Jesus was born just prior to Herod's death in 4 BCE, this marks the event as having happened in 26 or 27 CE, when Jesus was around 30 years of age, coinciding with the beginning of his ministry in his thirtieth year according to Lk. 3.23. If Jesus indeed ministered for two or three years, this statement would have located the event early in his ministry, rather than at the end. As the Fourth Evangelist is unlikely to have known about later controversies regarding the need to reconcile the event with the unitive Synoptic witness, this detail must

---

9. Of course, this does not imply anything about chronology or that an early Temple cleansing is historically preferable to a later one. It simply acknowledges two Markan references to a detail contained only in John – pointing to Johannine-Markan interfluentiality.

be regarded as unmotivated by rhetoric, and innocent as an unwitting chrono-logical clue to John's distinctive presentation. What is the case, however, is that Papias is reported in the *Ecclesiastical History* of Eusebius (3.39) as furthering an opinion by the Johannine Elder (plausibly, the author of the Epistles and the final editor of the Gospel), that Mark got down Peter's preaching adequately, but not in the right order. Given the likelihood of at least some familiarity between the Johannine evangelist and perhaps a public reading of Mark, John's presentation of an early Temple cleansing may have been designed to set the record straight. This is what Papias appears to have been getting at, and John's distinctive presentation appears intentional – corrective as well as augmentive.

From these considerations, the historicity of John's presentation of the Temple incident as an inaugural sign rather than a culminative offence is more plausible on the basis of historical realism. Given the likelihood of Mark's crafting of the Temple incident as a precipitative trigger to the last days of Jesus, along with all the other judgement teachings and Judean events, the 3-against-1 denigration of John's presentation fails to amass much historical weight. Upon Mark's outline Matthew and Luke have also built; therefore, in bi-optic perspective the critical weight of the discussion shifts toward the Johannine rendering. In addition, the unwitting detail as to the early dating of the event locating it around 27 CE, combined with the second-century reference to a first-century Johannine critique of Mark's order, bolsters the Johannine rendering as having greater historical plausibility than the Markan. Therefore, in the light of an early Temple cleansing as an inaugural prophetic sign, Jesus' movement to and from Jerusalem in John 5-10 – including his hostile reception by the Judean authorities – makes historical as well as narratological sense. It bears a closer resemblance to historical realism rather than to theological construc-tionism.

3) Jesus' Travel to and from Jerusalem and his Multi-Year Ministry
Related to the timing of the Temple cleansing is the question whether Jesus travelled to Jerusalem *only once* during his ministry as rendered in the Synoptics – whereupon he was arrested, tried and killed – or whether he had visited Jerusalem more than once during his ministry as presented in John. Related, of course, is the question of whether he ministered over three or more Passover seasons – as portrayed in John, or whether he only ministered over one Passover season – as portrayed in the Synoptics. On both of these accounts, the Johannine rendering is far more plausible and historically likely. Put negatively, it is entirely unbelievable that a charismatic and devout Jewish leader would have not gone to Jerusalem several times a year. Not only for the festivals, but for other reasons as well, observant Jews in Jesus' day would probably have gone to Jerusalem as many as three or four times a year, so the impression that between his baptism by John and his death Jesus visited Jerusalem only once is unrealistic. Within the Johannine narration of the trips to and from Jerusalem, events along the way are also reported (having to travel

through Samaria, Jn 4.3-4, for instance) bolstering the sense of Johannine realism here. Thus, John's rendering of multiple visits to Jerusalem in contrast to the Synoptic accounts is far more plausible.

On the three mentions of the Passover in John (Jn 2.13; 6.4; 11.55), these might not have been intended to be markers of either chronology or theology. Rather, each of them possesses a strong sense of political realism, and each bears with it a clear association of an impending showdown with the Romans at the great nationalistic festival – the Passover. The nearness of the Passover in Jn 2.13 is followed by a prediction of the destruction of the Temple (and the body of Jesus), an event fulfilled in 70 CE by the Romans; the nearness of the Passover in Jn 6.4 introduces a potential revolt in the wilderness with the crowd gearing up to make Jesus a Prophet-King like Moses at the expense of the Roman occupiers in Jerusalem (Jn 6.14-15); and in Jn 11.55, the nearness of the Passover follows the dread-filled words of Caiaphas the High Priest as an unwitting prophecy of the death of Jesus. Put politically, Caiaphas declares that it is better for one man to die instead of the multitudes – fearing a pre-emptive crackdown by the Romans, wherein hundreds or thousands might have been killed. As he was High Priest that year, however, the statement is understood as a *double entendre* referring to the atoning death of Jesus – on behalf of the people, Jewish and otherwise, as a prophetic word to be fulfilled on the cross. The mention of the Passover's nearness in John thus possesses overtones of impending political realism. It alludes to confrontations with Rome – indeed, ones borne out in the history of Jesus' career and the fate of Jerusalem, including Messianic zeal in the wilderness – three associations deserving of critical consideration.

Nonetheless, Jesus *is* presented as ministering over three Passover seasons in John, even if John 6 were to have been added to the final edition of the narrative, so chronological implications are unavoidable. Given the fact that the Jesus movement took some time to gather momentum, and given the fact that Jesus' followers apparently grew in their development and commitment to his cause, the presentation of Jesus' ministry having lasted for more than one year – at least two or three years – is more historically plausible than the Synoptic presentation. And, given the fact that it is far more realistic to imagine a progressive Jewish leader travelling to and from Jerusalem as an itinerant preacher and healer, and the Johannine rendering of multiple visits to Jerusalem is also historically preferable over that of the Synoptics. In John, Jesus travels from Galilee to Jerusalem at least four times (2.13; 5.1; 7.10; 12.12), although he is presented as taking other trips through Judea, as well. In these ways at least, the Johannine rendering of Jesus' ministry as having spanned a larger period of time and a broader geographical scope than that of the Synoptics deserves stronger consideration as a factor of greater historical realism.

4) *Early Events in the Public Ministry of Jesus*
Given the likelihood that the first edition of John was finalized between 80–85 CE, with some familiarity with Mark, its five signs (chs 6 and 21 were

part of the final edition) are precisely the ones *not* included in Mark or the other gospel traditions. Further, at several points the first edition of John seems to contain echoes of Mark, which suggest a dialogical relationship with the Markan tradition.[10] This being the case, the numeration of the first two signs performed by Jesus in Galilee (Jn 2.11; 4.54) appears to have served an augmentive role with relation to the beginning of Jesus' ministry as portrayed in Mark. Not that any critique was intended of the Markan narrative, but the emphasis upon the first and second signs served a means of saying that the exorcism of the man with an unclean spirit (Mk 1.21-8) and the healing of Simon's mother-in-law (Mk 1.29-31) were not the first ones Jesus performed in Galilee. Eusebius even describes John's interest as having written down the earlier parts of Jesus' ministry (*Hist. Eccles.* 3.24), and he cites Jn 4.44 as an emphasis that these events had transpired *before* John was thrown into prison (according to Mk 1.14). Therefore, internally and externally there is good evidence for John 2-4 playing a chronologically augmentive role with relation to filling out the story of Jesus as begun by Mark.

This being the case, what might the value of that traditional material be? The first sign shows something of the ministry of Jesus as being a celebrative one – echoing themes from the Dionysus tradition and its stories of free-flowing wine.[11] Whether or not a supernatural event such as this occurred in history, several features bear mention for their significance. First, the mother of Jesus plays important roles at the beginning and ending of Jesus' ministry (Jn 2.1-11; 19.25-7). This grounds the ministry of Jesus in a strong familial context, having implications for community life in subsequent situations. Second, the public ministry of Jesus is presented as beginning in an open and celebrative context – a suggestive setting regarding the life-producing character of his ministry. Note the ironic presentation of the stone purification jars, which have now fulfilled their telic function – bringing merriment and the abundance of life in ways a cultic system can only have hoped for. Third, the words of the steward, regarding saving the best for last, provide a proleptic clue as to the direction the story of Jesus is headed. On one hand, saving the best for last prefigures the glory of the final sign, to be fulfilled in the raising of Lazarus from the dead. On the other hand, it also refers to the exaltation of Jesus on the cross, perhaps alluding to the paradoxical glorification of the Son of Man. A fourth feature is also worthy of note. It was on behalf of Jesus'

10. As mentioned above, John's relation to the Markan tradition appears interfluential during the oral stages of their traditions, and augmentive and corrective to written Mark. Plausibly, where an early Temple cleansing and the Messianic disclosure of John may have been intended as a corrective to Mark, the presentations of early and southern events are designed as complements to Mark.

11. See parallels with Pausanias, *Description of Greece* (6.26.1-2); Pliny the Elder, *Natural History* (2.231); Philostratus, *Life of Apollonius of Tyana* (6.10); Lucian, *A True Story* (1.7); and 2 Bar. (29.1-8). While none of these stories are closely parallel to Jesus' turning the water into wine, they all associate the availability of wine as a wondrous sign of abundance and festivity.

first sign that his disciples believed, and one gets the sense that the wonder-working ministry of Jesus is about to take off with full force and 'significance'.

The second sign performed in Galilee causes one to wonder whether it is the second sign, proper, or whether the reference to Galilee might suggest other signs have been performed elsewhere. Indeed, this could be a reference to the Temple cleansing as a prophetic sign, and this is certainly suggested in Jn 4.45, as the Galileans had witnessed Jesus' Jerusalem performance as a sign. Whatever the case, the narration of the second sign builds upon the first sign performed in Cana of Galilee (Jn 2.11; 4.46), presenting these two together in association with each other. The significance of the sign is that it again demonstrates the wondrous powers of Jesus calling forth a believing response from the royal official's son. Parallel to the healing of the Centurion's servant in Q (Mt. 8.5-13; Lk. 7.1-10), this healing also is connected to Capernaum, and the improvement of the child is measured as happening exactly in timely accordance with Jesus' prophetic word of healing (at the seventh hour), even from afar (Jn 4.46-54). As a result, he too believed, as well as his entire household.

On an archaeological note, here, Luke mentions that this Centurion had been a patron of the Jewish nation, and that he had built the local Synagogue for the sake of the people there (Lk. 7.4-5). Whether or not these buildings are connected to the reported events in the story, there is to this day in Capernaum a set of three ancient foundations that at least suggest the historical realism of these accounts. To the north, the reconstructed Synagogue, presumably built upon the foundation of the earlier one, stands as an excellent monument of what first- and second-century CE Synagogues in Galilee were like. It has robust pillars for supporting a large roof, and the building would accommodate several hundred if they were standing. Just south of that site is the excavated foundation of what is thought to have been the house of Simon Peter. Given a strong history of pilgrimages to the site, the account in Mark 1 cannot be far off. The foundation of a third building, not far from the Synagogue, is that of a large house, which has a Roman bath system within it. Now, whether this indeed were the home of the royal official described in these narratives is impossible to ascertain. What is the case, however, is that the Johannine presentation of these events fills out a fuller picture of what Jesus' ministry might have been like. In that sense, it augments Mark's rendering with realistic complementarity.

5) Favourable Receptions in Galilee among Samaritans, Women and Gentiles
Despite the first two signs of Jesus playing a complementary role, this material and other presentations of Jesus' reception in John play a bit of a contrastive role with relation to Mark's narrative. Given the fact that Jesus' words in Mk 6.4 are echoed in Jn 4.44, the presentation of Jesus' open reception by the Samaritans and by the royal official and his household must be seen as providing a contrast to Mark. Despite the rejection of Jesus in his hometown of Nazareth (note also Nathanael's pessimistic words about Nazareth in Jn

1.46), at least part of the reason for including these signs is to show that Jesus was not entirely rejected in the north. Rather, in ironic contrast to being rejected by his own (Jn 1.11), many of the Samaritans believed in him (Jn 4.39-42), and from beginning to end so did the faithful among the Gentiles (Jn 4.46-54; 12.20-6). Therefore, Jesus' mention of the sheep he would gather that are 'not of this fold' (Jn 10.16) and the Prologue's declaration of the universal accessibility of the Light (Jn 1.9) are depicted in narrative form in the reports on Jesus' early ministry as presented uniquely in John.

This is also the case regarding Samaritans and women. Whereas Mark has no reference to Samaria or Samaritans, and whereas Matthew's Jesus demonstrates something akin to ethnocentric antipathy toward the Samaritans (Mt. 10.5), John gives special attention to the Samaritan mission of Jesus and shows many of the Samaritans coming to believe in him (Jn 4.3-42). While some scholars speculate that the origin of such narratives might have been connected with the mission of Philip, Peter and John to the Samaritans in Acts 8.14-25, such connections are insufficient to explain the origin of the material. Indeed, several archaeological facts corroborate the presentation of these events: the presence of Jacob's well in Sychar is an archaeological fact (Jn 4.5-6); several miles southeast from Sychar, the modern village of 'Ainûn, near ancient Sâlim' (Aenon near Salim; Jn 3.23), historically has had a series of springs in the area;[12] and Robert J. Bull has discovered the site of the Samaritan Temple on Mount Gerizim near Sychar.[13] From a historical point of view, Jesus is presented as extending his ministry to the Samaritan household as well as the Judean and Galilean ones, and it is likely that the Johannine tradition may have provided a formative basis for Luke's inclusion of Samaritan persons and themes in his presentation of Jesus' ministry (Lk. 9.51-6 – note that the sons of Zebedee are linked with this uniquely Lukan tradition; 10.25-37; 17.11-19).

Luke may also be indebted to the Johannine presentation of women, as he adds to his redaction of Mark several Johannine motifs featuring women and their proximity to Jesus.[14] Impressive in the Johannine record is the prominent role of women, notably: the mother of Jesus, who provides a familial inclusio at the beginning and end of his ministry (Jn 2.1-11; 19.25-7); the Samaritan woman, who becomes the first successful missionary in John – and to the Samaritans at that (Jn 4.3-42); Mary and Martha, who perform an anointing of Jesus and make a pivotal Christological confession (Jn 11.1-12.8); and Mary Magdalene, who not only becomes the first witness to the resurrection, but who also becomes the apostle to the apostles (Jn 20.1-23). Women figure more

---

12. See Raymond E. Brown (1966, p. 151).

13. See Robert J. Bull (1975, 1976–77).

14. In addition to borrowing many details from John, Luke's Johannine dependence may have accounted for such theological developments as his presentation of women, Samaritans and the Holy Spirit (Anderson, 1996, pp. 274–7).

prominently in John than in any of the other Gospels, and this is striking, given the likelihood that John is the last to be finalized, and given the impression that women's roles in leadership appear to have been eroded in the third and fourth Christian generations. Indeed, the Pastoral Epistles reflect the movement toward more of a male-oriented structure of leadership, for instance, and John's presentation appears to be going *against* the grain.

While the more favourable presentation of Samaritans and Gentiles in John functioned to serve the needs of emerging Christianity, the egalitarian presentation of women in John appears to have challenged some of those developments. When asking why this may have been so, the answer cannot involve one that reflects a growing trend or a rhetorically progressive interest. Rather, the Johannine narrative appears to be making the case for women yoked with Jesus in leadership on the basis of primitivity – the way it was back then, historically – as a countering to patriarchal developments. Parallel to the challenging of Petrine hierarchy in the name of Jesus' original intentionality for his church, the presentation of women in John bears likely historical plausibility precisely because it represents a time where the Jesus movement was more characterized by familiality and egalitarianism than by formalism and structural modes of leadership. Of course, John's presentations of Samaritans and Gentiles coming to Jesus may also have a fair degree of historical plausibility, but alternative explanations to the historicity of John's presentation of women in leadership are notably without merit. John's historical plausibility here stands firm.

6) *Jesus' Judean Ministry and Archaeological Realism*
In addition to the first two signs, filling out the early part of Jesus of Jesus' ministry as a complement to Mark, the other three signs in the first edition of John provide a southern and Judean augmentation of the Markan presentation of Jesus' Galilean ministry. Indeed, Mark mentions that Jesus had travelled more broadly than in the lake region alone, but all of his miracles are notably in the north, save the healing of blind Bartimaeus in Jericho on the way to Jerusalem (Mk 10.46-52) and the cursing of the fig tree in Jerusalem (Mk 11.12-14, 20-6). If the Johannine evangelist were familiar with Mark, as is at least arguable, the three Judean signs appear to have served the function of rounding out the rest of Jesus' ministry geographically. Significantly in terms of history and theology, the healing of the paralytic by the Pool of Bethzatha created a crisis in terms of Jesus' authority to heal on the Sabbath. This is presented as leading to a series of hostile debates with the Jewish leaders in Jerusalem over Jesus' authority. When claiming to be working on behalf of the one who sent him as a prophetic agent who does and says only what the Father commands him to do and say (Deut. 18.15-22), claiming unity with God, he is misunderstood as claiming to be equal with God in terms of status and is opposed on the basis of blasphemy. The Judean leaders make overstated claims about the Messiah needing to come from the south (Bethlehem) instead of the north (Nazareth), and ironically, they reject the Mosaic prophet in

seeking to adhere to the letter of the Mosaic Law. While these debates have been crafted so as to serve a rhetorical function within the first edition of the Johannine Gospel's outreach to Jewish audiences, the sense of religious threat and hostility by the centralizing religious leader regarding the rustic charismatic leader cannot be far from a lively sense of historical realism.

The healing of the blind man in John 9 is also highly stylized, so as to become an object lesson for later audiences whose 'claiming to know' might actually expose their unwitting religious blindness (Jn 9.39-41). Indeed, as J. Louis Martyn and others have shown, John 9 becomes something of a historical representation of the situation involving Johannine Christians engaged in a set of dialectical relationships with their Jewish family and friends, and the three passages reflecting Synagogue exclusion 'then and now' (Jn 9.22; 12.42; 16.2) undoubtedly reflect real tensions in the middle period of the history of the Johannine situation (esp. 70–85 CE). What cannot be said, however, is that the 'then' level of history never existed, or that *einmalig* narration ('once upon a time...') discounts a narrative's historical origins. Jesus indeed was killed in Jerusalem, and several waves of Jewish persecution of the Jesus movement are reported in Acts, including the martyrdom of Stephen (Acts 7) and Saul's actions before his conversion and name change in Acts 9. What is significant historically about the presentation of Jewish leaders, Jesus and the blind man is the *theological* foibles of how religious authorities negotiate dogmatic and traditional convictions in the light of Revelation and unexpected presentations of God's truth. In that sense, the realism of John 9 extends to every generation and religious situation where openness to the new is counterbalanced by faithfulness to the old. In Cognitive-Critical perspective, the Jewish leaders love the praise of men rather than the glory of God, and show themselves to be firmly stuck on James Fowler's Stage 3 level of Faith Development: Synthetic-Conventional Faith. The formerly blind man has nonetheless moved on to Stage 4 Faith: Individuative-Reflective Faith, and the hearer-reader of John is thus invited to do the same.[15]

The Lazarus narrative provides a culminative chapter in the ministry of Jesus, fulfilling the exclamation of the steward at the wedding feast that the best indeed is saved for last, and this event also becomes the occasion for Jesus' final threatening of the Jewish authorities. Interestingly, their final decision to find a way to put him to death is presented as a more subtle threatening of their religious authority than the blunt offence of the Temple incident in Mark. In Jn 11.45-57 the consternation of the chief priests and the Pharisees is expressed as fear that as a result of Jesus' continuing performance of signs, all the world would go after him and that the Romans would destroy their place and their nation. Interestingly, they also were threatened by Lazarus, and in Jn 12.9-11 a plot is devised to kill Lazarus too, because many were coming

---

15. John's Christological tensions are analysed more fully in Cognitive-Critical perspective in Anderson 2006b, using the Prologue as a case study.

to faith on his account. On the basis of something similar to the criteria of embarrassment and dissimilarity – perhaps a criterion of 'unlikely fabrication' – the Johannine explanation of the final motivation for putting Jesus to death requires more of a historically-rooted explanation. In the more straightforward Markan account, they make a plan to put Jesus to death because he has disturbed the Temple and has been preaching judgement themes – an obvious conjecture, of course. The Johannine presentation, however, requires a more engaged interpretation of religious authority, political power and sociological sensitivities. In these ways, the final sign of Jesus in John signifies the threat spiritual reality and power can be to those with political sensibilities, but like Nicodemus, having no grasp of the whence nor whither of the Spirit. In these ways, this presentation conveys a sense of spiritual realism whether or not all of the details conveyed originated in historical event.

At this point, some comment deserves to be made as to the historical tension between the problem of the wondrous and the fact of archaeological corroboration within these narratives. First, all three of these healings share a good deal of similarity with the healings of Jesus in the rest of the canonical Gospels. Other paralytics and blind men are healed in the Synoptics, and if Jesus did it there, who is to say the Johannine narratives are any less historical. The raising of Lazarus, though, is in a bit of a different category. Whether intended to do so or not, at least for hearers and readers of Mark and John together, this sensational miracle certainly outdoes the raising of Jairus' daughter in Mk 5.21-43. If such a feature were intentional, John's augmentive interest would indeed have played a role in its presentation. This raises a question, however, regarding the historical innocence of the narrative. If it were motivated by rhetorical interests, might it have had an origin other than historicity? Further, if such an event really transpired, how could the other three gospel traditions have not known about it? Geographical isolationism might explain part of the answer, but the fact that the most sensational miracle of Jesus is found only in one Gospel – John, the most theological and spiritual among the four, still presents problems of historicity beyond what this treatment can alleviate. It suffices to say that the wondrous within biblical narrative continues to be a problem for cause-and-effect modernist analysis, and in the case of the Johannine signs, this problem is both enduring and acute. What is significant, however, is the Johannine dialectical attitude toward the relation between faith and signs. Jesus is presented as rebuking the desire for signs – and then he goes and performs them (Jn 4.48-50); but he also declares, 'Blessed are those who have not seen, and yet believe', – right after he shows Thomas his flesh wounds (Jn 20.27-9). The point is that the evangelist's dialectical engagement with the tensions between signs and faith suggests that he has engaged personally the realities of both hopeful faith and profound disappointment. This dialectical engagement with both wonder and realism suggests proximity to the events rather than second-order reflection.

The second consideration is the fact that embedded within these signs is an impressive set of topographical details that are corroborated by the latest of archaeological findings. Some of this is mentioned above, but a brief reminder is in order. Whereas scholars of an earlier era deemed much of John's topographical detail as theologically motivated and having no basis in history, John has more archaeological detail than all the other Gospels put together. Where scholars of a half-century ago regarded the five porticoes in Jn 5.2 as a fabrication due to the mistaken impression that the reference was to a pentagonal shape, archaeologists have discovered the actual Pool of Bethzatha, which involves two pools with pillars supporting four porticoes on all four sides, plus an additional one in the middle between the two pools. Thus, the unlikely 'five porticoes' around this pool in Jerusalem are *exactly* what is depicted in John 5. And, given that the Pool of Siloam has an explicit reference to its theological meaning (Siloam means 'sent' – Jn 9.7), scholars in eras past have argued that because the pool had a theologically associated name, its origin lay not in history but in theology. Within the last two years, however, the Pool of Siloam has indeed been discovered in Jerusalem, and it appears to have been a large wading pool with several levels on which to stand. One might question the events, but the setting and its depiction have been recently corroborated by archaeological facts.

Surrounding the Lazarus narrative, archaeological details are not as pertinent (although other details in Jerusalem are, including the Praetorium of Pilate in Jn 18.28, and the references to *Gabbatha* and the *Lithostrōtos* in Jn 19.13), but the Johannine presentation of the anointing by Mary is. In Jn 12.1-8, several details of the presentation are worthy of historically plausible consideration when compared with Mk 14.3-9. First, the anointing of Jesus' feet rather than his head is an unlikely move to have made without a historical or traditional reason for doing so. A head anointing would have moved the mundane to a royal association, but a move in the other direction is unlikely to have been concocted. Luke apparently follows John in this move, departing from Mark, which bolsters the likelihood of Lukan dependence on the Johannine tradition (Lk. 7.36-50). Second, the Johannine rendering includes non-symbolic, illustrative detail common to the Markan tradition (such as the 300 *denarii*, Mk 14.5; Jn 12.5), suggesting proximity to the oral rendering of the event and interfluential contact between the two traditions. Third, John also contains several details implying first-hand knowledge of the event. An empirical reference is made to the smell of the perfume filling the room (Jn 12.3), and statements are made about perceptions (wrong ones) of Judas' intentions and actions. Fourth, the particulars of the woman performing the anointing are known to the narrator. She is connected with the raising of Lazarus, and this event is presented as an expression of gratitude for the raising of her brother, rather than a random act performed by an unnamed woman along the way. Fifth, the tradition is presented as a familiar one to the hearer/reader elsewhere, as this particular Mary is even introduced in Jn 11.2 as the one who had performed the anointing, even though it does not happen until the next chapter. In these and other ways, the Johannine presentation of the anointing of Jesus bears a remarkable degree of historical plausibility as compared to alternative presentations.

A mistake is sometimes made regarding John's Judean and Jerusalem-based narrations: namely, that the evangelist must have been a Judean rather than a Galilean. This is by no means a compelling inference. A good deal of northern detail is also included in John, so it is not as though only southern details are included. A more plausible explanation is the likelihood that tradition from other sectors besides those reported in Mark was known by the Johannine evangelist, and part of his selective interest (Jn 20.30; 21.25) is to include accounts that had not been covered by Mark (Kundsin, 1925). The presence of archaeological material in the Judean accounts may also have reflected an interest in cultivating a sense of topographical realism for the hearer/reader, and based on the latest archaeological discoveries, these details appear not to be rooted in theological motives, but in historical knowledge, proper. In that sense, the southern signs of Jesus fill out the Markan picture geographically, just as the first two signs fill out the Markan picture chronologically.

7) *The Last Supper as a Common Meal and its Proper Dating*
The presentation of the last supper in John as a common meal rather than a Passover meal bears greater historical plausibility than the presentation in the Synoptics on the basis of the criterion of dissimilarity. Given the fact that the words of the institution of the Lord's Supper are presented by Paul in his moving a common meal to a symbolic meal of remembrance in 1 Cor. 11.17-34, the move from an informal setting to a more formal celebration can clearly be seen. What is not the case is that all Christian common meals moved toward formalization at the same time or in the same ways. Indeed, the fellowship meals of Acts 2.43-7 and elsewhere appear to have been alimentary meals, rather than symbolic or formalized meals, and yet the presentation of the Lord's Supper as a Jewish Passover meal probably functioned to legitimate the formalization of a Christian equivalent, which came to be celebrated not only at the Passover season but with greater frequency as an emerging part of Christian worship. One can even observe Luke's embellishment of the meal's formalization in that while Mark emphasizes the contents of the cup – Jesus' *blood* of the covenant to be ingested, Luke emphasizes the container of the contents – the *cup* of the covenant to be received (Mk 14.24; Lk. 22.20). While this move toward formalization in Luke is clear, it cannot be construed simply as a later development versus an earlier one. Luke's modification bears an impressive similarity to Paul's words of the institution in 1 Cor. 11.23-5, and Paul's letter was probably finalized a decade or more before Mark was. Nonetheless, the fact that John's presentation of the Last Supper contains no words of the institution, but rather an appeal toward serving one another (Jn 13.1-17), suggests John's primitivity and historical neutrality. It also need not suggest a critique of formalism, as it is not clear how widespread the move

from common meals to symbolic and ritual meals might have been. Indeed, some groups might never have made the move to a symbolic meal of remembrance before the turn of the first century, so the presentation of events in John 13 might reflect sacramental innocence rather than a formalistic critique.

At this point, a comment on the dating of the last supper is in order. John presents the meal as happening on the day *before* the Passover (presumably Thursday, Jn 13.1), while Mark presents it as happening on the evening *of* the Passover (presumably Thursday, Mk 14.16-17). Standard explanations include the conjecture that John has placed the supper on the day of preparation – the day on which the Passover lambs were killed (Mk 14.12; Lk. 22.7) – implying that John's narrative is not rooted in history but in the 'Paschal theology of the evangelist'. This view has several major problems to it. First, the detail about the day of preparation on which the lambs were killed is *not* in John. It can be found in Mark and Luke, but it is by no means certain that the Johannine evangelist knew of that detail, or if so, that it bore any significance to him. Second, an inferred 'Paschal theology' in the thought of the evangelist is little more than a conjecture, and it is largely a false one. John's primary soteriological construct is revelational, not sacrificial, and assuming that *anything* was adapted in order to conform to a so-called Paschal theology is at best a move of speculation rather than substance. Third, John's presentation of events comes across with impressive realism, as the Jewish leaders refused to enter the house of Pilate because they wanted to be able to eat the Passover the next day (Jn 18.28). On this account, Mark comes back into agreement with John and declares the day of the crucifixion to be the day of preparation (Mk 15.42; Jn 19.31), and John uniquely contributes the detail that the Passover and the Sabbath converged on that year (Jn 19.31). If this were the case, the Passover meal of the Markan rendering would have taken place *after* the date of the crucifixion (the day of the preparation, Mk 14.12-17; 15.42), and if Jesus were indeed raised on the first day of the week (Mk 16.1-2; Jn 20.1), providing the Sabbath was a 'high day' (Passover, Jn 19.31) that year, this would have meant that Jesus was in the tomb overnight instead of over three days. For these and other reasons, the more pronounced cultic innocence of the Johannine presentation of the last supper shows a greater degree of historical plausibility, and even Mark's own account poses a challenge to the last supper having been a full Passover meal.

8) Jesus' Teaching about the Way of the Spirit and the Reign of Truth
Given the likelihood that the Jesus of history was a charismatic preacher, challenging institutions and legalistic structures in the name of a loving God and the empowerment of the Spirit, the Johannine presentation of Jesus as sending the Holy Spirit and emphasizing the Spirit's truth-effecting work essentially coheres with such an impression. Whereas the later Matthean tradition adds passages to Mark that contribute structure and means of accountability to serve the needs of the emerging church (Mt. 16.17-19; 18.15-20), the later Johannine tradition seeks to restore a vision of the reality

of the Holy Spirit's work, and it champions a Spirit-based ecclesiology and the dynamic unfolding of the divine will for Jesus' followers. While John's presentation of the *Paraklētos* appears to be a central part of the later material added to the first edition (Jn 15-17), and while it certainly resembles the theological and spiritualizing work of the evangelist, this is not to say that its origin was late-and-only-late. Indeed it can be argued that the pneumatic work of the Jesus of history is well represented even in the Johannine paraphrase of Jesus' last will and testament for his church (Jn 17), and this impression is confirmed by considering Johannine parallels to the way of the Kingdom as furthered by the Synoptic Jesus.

Just as the Synoptic Jesus came heralding the dynamic and pneumatic reign of God, the Johannine Jesus argues that the Spirit is like the wind that blows where it will, and that while people do not know where it comes from or where it is headed, its impact and power are real indeed. Likewise, just as the Synoptic Jesus called for a means of transcending human loyalties and structures in the name of the spiritual reality of the ways of God, so the Johannine Jesus calls for worshipping in Spirit and in Truth because God is Spirit, and it is such persons that God seeks to draw into authentic worship – independent of form and location (Jn 4.21-4). And, just as the Synoptic Jesus declares prolific accessibility to the power and presence of God, the Johannine Jesus embodies that reality and promises to send the Holy Spirit, who will continue his work with spiritual unencumberment (Jn 14-16). Despite the fact that John's presentation of the spiritual work of Jesus and the Holy Spirit are couched in Johannine language and paraphrase, they also cohere with the pneumatic ministry of the Jesus of history – even as represented by the Synoptics. John takes those impressions even further, though, and in that sense, the Johannine rendering of the pneumatic work of Jesus and the Kingdom makes an impressive contribution to a fuller understanding of the mission of Jesus in its emerging *and* original forms.

Overall, the distinctively Johannine contributions to the Jesus story do not simply reside in the category of theology or drama in terms of their value; they also contribute to the quest for historicity regarding the ministry of Jesus and developing memory about those events. Given that Matthew and Luke built *upon* Mark, but that the first edition of John built *around* Mark, some of John's distinctive presentations can be seen to have intentionally been aimed at filling out the picture (early material and southern material), and also at setting the record straight here and there. Matthew and Luke do something similar, but the fact of John's dialogical autonomy provided a greater resource of independent tradition as well as a more autonomous and individuated perspective from the earliest stages of traditional development to the last. This being the case, the Johannine perspective as a bi-optic alternative to the Markan traditions deserves critical consideration, despite its late finalization and theological development. What cannot be said is that John has no contribution to make to the historical quest for Jesus, or that theological and literary interests can account for the presence of *all* of John's distinctive material. This autonomous tradition may have been wrong or misguided, but much of its intentionality – explicitly and otherwise – is to testify to what has been *seen and heard* from the beginning, that later generations might believe *without* having seen (Acts 4:20; 1 Jn 1:3; Jn 20:29).

Findings

When the particular historical contributions of all four gospels are considered in bi-optic perspective, several things become clear. First, given the facts that over 30 accounts bear multiple attestation in all four gospels, that John has at least 44 contacts with memorable sayings in Mark, and that John and the Q tradition share contacts at over a dozen places (independent, of course, of Mark), it must be acknowledged that, although John is highly distinctive and individuated, John is not entirely unique among the gospels. Rather a good deal of information can be gained from considering John within the mix of multiple attestation between the four traditions, and to overstate John's individuality overlooks the facts. Second, it also must be said that the Synoptics still must be considered as contributing the bulk of historical information about Jesus, despite John's reconsidered historical viability. The reader might be surprised at this point, as the thrust of the present work is to assess critically the dismissal of the historical contribution of John. The historical contribution of the Synoptics cannot be overlooked, however, and the above analysis outlines some of the major ways in which the Markan traditions contribute indispensably to the historical quest for Jesus. Finally, though, the Johannine tradition makes its own set of contributions to the historical quest for Jesus, and in many ways John complements and augments the Markan narrative helpfully. Some of John's theological concerns may also contribute to historical understandings of originative events, their perceptions, and the development of memory about them. This being the case, history must be considered alongside theology, and vice versa. Overall, though, the above analysis shows that a more nuanced approach to the historical quest for Jesus in bi-optic perspective is a superior critical alternative to a disjunctive approach, excluding the Johannine tradition from the equation. In many ways, John's tradition provides a key to understanding the larger pictures involved – not only of theological, but also of literary and historical interest.

Part V
Modern Foundations Reconsidered –
Implications for the Critical Investigation of John,
Jesus and History

'In the area of philosophy there might be a kind of "dialectical method"; for the New Testament there can be only *one* method, the *historical*. However, insight into what is really meant by dialectical theology could lead to a deeper insight into the nature of history and thus modify, enrich or clarify the method of historical investigation.

What, then, is meant by *dialectic*? Undeniably it is a *specific way of speaking* which recognizes that there exists no ultimate knowledge which can be encompassed and preserved in a single statement.'

Rudolf Bultmann, 'The Significance of "Dialectical Theology" for the Scientific Study of the New Testament,' in his *Faith and Understanding* (ed. Robert Funk; trans. L. P. Smith; London: SCM Press, 1969, p. 146)

While the above analyses are intended to pose a sustained and vigorous critique of particular aspects of the so-called 'critical consensus' regarding investigations of John, Jesus and history, one's intention is not to replace critical views with uncritical ones or to supplant modernist criticism with post-modernist analysis. Nor is it to abolish or defend traditional views. The intention is to perform the critical task well, hammering hard on all claims – traditional *and* modernist – believing such is required of sound interpretation. If critical scholars are scandalized by the assessment of critical views critically, one questions the degree to which they are indeed 'critical' scholars, for the trademark of critical scholarship is to welcome all good questions, assessing claims on the basis of their merits rather than their implications. Nonetheless, implications do matter, and considering the outcomes as well as inputs of one's findings is important work to do. First, however, a sympathetic note for the modernist project is in order.

A. *A Sympathetic Note for the Modernist Project*

Despite the critical approach to the above issues, the goal is not to overturn modernist Jesus and Johannine studies, but to infer the strengths and weaknesses of a multiplicity of approaches and claims in order to sift through the weaker ones and to identify the stronger ones. These, then, become fitting material on which to build one's interpretive and analytical work. In that sense, the present hope is to contribute to critical scholarship by testing critical perspectives and approaches, in hopes of strengthening that which is worthy and diminishing that which is not. The goal is the seeking of truth, believing that even its approximation will always be liberating (Jn 8.32).

1) *Real Problems of Presentation and Interpretation*
Nonetheless, interpreters owe a great debt to the modern investigations of John, Jesus and history, as they have time and again shone the light hard on real problems of presentation between the gospel traditions and their resulting interpretations. As the various planks in each of the modernist platforms show, real problems exist between the similar-yet-dissimilar presentations of Jesus in John and the Synoptics, and these problems cannot be ignored. Like the so-called 'Synoptic Problem', the 'Johannine Problem' has been addressed with a variety of literary, historical and theological approaches, each having varying degrees of merit. New sets of solutions to familiar problems, however, produce new sets of problems, and the present study reflects an attempt to address new sets of problems emerging from various approaches without losing sight of the original issues they sought to address. One way forward involves asking better questions, whence better answers come.

This being the case, as questions of one or two centuries ago determined the analytical approaches to genuine problems, posing a suitable way forward hinges upon asking better questions. For instance, 'How could John be correct if the Synoptics disagree, 3-against-1?' is better asked: 'Why does John differ from Synoptic presentations rooted in Mark; is it a factor of historical knowledge, rhetorical design, or theological perspective?' And, 'How could claims of supernatural wonders be regarded as true in the scientific and naturalistic era?' is better asked: 'What are the originative and developing factors in an event being presented as wondrous; how did earlier impressions and later understandings affect particular presentations of Jesus' signs?' And, 'How could a theologically loaded presentation reflect anything historical?' is better asked: 'What is the relation between theological insight and historical event; do we have a theological attribution of meaning to a historical event, or do we have a crafting of events in the light of later, theological and rhetorical interests?' The point is that reflective approaches to these real problems are more likely to contribute a fuller set of understandings rather than pushing conclusions to either/or disjunctive stances.

2) *Overstated Claims – In One Direction or Another*
In sympathy with critical approaches to interpretive problems, unreflective assertions of John's accuracy on the basis of eyewitness claims (Jn 19.34-5; 21.24-5) and dogmatic attempts to harmonize differences between the Gospels have led to the insistence upon rational, critical and scientific means of analysis to provide a way forward. This is especially the case regarding John's high Christological claims and theological assertions. Overstated claims regarding John's presentation of Jesus' preexistent divinity, particularistic soteriology and wondrous semeiology, as well as misappraisals of John's apparent sacramental instrumentalism, determinism and anti-Semitism have at times been argued and substantiated upon rhetorical claims regarding John's historicity and eyewitness authority. This has understandably caused scholars to examine the substantiation and to ask whether it indeed serves a solid basis upon which to ground one's theological claims.

   John's Christology, of course, deserves to be investigated in its own right, and the present project largely leaves that interest aside in order to focus directly upon historical ones. And yet, while positive claims regarding John's historicity overstate the evidence and its implications, the same must be said for overstating one's negative claims regarding John's ahistoricity – or even flawed historicity. This is why the present study is needed, and why it is needed now. A dogmatic inference of the de-historicization of John and the resulting de-Johannification of Jesus is no intellectual improvement over dogmatic claims in favour of a hyper-historicization of John and an exclusively Johannine portraiture of Jesus. Rather, more nuanced approaches to these matters are needed, and the present study hopes to contribute a plausible and fruitful set of ways forward on such matters.

3) *Enduring Challenges of Supernaturalism for Scientific Inquiry*
The problem of supernaturalism (or even supra-naturalism) will always be a struggle for cause-and-effect analysis, and this is especially the case in the

scientific era. The great value of the scientific method is that problems can be identified, hypotheses can be posed and tested, and fair judgements can be made by sober minds on the basis of observable evidence and rational coherence. Something of aesthetics and serviceability also plays a role here, especially in the contagion of a forwarded view, but the scientific method is here to stay, and that raises questions about how to understand the character of naturalism and its limitations, given trans-temporal and cross-cultural appeals to wonder. For this reason, the miraculous elements in all four gospel traditions will remain a source of intrigue and problem, especially in the scientific era.

Perhaps a note on the overstatement of claims is also worth noting here. While some interpretations of the miraculous in Bible times are more nuanced and experientially adequate, more strident interpretations fail to correspond to general human experience. Whereas earlier days of Modernism declared a greater degree of certainty regarding laws of nature and limitations of the supernatural, recent cosmological views involving quarks, chaos theory and quantum mechanics have caused the best of scientists to challenge mechanistic cosmologies and entirely predictable understandings of nature. A great deal of research has been performed over the last two or three decades shedding new light on the science-religion problem, and many of the best scientists and historiographers are reluctant to declare with certainty any claim about what could *not* have happened regarding an earlier claim to historicity.

On this matter, Bultmann's epoch-making work suffered in its bondage to a narrow view of scientific naturalism – a perspective that even the best of scientists in his day would have rejected. Due to his interest in theology, he was willing to sacrifice nearly all reportings of the wondrous in the gospels to inferred history-of-religions origins, rather than Jesus-of-history events. Indeed, the evangelists and their redactors were all collectors of meaningful material, and even historical memory accumulated mythic forms of construal and conveyance along the way, but can it really be claimed that a purported event cannot have happened? Especially when the multiply attested traditions vary with each other – perhaps representing bi-optic impressions from start to finish – such accounts are less susceptible to historiographic elimination. They remain as problems to be considered, and Cognitive-Critical analysis may provide a helpful set of ways forward.

Along those lines, it cannot be claimed that all appeals to the wondrous involved the breaking of natural laws. Indeed, that natural outcomes may be experienced as wondrous, and even a coincidence, or a genuinely therapeutic outcome, rightly deserves to be regarded as a gift of grace. Empirical research done by medical scientists at Harvard within the past decade,[1] for instance,

---

1. See the results of empirically based, double-blind experiments identifying positive correlations between more intensive forms of prayer and physical healing performed by the Harvard School of Medicine and other institutions in Theodore J. Chamberlin J. and Christopher A. Hall, eds (2000). Given the advances in the science-religion dialogue, 'science' itself has come a far distance from the nineteenth-century mechanistic and woodenly naturalistic cosmologies of earlier eras (see Gadamer

has performed double-blind experiments regarding the relation between prayer and healing, and their findings have been significant. They have noted an increased correlation between intensive prayer and healing outcomes, empirically, and whether it was a factor of auto-suggestion or psychic energy, the point is that medical science is itself coming to a more nuanced view regarding the science and religion dialogue. This being the case, the scientific investigation of the New Testament – a venture this study aspires to embody – is itself being afforded a new set of options and perspectives unavailable to more closed and brittle understandings of wonder and causality.

4) *Merited Authority and its Appropriations*

A liability to the Modern era is that its measures of authority can and will be appropriated by those with ulterior agendas. This was certainly the case in the pre-critical era, as the 'divine inspiration of Scripture', the 'divine right of kings', the 'fundamentals of the Christian faith', the 'authoritative canons of the church' and even the 'personally revealed insight' have been used to fight religious and ideological battles – and even political ones – in Christian Europe and America. After the Thirty Years War in Europe and the Civil War in England, however, the intellectual consciousness of Western opinion shifted to rational and scientific ways forward, over religious ones. And, for the last three and a half centuries, the modernist program has delivered admirably, including a set of critical approaches to biblical analysis and historicity quests. However, just as extended appeals to religious authority diminished the authority of religion, extended appeals to rationalist and modernist authority have tended to do the same. In that sense, the very merits of an authority, if hyper-extended or overstated, function to diminish that authority.

Nonetheless some critical claims to 'scientific' interpretation have been forwarded as factors of rhetoric, rather than as factors of modest, evidence-based analysis. The claims of Strauss against Schleiermacher in the nineteenth century, for instance, claiming that Bretschneider was 'the man of science' versus his targeted opponent, appropriated the full weight of scientific authority behind his critical examination of Jesus. In doing so, Strauss leveraged a wedge between critical and traditional gospel analysis, but the disjunction was overstated. Indeed, many a modern interpreter has been tempted to side with the authority of science and criticalism versus tradition and fideism, but a more adequate epistemological approach is to welcome truth and evidence from all sides and in all forms, aspiring to improve one's understandings at every step of the way. The point is that this approach embodies the best of traditional and critical interpretations alike.

1989, Ricoeur 1965 and Polanyi 1946 and 1962 for epistemological ways forward). Wonder in biblical narrative is still a problem to be addressed critically, but scientific scholars have come to incorporate religious anthropology, Mediterranean sociology, social-science studies and cognitive-critical analysis (among other disciplines) as providing useful tools for analysis rather than feeling compelled to reject every aspect of wonder-appeal from historiography proper.

5. Critical Analysis as a Way Forward

As a way forward, critical analysis aspires to employ the best of methods and of findings – testing given foundations and hypotheses and building upon them when deemed sound, but improving upon them when deemed lacking. In that sense, the present exercise is intended to be a historical-critical project in the light of the most compelling of literary, historical and theological analyses. If a shift in paradigm were to develop, the following elements might be serviceable. First, historical *and* theological elements must be considered in all four gospel traditions, not just John. Given the theological interests of the Markan Gospels and Origen's assertion of John's *somaticality* (*Comm.* 1.9), Clement's dictum might be restated as follows:

> The Synoptics wrote down *pneumatic* records of Jesus' ministry – emphasizing its furthering the Kingdom of God by works of spiritual power and authority; but last of all John wrote a *somatic* gospel – adding the flesh and bones of the ministry of Jesus as a means of filling out the gospel record, in order that the world might in the end *believe.*

Second, ways of re-envisioning history itself will help in the ascertaining of what might be historical in the Gospels and what might not be. Third, accounting for John's distinctive origin and development, plus a workable theory of interfluential engagement with Mark and the other Gospels, is required. This must be done while at the same time attempting to account for the fact of John's pervasive autonomy. Fourth, Cognitive-Critical analysis deserves to be performed on the origin and development of gospel traditions. It is not only valuable to consider what sort of packaging a conviction was expressed within, but it is also important to understand how such a conception developed and why it was chosen. Finally, a more *nuanced* approach to John, Jesus and history deserves to be embraced, and such a view would not simply choose between John and the Synoptics at every turn; it would favour one presentation or another where the evidence is strongest, but it would also benefit from alternative perspectives dialectically. In short, such a paradigm would not supplant the modernist and critical approaches with something different; it would aspire to produce a more adequate set of critical approaches, availing fruitful inquiry at the beginning of the new millennium.

B. *John and the Synoptics – A Nuanced Appraisal of the Bi-Optic Traditions*

Given the facts that a triumphalist view of John's historicity is hopelessly flawed and that the denigration of John's historicity is fraught with insurmountable problems, an alternative is sorely needed. If any aspect of the above analysis seems worthy, a more nuanced approach to the John-Synoptic problem will be preferable, resulting in a more measured set of judgements regarding aspects of historicity in all four gospel traditions. Rather than seeing John as a problem to be eliminated, however, John may provide a key to understanding not only the subject of the Gospels – Jesus – but also central elements of how all four gospel traditions developed. Following is a nuanced appraisal of John and the Synoptics as bi-optic traditions.

1) *John the Problem; John the Key*

Contrary to the nineteenth-century critical scholars' approach to John as a problem to be eradicated, John is better conceived as a resource to be exploited. Therefore, a more critically adequate stance is to consider the distinctive contribution of John in terms of its autonomous origin and development, seeking to understand the epistemological origins of all aspects of John's tradition. Given the fact that John represents an independent perspective on the Jesus of history, albeit developed through a theologically engaged reflection, John offers rich elements of contrastive texture to the otherwise monochromatic presentations of the other Gospels. Rather than conceive of John as an intrusion upon the quest for the Jesus of history, a more measured analysis of John's potential and actual contribution will enhance Johannine and Jesus studies alike.

In particular, when the individuated-yet-dialogically-engaged character of John's witness is taken into account alongside the other Gospels, some interesting openings emerge. What had been thought to be open-and-shut-cases regarding Synoptic analysis become opened to fresh considerations when considered in the light of the developing of the Johannine tradition. In fact, notable weaknesses with recent historical Jesus studies have resulted from leaving John out of the mix, and a more nuanced incorporation of Johannine studies into Jesus studies might not just add a fresh insight or two; it might provide the key to unlock some hitherto closed doors.

For instance, the duplicative feeding narratives in Matthew and Mark are informed by John's more unitive witness. The problem of a single-year ministry of Jesus with a one-time visit to Jerusalem in the Synoptics is alleviated by the Johannine realism of a ministry spanning several years and including several visits. And, reasons for the religious authorities' having been threatened by Jesus (other than an obviously problematic Temple disturbance) emerge when the Johannine perspective is taken into consideration. Likewise, questions of Luke's departures from Mark and agreements with John become explicable in the light of a fresh theory of inter-gospel relations, as do the impressive similarities-yet-difference between John and Mark – the bi-optic Gospels. In these and other ways, John becomes not a problem to be managed, but a key to unsolved questions, to be used as a resource for Gospel and Jesus studies alike.

2) *History and Theology in All Four Traditions*

An important consideration here is the fact that all four gospel traditions are both historical and theological, and both historical and theological ventures contribute also to each other. In that sense, Mark is deeply theological as well as historical, so the interpreter must consider also what sorts of theological and programmatic interests might have motivated his ordering of units and materials in the crafting of his Jesus narrative. Something of Mark's culminative work in constructing the Jerusalem showdown as he did, and the Johannine presentation of a plausibly early Temple cleansing throws Mark's editorial work into sharp relief. In that sense, coming to understand that not all of Mark's moves were necessarily made for historical reasons alleviates some of the apparent contradictions between the Gospels. There were a variety of reasons behind which each of the evangelists gathered and crafted the material that they did, and a more balanced appraisal of historical, literary and theological interests is sure to be profitable all around.

While John's interests were clearly theological, however, this does not mean they were not also historical. This is one of the most critically flawed dichotomies in recent biblical studies, as one interest does not necessarily exclude or eclipse the other. It is also a fact that there are many types of historical interests to consider. One interest is what happened. Another is what that means. Another interest still is how perceptions of what happened represent former realities and how they also construct new ones. In all these ways, the Johannine witness shows that delimiting 'history' to a single definition and form – used to include and exclude material from canons of historical consideration – itself violates the many forms of historiography embraced by an ancient writer.[2] More profitable would be an exploration of the various forms of historiography exercised by ancient writers, seeking to learn what we can from each that appears to have been employed by the Gospel writers. Such a venture then informs theology, and the history-theology dialogue continues to be a fruitful one.

3) *A Common Subject; A Diversity of Portraiture*

Despite having a common subject – Jesus, the four canonical gospel traditions (and five, if Q is included in the mix) all have distinctive sets of perspectives to contribute. Mark shows him as a Jewish Rabbi, taking his band of followers on itinerant tours of ministry and calling them to count the cost of discipleship while at the same time calling them to follow him. The Q tradition shows Jesus as a purveyor of wisdom about the Kingdom of God – addressing some perplexities and creating new ones, as a means of calling humanity to the life of faith. Luke presents Jesus as a just man – one caring for the needs of the poor, women and Samaritans, and one who promises the empowerment of the Holy Sprit in the lives of believers. Matthew shows Jesus as the ultimate teacher of righteousness, challenging Pharisees as to their hypocrisy and fulfilling the Law radically. John presents Jesus as the revelatory agent from heaven, who leads humanity from darkness and death into light and life if they will but open their hearts and minds in a believing response to the divine initiative. Despite a common subject, these perspectives are impressively diverse.

---

2. On ancient historiography, Richard Burridge (1992; 2nd edn 2004) has contributed helpfully in showing the characteristics of Greek *bioi*. Craig Keener (2003) has impressively built on this work in his massive two-volume commentary.

What are the reasons for gospel distinctives? Are the differences simply factors of historicity, or are others matters involved? Within every Jesus narrative at least three elements are involved. First, tradition forms a foundation and sets the questions to be asked as well as the answers to be provided. Indeed, underlying the gospel narratives are a variety of traditions – sometimes multiple within a single Gospel, and sometimes reflecting differences of early impressions as well as later reflections. Second, the theological and historical work of the evangelist is responsible for gathering and arranging tradition into an ordered whole. Even if an evangelist is 'the tradition, himself', as some have said of John, selection and arrangement also play crucial roles. Finally, the situation and targeted audience of the narrator's work, along with editorial help along the way, influence the final stages of a developing gospel tradition. Each of these levels is both theological *and* historical, and they must have contributed to the diversity of portraiture among the Gospels, despite their common subject. It also must be said that this is a good thing, on the whole. Were any of these perspectives missing, the whole would be the less.

4) *A Variety of Presentation; A Coherence of Impression*
Even with John contributing to the mix, despite the variety of presentation among the Gospels, they convey a remarkable coherence of impression. This can especially be seen in the elements of multiple attestation between John and the various gospel traditions. Even though John's differences have been extensive and significant, it must be acknowledged that John's portrait of Jesus coheres more with the Jesus of the Synoptics that it does with the Odes of Solomon, the writings of Homer, the book of Exodus, the biography of Apollonius and even the Gospel of Thomas. In that sense, the impressive thing about John's distinctive tradition is the way it nonetheless coheres with the Markan traditions.

In particular, the multiply attested Jesus, catapulted into public ministry by John the Baptist, cleanses the Temple, heals the sick and raises the dead, teaches about the Kingdom of God and the Way of the Spirit, challenges religious authorities and receives hostile treatment in return, travels with a group of twelve disciples and others, including women, feeds the multitude and delivers his followers on the lake, marches to Jerusalem, is welcomed by the crowd triumphally, dines with his disciples and predicts his betrayal, goes to the garden and is there arrested, is tried before Jewish and Roman tribunals, is sentenced to death by Pilate, dies on the cross, is buried and is attested by post-resurrection encounters of his followers. This basic commonality of elements (plus a few others if a more detailed analysis were performed) produces an impressively coherent portrait of Jesus, despite the variety of presentation. In that sense, despite John's distinctives, the larger quest is not scandalized – even with the Johannine witness directly on the table.

5) *Dialectical Memory and Dialogical Engagement*
A notable flaw in historical analysis is to assume that an eyewitness account will have no variation from the facts or subjectivity of perception to it.

Therefore, if two witnesses disagree, one of them must by wrong or must be lying – so the thinking goes. Empirical forensic analyses demonstrate, however, that eyewitness memory can be variable and flawed, and that when eyewitness accounts of the elderly are presented alongside those of the young, they are not necessarily more accurate. The elderly tend to miss particular details, or to add ones that they might have encountered elsewhere, introducing alternative memory into the story as a means of filling a gap. Likewise, the elderly are more likely to be stereotypical in their characterization of suspects, and they are especially prone to label an innocent bystander as guilty, or even a person of similar association rather than identical appearance.[3] The point here is that proving or disproving a detail's veracity may say little about whether a tradition is rooted in eyewitness testimony or commonsense conjecture. A variety of dialectical factors may have been involved, including selective memory and emerging associations.

It is also a fact that memory of 'what happened' will always be impacted by developing understandings of the meaning of 'what happened' within later situations and generations. This being the case, any narrative will accrue elements of its evolving history of narration along the way, and while this is interesting, it does not remove the tradition from the genre of historiography. *All* historiography is subjective, in that humans are centrally involved in the making of meaning from first impressions to last ones. Therefore, recency and primacy effects must be considered as factors of historical memory and its development. For instance, if Mark contains a collection of units from Peter's preaching, crafted to address the needs of the church (Papias' way of saying that he got at least some of it down correctly, but not necessarily all of it; Eusebius, *Hist. Eccles.* 3.39), this is precisely what is observable in the Johannine narrative as well. So, in both of the bi-optic Gospels, history is made relevant, instructively and rhetorically, for later audiences.

For the pre-Markan tradition, emphases upon the hiddenness of the Kingdom, the Messianic Secret, the Way of the Cross, the cost of discipleship, the celebration of the Lord's Supper, and the hope for the *Parousia* probably reflect crafting the material to address the needs of emerging audiences. Likewise in John, the witness of the Baptist, the controversies between Jesus and Judean leaders, translations of Palestinian language and customs for Gentile audiences, reports of original and ongoing persecutions of Jesus followers, foibles of Roman leaders and Peter and emphases upon the incarnation involved emphases likewise targeted at emerging audiences as well. In that sense, like fiction and all forms of narrative, historiography itself is a fundamentally dialogical process. Out of formative reflective dialogues with pivotal events in the past memory emerges, but not in a vacuum. Memory develops as perceived significance grows and wanes in the light of emerging situations and experiences. Finally, the past only becomes 'history' as it is seen

---

3. See, for instance, the impressive work done by A.D. Yarmey (1984, pp. 153–4).

to be relevant to later situations and is called into action as an orienting force – challenging or inspiring the present on the basis of the past – but also driving toward the future. In the making of meaning, all levels of tradition and their participants are involved. What *cannot* be said is that alternative memory has no root in history. In that sense, what is needed is not only a fresh appraisal of gospel traditions, but a radical analysis of the meaning and character of the historical enterprise, itself. Therefore, from dialogue to dialogue, the character and structure of gospel memory deserve a new and sustained analysis in the light of latest scientific understandings of cognition, perception, experience and the resulting reflective process.

C. The Dialogical Autonomy of John and Modern Foundations Reconsidered

To be fair, the de-historicization of John and the de-Johannification of Jesus, as modern foundations of how to approach issues related to John, Jesus and history, have been limited by the lack of suitable approaches to enduring questions regarding matters Johannine – literary, historical and theological. While the present work cannot develop all approaches to these matters in equal detail, it can build upon other treatments elsewhere within a larger synthesis. That being the case, the dialogical autonomy of John is constructed upon two foundational axes: first, a pervasively autonomous tradition, going back to Jesus in its own distinctive way; and secondly, one that is accompanied by a set of dialogical engagements along the way. Each of these involves distinctive forms of dialogical reality, supported by particular evidence and analysis, and yet each of them also relates to the others in terms of the unique development of Johannine tradition. It is in the light of this larger synthesis that modern foundations regarding John and the quest for Jesus deserve a fresh reconsideration.

1) *Intra-traditional Reflection – First Impressions and Later Understandings*
When thinking about the sort of historical project the Gospel of John represents, several features deserve consideration. Fulfilled understandings are mentioned, suggesting earlier misunderstandings and later fuller understandings: the prophecy about rebuilding 'this temple' in three days (Jn 2.22) is understood more fully after the resurrection; the Jewish leaders do not understand that the one whom Jesus claimed had sent him was the Father (Jn 8.27), but the reader knows; the disciples did not realize that his entering Jerusalem on a donkey fulfilled the Zechariah prophecy (Jn 12.16), but later they discovered it; at the last supper no one around the table understood what Jesus was saying to Judas (Jn 13.28), but they caught on later; the disciples did not recognize Jesus on the shore (Jn 21.4), but the Beloved Disciple did and pointed him out to Peter. In all these presentations, earlier understandings give way to fuller and later ones.

It is also the case that events and even surprises are reflected upon dialogically, suggesting that an unfolding set of meanings continue to be discovered as fulfilments of meaning within the tradition. The work of the *Paraklētos* not only comforts Jesus' followers in later generations, but guides them into all truth and reminds them of what Jesus has said in the past in ways that become relevant for the present (Jn 14.26; 15.26; 16.8-15). This being the case, the sort of 'history' represented by the Johannine project values originative meanings insofar as they are fulfilled in eventual ones. The drawing of connections between an earlier memory and the present situation becomes the marker of meaningful historical memory, and the narrator and audience alike are ongoingly involved in the making of meaning. Certainly the Fourth Evangelist would have embraced Ricoeur's concept of 'the surplus of meaning' as descriptive of his own experience and his understanding of how the present and future are well served by the past. Therefore, paraphrasis and alternative representations of earlier themes and memories would not have been regarded a historical 'problem' – they would have been descriptive of the historical process valued and practised by the Johannine evangelist. John's intra-traditional dialogue thus deserves consideration in helping the modern critic understand the type of historiography that was being performed, instead of judging it positively or negatively by an alien standard.

2) *Inter-traditional Engagement – Dialogical Relationships Between Gospel Traditions*

While John's intra-traditional dialogue is apparent, the Johannine tradition also shows signs of being involved dialogically with other parallel traditions. Within the interfluential stages between the early Johannine tradition and the pre-Markan tradition, several features can be inferred. Descriptions of places and details, uses of Scripture, and narrating significant aspects of the words and works of Jesus were here interfluentially engaged. Even some dialogically corrective engagement may have existed between Petrine and Johannine traditions (or whoever the preachers underlying the traditions of Mark and John might have been; although see Acts 8.14-25 for a plausible example of such interaction) on such themes as the character of the Kingdom and its advance, the relation between faith and signs, Jesus' teachings on the *Parousia*, Messianic disclosure and the character of leadership. With the rendering of written Mark, the first edition of John appears to fill out the picture and to set a few things straight in terms of chronology and presentation, and while Luke and Q appear to have employed the Johannine oral tradition as a source – certainly the Johannine Epistles did. The later Matthean and Johannine traditions can be seen to be involved in an ongoing set of dialogues on consonant apologies for Jesus as the Jewish Messiah and somewhat dissonant presentations on charisma and structure in Christian leadership.

Of course, such a possibility creates a new set of problems for interpreters if John's narrative is credited with historical weight and Markan familiarity. Would inter-traditional complementarity or correction call into question the veracity of all four gospel traditions?[4] It might be simpler and more comfortable to go back to the chopping block and sacrifice John for the sake of the Markan traditions. And yet, critically, John's tradition demands engagement and renewed consideration. Perhaps the problem lies with our understanding of memory and historicity. Seeing historical memory as hermeneutically driven helps us appreciate the relation between subjectivity and objectivity in the construction of historical narrative. Memory is always selective, and a plurality of impressions itself contributes to the historical realism of the bi-optic traditions. Seeing John as autonomous-yet-engaged dialectically not only with other written traditions but with oral ones, and even secondary orality – what was heard about what was written or said about what was heard or written – indeed may have played a role in the inter-traditional set of dialogues. Especially John makes that plausible reality apparent.

3) *Cognitive Dialectic – Conjunctive Approaches to Historical and Theological Challenges*

The most fascinating feature of interpreting John's theology over the last two millennia has been the attempts to deal with John's apparent contradictions and tensions. Jesus is equal to the Father and also subordinate to the Father; Jesus is human as well as divine; Jesus judges no one but has been sent for judgement; eschatology happens now and also on the last day; the hour of Jesus is not yet come, but now it is fulfilled; the signs are embellished but also existentialized; salvation happens exclusively through Jesus, but the saving light of Christ illumines all humanity; no one can come to Jesus without being drawn by the Father, yet all who believe become the children of God; the institution of the eucharist is missing, yet one has no life without ingesting the flesh and blood of Jesus; and Jesus and his disciples were baptizing, but Jesus did not, only his disciples did – just to name a few. While other forms of dialogue abound within the Johannine tradition, these reflect the cognitive dialogue of a dialectical thinker, looking at something from one side and then another.

In terms of James Fowler's Stages of Faith (1981), the Johannine evangelist's thought process exhibits a Stage 5 Conjunctive level of faith. Having moved from Stage 3 Synthetic-Conventional Faith to Stage 4 Individuative-Reflective Faith, the evangelist has come to hold various aspects of the truth together in

---

4. This was the concern of P. Gardner-Smith (1938); if the Fourth Evangelist were indeed familiar with the Synoptics, he would have been disagreeing with them at nearly every turn, despite many similarities. Of course, there are also degrees and manners of familiarity. Despite his arguing that John is dependent upon Mark, C.K. Barrett (1978) must admit that such a dependence was nothing like the literary dependence of Matthew and Luke upon Mark; the similarities between Mark and John are too few and inexact. If, however, familiarity with Mark might have been a factor of the Fourth Evangelist's having heard it read in a meeting for worship, as suggested by Ian MacKay (2004), such a history of inter-traditional engagement is not at all unlikely.

tension, and no Christological or theological analysis of John (or even Christian theology, for that matter – given John's indelible impact upon it) can be adequate without considering this epistemological feature. Especially when contrasted to the Johannine Epistles, the evangelist's both-and approach to things, rather than an either-or stance, must be taken into consideration. The point here is that this feature also applies to aspects of Johannine history as well as Johannine theology. A dialectical presentation of history appreciates events and their originative meanings, but it is also mindful of developing and newer meanings along the way. In that sense, a dialectical approach to historiography may come across as disturbing to a modernist historian, but just as the theologian must let John be John (Dunn, 1983), so must the historian. Cognitive dialectic affects the very meaning of history itself.

4) *Dialogical Narrative – Engaging the Reader in an Imaginary Dialogue with One's Subject*

In addition to theology and history, the literary aspects of John's dialogical character must also be considered critically. Here the narrator sets out to engage the reader in an imaginary dialogue with the subject of the narrator – Jesus, and various ploys are used. At the outset, the audience is told about the Word of God, communicated to the world as a message of illumination and redemption, inviting a response of faith from those who are the objects of God's love. The reader is then introduced to a variety of bases upon which to believe that Jesus was authentically sent from God: witnesses declare his authenticity, signs perform the divine power of his commission, and the fulfilled word of prophecy and Scripture confirm that he indeed is the Jewish Messiah. Along these lines, a believing response to the divine initiative is the way the Johannine evangel presents its apologetic goal (Jn 1.11-13; 3.16; 20.31). The text invites the reader to move from being an outsider to being an insider to the community of faith by exercising such a response (Anderson, 2000b).

From a narrative perspective, however, a highly effective dialogical ploy is also used extensively in John. When the initiative shifts from God or God's agent to humanity or a discussant involved in a dialogue with Jesus, the dialogical mode shifts from a revelational mode to a rhetorical mode of dialogical engagement. Here, the discussant is presented as coming to Jesus with a question or a wise-sounding claim, only to be exposed as non-comprehending and naive. Misunderstanding is always rhetorical in narrative, and the presentation of misunderstanding discussants functions to expose their views as false and insufficient, pointing instead to the way of the revealer. Rhetorically, the reader becomes engaged in the questions and roles of the discussant, leading to being drawn into an imaginary dialogue with Jesus. In that sense, every reader becomes Nicodemus – a religious leader who is clueless about the way of the Spirit; or the Samaritan woman – whose personal life is a source of anxiety and concern; or Pilate – who fails to understand the power of truth; or Peter – who struggles to comprehend servant leadership and pastoral responsibility. The literary dialogue between the text and the reader ultimately functions to lead the reader beyond the text to its subject – Jesus, and when that happens, the Johannine narrative has indeed moved from encounter to encounter.

5) *Dialectical Hermeneutics – An Interdisciplinary Quest for History and Meaning*
From the dialogical autonomy of the Gospel of John we gain a sense of dialectical hermeneutics, wherein the life of the reader is drawn into the world of the text – calling back and forth from one form of reality to another. This dialogical process is essentially what history is, for historicity itself is ordered by highly subjective interests rather than solely objective ones. Put otherwise, there is no such thing as purely objective history. The very process of historiography distinguishes events of greater importance from lesser ones, and that is itself a subjective venture. Objectivity, of course, becomes a measure of a historical claim, but the historical quest is from beginning to end a quest for meaning, wherein the past is measured by its significance for the present.

In terms of John's contribution to the historical quest for Jesus, it should be noted that while chronological and topographical issues will be involved, these are never the first interest of historical meaning. Rather, it is the enduring significance of an event that determines the historic value of places, names and dates. In pursuit of that interest, any and all disciplines that contribute to the understanding of context, development, perception, culture, cognition, experience and memory should be pursued. In the historical quest anything that is true will be of value; the question is *how* to approach the venture. As a dialectical hermeneutic, not only are present questers concerned with engaging and understanding the past and its unfolding meanings, we are also involved in an interdisciplinary dialogue wherein we borrow and learn from other fields the best approaches, tools and perspectives for the pursuit of truth and the making of meaning. In that sense, no good question is off limits, and no profitable discipline should be disregarded. Indeed, given the great multitude of approaches to the investigations of John, Jesus and history, there's bound to be good interdisciplinary fellowship along the way.

Findings

In reconsidering the modern foundations regarding John and the quest for the Jesus of history, a critical appraisal of critical perspectives must be balanced with a sympathetic appreciation for the need of a nuanced approach. Strengths and weaknesses of all approaches abound, and what is needed is a nuanced approach to the issues involved. Indeed, there is far more material for consideration in the material common to John and the other Gospels than is often granted, and there are significant ways in which distinctive contributions are made by the Markan and Johannine traditions alike. A more nuanced appreciation for the ways that each of these bi-optic traditions contributes to the historical quest for Jesus deserves fresh critical consideration, and as a dialogical set of realities differences are not necessarily mutually exclusive. For this reason a profitable set of approaches to the enduring Johannine questions deserve to be considered and implemented where found suitable. The dialogical autonomy of John combines its individuated perspective on the Jesus of history with dialectical operations throughout its development. From dialectical reflection on the past, to interfluential dialogues with other traditions, to dialogical engagements with the reader, John's dialogical autonomy finally invites the reader into a dialogical response of faith to the divine initiative. Where this happens with authenticity, history is not only understood, but in Johannine perspective, the meaning of history is fulfilled.

CONCLUSION

John and the Quest for Jesus – A Nuanced View

Just as John played a central role in the creation of theological controversies in the Patristic era regarding Jesus as the Christ, John has created also some of the most intense historical-critical controversies in the Modern era regarding the historical quest for Jesus. Whereas John's dialectical approach to truth was effectively yoked to providing a conjunctive way forward in the formation of Christian theology, John has not yet been integrated into a plausible way forward regarding the historical quest for Jesus. Part of the reason for this fact is that John has been exiled from the canons of historicity by critical scholars. They have indeed identified real problems to which they pose the solution of the de-historicization of John. This results, then, in excluding John from the historical quest for Jesus, making that enterprise an exclusively Synoptic one – until more recently, when ironically extracanonical gospels are welcome, but John is not. The problem is that the de-Johannification of Jesus produces an impoverished portrait of Jesus, devoid of fuller contrasts and textures. This enterprise may serve the work of sound-bite descriptions of Jesus and his mission, or producing a modern Jesus instead of a historical one, but the quest for Jesus is itself diminished by such a move.

The fact is that *none* of the planks in the two platforms of the de-historicization of John and the de-Johannification of Jesus is especially solid. They provide solutions to real problems, but in no case is the extreme option the most suitable way forward from a critical standpoint. Also given the fact that the best of Johannine scholars fail to assent to the so-called 'critical consensus' on these points, the critical conclusion must be that the 'critical consensus' is *neither*. As a literary-critical and historical-critical way forward, a fresh synthesis is proposed that considers the dialogical autonomy of John developing as an individuated Jesus tradition, but developing in its own dialogical ways. These dialogical engagements include a dialectical thinker who reflected dialogically upon his tradition, engaged dialectically other traditions, and addressed his emerging audiences with a dialogical presentation of the Jesus story.

In the light of a new synthetic approach to literary, historical and theological Johannine questions, the history of the Johannine tradition and its differences with the Synoptic traditions are not as insoluble as they have often been construed to be. Inferring a distinctive set of relations between the Johannine and each of the Synoptic traditions provides a database of contacts – or at least similarities and differences – lending itself to a fresh set of approaches to enduring problems. It must be said that the motivation for posing such a construct is not primarily the recovery of historiographical possibilities, but such venues present themselves as new ways forward open. In the spirit of scientific critical analysis, the various models here proposed also welcome critical scrutiny. All scholarship is a work in progress – benefiting from critical engagement and new discoveries – so suggested improvements are welcome indeed.

As the above study suggests, critical biblical scholarship requires a more nuanced view of John and the quest for Jesus, and the present work aspires to make such a contribution. Indeed, John's dialectical approach to truth has provided the way forward in addressing John's Christological tensions; perhaps John's dialogical autonomy will provide a way forward in pursuing the quest for the Jesus of history and also the historical character of John – the enigmatic Gospel. How, though, do modern historiographers deal with enigmas? Monological thinkers tend to crush them, or to explain them away, but the most skilled of historians keep them within the mix. Perhaps an insight from the exegetical master of the twentieth century, Rudolf Bultmann, might yet provide us a way forward (see above, p. 175).

If philosophical and theological thinking are best explored dialectically, why not expect the same with reflective historiography? If the challenge of the Patristic era was to overcome monological approaches to theological truth (especially with regard to John's contribution to Christological controversies), the challenge of the modern era is to transcend monological approaches to historical truth (especially with regard to John's contribution to Jesus-quest controversies). If gospel historiography can be seen as a more dialogical enterprise – from epistemic origins to tradition-critical analyses – the John *versus* Jesus dichotomy might yet be supplanted by a more conjunctive and nuanced approach.

Might this lead to a *fourth* quest for Jesus? Only time will tell.

APPENDIX I

A Two-Edition Theory of Johannine Composition

While a theory of composition works necessarily from earlier to later, the strongest evidence will often be a factor of identifying first the apparent later material that was added to earlier material. Therefore, the following elements of this two-edition theory of Johannine composition ascend in order of certainty as well as chronology.

A) *The Formation of the Johannine Tradition (30–85 CE)*

- The Johannine tradition develops in its own way as an independent Jesus tradition.
- Material is formed in its own patterns, perhaps developing with *Amēn Amēn* sayings, *egō eimi* sayings, signs narrations, dialogues, and Scripture references.
- The Johannine Passion narrative develops in its own distinctive way.
- Connections between signs and discourses emerge with signs being expanded in the dialogues and discourses.
- Some interfluentiality between the pre-Markan and early Johannine tradition emerges, especially involving graphic detail and some points of content.
- John's oral-traditional material becomes a source for Luke/Acts, and possibly the Q tradition.
- Some material may have been produced in written form, and duplicate sections may have been gathered together.

B) *The First Edition of the Johannine Gospel (John A) is written by the Johannine Evangelist (80–85 CE)*

- In desiring to augment, complement and correct Mark, the first edition of John was written as (chronologically) the second Gospel.
- Beginning with the ministry of the Baptist, John A contains five signs designed to convince Jewish family and friends that Jesus was the Messiah. These signs are the five that are not in Mark (chs 2, 4, 5, 9, 11) or any of the other Synoptic traditions.

- Most prevalent are the intense dialogues with Jewish leaders, seeking to show that Jesus was indeed the authentic prophet like Moses (Deut. 18.15-22).
- The first two signs fill out the early part of Jesus' ministry, and the latter three signs fill out the Judean ministry of Jesus, building around Mark.
- The Johannine Gospel is written that the reader might believe that Jesus is the Jewish Messiah (Jn 20.31).

C) *The Johannine Epistles are written by the Johannine Elder (85–95 CE)*

- 1 John was written as a circular to various Johannine churches exhorting them to love one another and to maintain solidarity with Jesus and his community of faith, following at least one schism.
- 2 John was written to a church exhorting its leadership not to receive docetic preachers.
- 3 John was written to a church leader, Gaius, suffering the inhospitality of Diotrephes, plausibly a hierarchical aspirant rejecting Johannine Christians and any who take them in.

D) *Interim Period between the Two Editions of the Johannine Gospel (85–100 CE)*

- The Beloved Disciple continues to preach and teach (and perhaps write) locally or more extensively.
- Emphases upon antidocetic correctives (costly discipleship) emerge in the Johannine teaching as a factor of Gentile believers desiring to assimilate under Roman demands of emperor worship.
- Some dialogue emerges between Johannine and Matthean Christianity (or its purveyors) regarding aspects of church leadership and organizational development.
- The Beloved Disciple dies, leaving his final witness to be gathered and distributed by another.

E) *The Johannine Elder compiles and finalizes the Johannine Gospel (John B) and sends it off as the witness of the Beloved Disciple, whose 'witness is true' (100 CE)*

- The Prologue (Jn 1.1-18) is added as an engaging confessional introduction to the Johannine narrative.
- Chapter 6 is inserted between chs 5 and 7 (following 'Moses wrote of me,' at the end of ch. 5; the unit fits well after the second healing sign mentioned at the beginning of ch. 6; ch. 5 originally continued into ch. 7). The editor added v. 71 to take the focus off of Peter.

- Chapters 15–17 are inserted between chs 14 and 18 (14.31 originally flowed into 18.1).
- Chapter 21 is added as a second ending, and the final two verses were crafted to imitate the original ending of ch. 20.
- The editor/compiler also adds 'Beloved Disciple' and 'eyewitness' passages to affirm the Gospel's authority.
- He then sends it off to the churches as the witness of the Beloved Disciple, whose testimony is true – a distinctively ideological claim, seeking to affirm how Christ desires to lead and unify the churches through the work of the Holy Spirit (at least partially as a corrective to Diotrephes and his kin).
- In this later material most of John's incarnational (anti-docetic) material and ecclesial emphases can be found.

F) *Post-Johannine Influences continue into the second century* CE

- The spurned Johannine Docetists took with them at least some portions of the Johannine Gospel and developed into at least one strand of second-century Christian Gnosticism – perhaps those represented by Heracleon, who wrote the first commentary on John. In addition, Johannine connections with Thomasine and other Gnosticizing traditions may have evolved during this time.
- Johannine influences appear also to have been formative for the Montanist movement in Asia Minor, but these trajectories need not have involved spurned Docetists. They simply may reflect the fact that the Johannine emphasis upon the ongoing work of the Holy Spirit in the church deserved to be taken seriously by committed Christians, and this represents something of the intentional focus of the later Johannine material.
- Other aspects of John's influence upon the mainstream Christian movement in the second century resulted in an immense impact on the early church, and the greatest number of second-century gospel fragments are from the Gospel of John. The Bodmer Papyrus dates a Johannine fragment as early as 125 CE, so John can no longer be regarded late-and-only-late.
- Both Polycarp and Papias claimed to have been influenced by the Johannine Elder, and it is likely that the Johannine influence continued on for some time through them and others. By the time of Irenaeus, the Johannine tradition's authority becomes yoked to his interests in defeating the Valentinians and Marcionites, and the Johannine memory was used to bolster the movement it once challenged.

Appendix II

A Historical Outline of Johannine Christianity

The Johannine situation spanned three major periods with at least two crises in each, a total of six crises. A seventh may be added – as dialectical engagements with Synoptic perspectives on Jesus' ministry may be inferred – but these overlapped all three major periods. While these crises were largely sequential, they were also somewhat overlapping. Social movements rarely enjoy the luxury of engaging only on one front at a time, nor does one crisis wait until another has passed before presenting itself. The Johannine situation involved several sorts of dialogical relationships, in different settings, and it deserves to be considered in longitudinal perspective over a 70-year time-span.

A. *Early Period* – A Northern Palestinian Setting of the Johannine Tradition's Development (30–70 CE)

Crisis I: *North–South Tensions over Authentic Worship and what God Requires* (Jn 2-5)

- The *Ioudaioi* are described in some parts of John as Judeans (chs 11–12) or from Jerusalem (chs 1–2).
- Jesus is rendered as a northern prophet like Moses (Samaritan, Galilean or both?).
- The Jerusalem-centred leaders overlook Jesus' Messiahship because he comes from the north (Nazareth) rather than the city of David (Bethlehem).
- Samaritans and Galileans are privileged in John, and yet authentic worship is independent of place and form.
- The Jerusalem-centred religious authorities reject the revealer and become typologies of the unbelieving world.

Crisis II: *The Ministry of Jesus versus the Ministry of John the Baptist?* (Jn 1, 3 and 10)

- The Fourth Evangelist (and some of the other disciples of Jesus) may have left John to follow Jesus; John's ministry remains important.
- John's baptism in the free-flowing Jordan posed a striking contrast to

constrictive means of ritual purification – liberal accessibility of the Spirit – likewise, Jesus' ministry!

- Baptist adherents were pointed to Jesus in the eulogizing of Jesus by the departed hero.
- The baptism of Jesus is emphasized over John's as a factor of setting the record straight among those who knew the latter but not the Holy Spirit (Acts 18.24-19.7).
- Hence, water does not suffice (Jn 3.5), and Jesus himself did not baptize, although his disciples did (Jn 4.2).

Transition A: From the Early Period to the Middle Period, including a Move to Asia Minor or one of the Gentile-Mission Churches

B. Middle Period – Asia Minor I, The Formation of the Johannine Community (70–85 CE)

- The evangelist moves from a Palestinian setting to one of the mission churches (Asia Minor?).
- Dialogues with local Jewish communities continue; they do not begin.
- Explanations of Jewish customs and Hebraic phrases are 'translated' for a Gentile audience.
- Gospel material becomes further organized into teaching units, including signs and discourses together.
- An interfluential engagement with the oral Markan material gives rise to an augmentation and correction of Mark.

Crisis III: *The Local Synagogue and Antichristic threat 1* (Jn 9.22; 12.42; 16. 2; 1 Jn 2.18-25)

- John's Christianity moved from Palestine to one of the mission churches (Ephesus).
- The Jamnia Council codifies local practices rather than jump-starting all marginalization of Jesus-adherents.
- Christians are marginalized from the Synagogue; the *Birkat ha-Minim* curses 'Nazarenes'.
- Accusations of 'ditheism' lead to at least some expulsion, but more characteristically, socio-religious pressure (Jn 9.22; 12.42; 16.2).
- Some Johannine community members are recruited back into the Synagogue, producing the first Johannine schism.

Crisis IV: *Emperor Worship and its Implications*: Pilate, the Confession of Thomas, 'the Second Beast' and '666' (Revelation 13; Jn 20.28; even 1 Jn 5.21?)

- Domitian required Emperor worship as a sign of loyalty to the Empire (to reverence Caesar's statue, offer incense, say 'Caesar is Lord', deny Christ, etc.).
- 'Lord and God' was required of officials (notice the striking confession of Thomas, Jn 20.28).
- Jews had been given a dispensation.
- Gentiles saw little wrong with emperor laud.
- Synagogue separation meant vulnerability before Rome.
- Christians were to confess Caesar or die (stay away from idols – 1 Jn 5.21).

Transition B: From the Middle Period to the Later Period – Emerging Communities in Johannine Christianity

C. *Later Period* – Asia Minor II, The Expansion of Johannine Christianity (85–100 CE)

- The first edition of John is finalized, but the evangelist continues to preach, addressing the needs of the community.
- Other communities begin to form, though, and the Elder addresses them, as well.
- Concerns with Jewish and Roman issues continue, but docetizing preachers and hierarchical tendencies raise new concerns.
- The Elder finalizes the witness of the Beloved Disciple after his death and circulates it among the churches.

Crisis V: *Docetizing Gentile Christians and Antichristic threat 2* (1 Jn 4.1-3; 2 Jn 7; the Gospel's second-edition material – Jn 1.1-18, chs 6, 15-17, 21, Beloved Disciple and 'eyewitness' passages)

- Some Gentile Christians believed it was not a problem to worship Caesar.
- Jewish Christian leadership emphasized 'one Lord' who suffered and died for us.
- The Docetists argued Jesus did not suffer, he merely appeared to.
- John's leadership emphasized Jesus' suffering and disciples' willingness to do the same.
- False teachers (teaching assimilation with Rome) are opposed by John's leadership.

Crisis VI: *Institutionalization within the Late First-century Church* (3 Jn 9-10; second-edition material – *Paraklētos* passages; juxtaposition of Peter and the Beloved Disciple)

- The Johannine leadership felt the apostolate had been hi-jacked by structuralists and sought to provide a Spirit-based (historical) corrective.
- *This* is why Diotrephes was threatened.
- The juxtaposition of Peter and the Beloved Disciple and the *Paraklētos* passages set the record straight (Jesus' original intention).
- 'His witness is true!' bears with it ideological (ecclesiological) implications.
- The Elder thus circulates the Gospel ca. 100 CE as a witness to Jesus' will for the church and as a source of encouragement.

Crisis VII: *Dialectical Engagements with Synoptic and Prevalent Christian Renderings of Jesus' ministry* (30–100 CE, spanning all three periods)

- Correcting the valuation of Jesus' works (revelatory signs, *not* 'ate and were satisfied', Jn 6.26).
- The Kingdom goes forward as a function of truth (Jn 18.36-7, *not* power, even thaumaturgic power).
- Jesus is the light of the world (versus his followers, Jn 8.12).
- Moses and Elijah are present in Jesus, *not* in the ministry of John the Baptist or at the transfiguration (Jn 1.19-23).
- The second coming of Christ was not necessarily what he predicted (in Mark 9.1); rather, what he actually said (to Peter, by the way) is '*What is it to you* if he lives until I come again...*you follow me!*' (Jn 21.18-24).

D. *Post-Johannine Christianity* – The Johannine Gospel Impacts the Mainstream Christian movement *and* Alternative Ones (100 CE→)

The Johannine Gospel was taken by expelled Gentile (docetizing) Christians into their movement, leading to the formation of Gnostic Johannine Christianity (Heracleon *et al.*). Some Johannine influence goes toward influencing Christian enthusiasm reflected in the Montanist movement (with Montanus calling himself the '*Paraklētos*', the inclusion of women in ministry, and the desire to restore the spiritual vitality of the Church).

Most of John's influence impacted the mainstream Christian movement, so that by the turn of the second century CE, more copies/fragments of John have been found than any other gospel narrative. The Gospel of John became the most popular Christian document in second-century Christianity, among orthodox and heterodox communities alike.

BIBLIOGRAPHY

Adam, A.K.M. (ed.)
    2000   *Handbook of Postmodern Biblical Interpretation* (St Louis: Chalice Press).
Albright, William F.
    1956   'Recent discoveries in Palestine and the Gospel of St John', in W.D. Davies and
              D. Daube (eds), *The Background of the New Testament and its Eschatology;
              In Honour of Charles Harold Dodd* (Cambridge: Cambridge University Press):
              153–71.
Allison, D.C., Jr.
    2003   'The continuity between John and Jesus', *JSHJ* 1.1: 6–27.
Anderson, Paul N.
    2007   'On guessing points and naming stars – the epistemological origins of John's
              Christological tensions', in Richard Bauckham and Carl Mosser (eds), *The
              Gospel of St. John and Christian Theology* (Grand Rapids: Eerdmans).
    2006   'Aspects of historicity in John – implications for the investigations of Jesus and
              archaeology', in James Charlesworth (ed.), *Jesus and Archaeology* (Grand
              Rapids: Eerdmans): 587–618.
    2004a   'Jesus and transformation', in J. Harold Ellens and Wayne Rollins (eds),
              Psychology and the Bible; A New Way to Read the Scriptures (vol. 4;
              Westport/London: Praeger Publishers): 305–28.
    2004b   'The cognitive origins of John's Christological unity and disunity', in J. Harold
              Ellens and Wayne Rollins (eds), *Psychology and the Bible; A New Way to Read
              the Scriptures*, (vol. 3; Westport, CT: Praegers/Greenwood Publishers): 127–48;
              also published in *Horizons in Biblical Theology* 17 (1995): 1–24.
    2002a   'A response to Professors Borg, Powell and Kinkel', *QRT* 98: 43–54.
    2002b   'Interfluential, formative, and dialectical – a theory of John's relation to the
              Synoptics', in Peter Hofrichter (ed.), *Für und wider die Priorität des
              Johannesevangeliums* (TTS, 9; Hildesheim, Zürich, and New York: Georg
              Olms Verlag): 19–58.
    2001   'John and Mark – the Bi-optic Gospels', in Robert Fortna and Tom Thatcher
              (eds), *Jesus in Johannine Tradition* (Philadelphia: Westminster/John Knox
              Press): 175–88.
    2000a   'On Jesus: quests for historicity, and the history of recent quests', *QRT* 94: 5–39.
    2000b   *Navigating the Living Waters of the Gospel of John: On Wading with Children
              and Swimming with Elephants* (Wallingford, PA: Pendle Hill Press).
    1999a   'The Having-Sent-Me Father – Aspects of agency, irony, and encounter in the
              Johannine Father-Son relationship', *Semeia* 85: 33–57.
    1999b   'Response' (to reviews of *The Christology of the Fourth Gospel* by Robert Kysar,
              Sandra M. Schneiders, R. Alan Culpepper, Graham Stanton and Alan G.
              Padgett: 38–61), *Review of Biblical Literature* 1: 62–72.
    1997   'The *Sitz im Leben* of the Johannine Bread of Life Discourse and its evolving
              context', in Alan Culpepper (ed.), *Critical Readings of John 6* (BIS, 22; Leiden:
              E.J. Brill): 1–59.

| | 1996 | The Christology of the Fourth Gospel; Its Unity and Disunity in the Light of John 6 (WUNT II, 78; Tübingen: J.C.B. Mohr (Paul Siebeck); Valley Forge, PA: Trinity Press International, 1997). |

1996 *The Christology of the Fourth Gospel; Its Unity and Disunity in the Light of John 6* (WUNT II, 78; Tübingen: J.C.B. Mohr (Paul Siebeck); Valley Forge, PA: Trinity Press International, 1997).

1991 'Was the Fourth Evangelist a Quaker?', *QRT* 76: 27–43.

Anderson, Paul N., J. Harold Ellens and James W. Fowler

2004 'Cognitive-critical analysis – a way forward in the scientific investigation of gospel traditions', in J. Harold Ellens and Wayne Rollins (eds), *Psychology and the Bible; A New Way to Read the Scriptures* (vol. 4; Westport, CT: Praegers/Greenwood Publishers): 246–76.

Ashton, John

1997 (ed.) *The Interpretation of John* (2nd edn; Edinburgh: T&T Clark).

1994 *Studying John* (Oxford: Oxford University Press).

1991 *Understanding the Fourth Gospel* (Oxford: Clarendon).

Askwith, E.H.

1910 *The Historical Value of the Fourth Gospel* (London: Hodder & Stoughton).

Attridge, Harold W.

2002 'Genre bending in the Fourth Gospel', *JBL* 121: 3–21.

1980 'Thematic development and source elaboration in John 7:1-36', *The Catholic Biblical Quarterly* 42: 161–70.

Auerbach, Erich

1953 *Mimesis: The Representation of Reality in Western Literature* (Willard R. Trask, trans.; Princeton: Princeton University Press).

Aune, David E.

1991 'Oral tradition and the aphorisms of Jesus', in Henry Wansbrough (ed.), *Jesus and the Oral Gospel Tradition* (Sheffield: JSOT Press).

Bacon, Benjamin Wisner

1918 *The Fourth Gospel in Research and Debate* (2nd edn; New Haven: Yale University Press).

Bailey, J.A.

1963 *The Traditions Common to the Gospels of Luke and John* (NovTSup, 7; Leiden: E.J. Brill).

Bakhtin, Mikhail M.

1990 *Art and Answerability; Early Philosophical Essays by M. M. Bakhtin* (Michael Holquist and Vadim Liapunov, eds; Vadim Liapunov and Kenneth Brostrom, trans.; Austin: University of Texas Press).

1981 *The Dialogic Imagination,* (Michael Holquist, ed.; Austin: University of Texas Press).

Ball, David Mark

1996 *'I Am' in John's Gospel; Literary Function, Background and Theological Implications* (JSNTSupS, 124; Sheffield: Sheffield University Press).

Ball, R.M.

1985 'St John and the institution of the Eucharist', *JSNT* 23: 59–68.

Barbour, Ian

1997 *Religion and Science; Historical and Contemporary Issues* (New York: HarperSanFrancisco).

Barnett, Paul W.

1986 'The feeding of the multitude in Mark 6/John 6', *Gospel Perspectives*, David Wenham and Craig Blomberg (eds) (vol. 6; Sheffield: JSOT Press): 273–93.

1981 'The Jewish sign prophets – A.D. 40–70: their intentions and origin', *NTS* 27: 679–97.

Barrett, C.K.

1982 'History', *Essays on John* (London: SPCK): 116–31.

1978   *The Gospel According to St. John* (2nd edn; London: SPCK; Philadelphia: Westminster).

1973–74   'John and the Synoptic Gospels', *The Expository Times* 85: 228–33.

1972   'The dialectical theology of St John', *New Testament Essays* (London: SCM Press): 49–69.

Barth, Fritz

1907   *The Gospel of St. John and the Synoptic Gospels* (New York: Eaton & Mains).

Barton, Stephen

1993   'The believer, the historian and the Fourth Gospel', *Theol* 96: 289–302.

Bauckham, Richard

2003   'The eyewitnesses and the gospel traditions', *JSHJ* 1.1: 28–60.

1998   'John for readers of Mark', in Richard Bauckham (ed.), *The Gospels for all Christians: Rethinking the Gospel Audiences* (Grand Rapids: Eerdmans): 147–71.

1993a   'The Beloved Disciple as ideal author', *JSNT* 49: 21–44.

1993b   'Papias and Polycrates on the origin of the Fourth Gospel', *JTS* 44: 24–69.

1978   'The Sonship of the historical Jesus in Christology', *SJT* 31: 245–60.

Baur, F.C.

1999   *Kritische Untersuchungen über die kanonischen Evangelien, ihr Verhältnis zueinander, ihren Character und Ursprung.* (1847, 2nd edn; Hildesheim: Georg Olms).

Berger, Klaus

1997   *Im Anfang war Johannes: Datierung und Theologie des vierten Evangeliums* (Stuttgart: Quell).

Birdsall, J.N.

1960   *The Bodmer Papyrus of the Gospel of John* (London: The Tyndale Press).

Blomberg, Craig L.

2002   *Historical Reliability of John's Gospel; Issues and Commentary* (Downers Grove: InterVarsity Press).

1993   'To what extent is John historically reliable?', in Robert B. Sloan and Mikeal C. Parsons (eds), *Perspectives on John: Method and Interpretation in the Fourth Gospel* (Lewiston: Mellen, 1993): 27–56.

Boismard, Marie-Emile

1992   *Moses or Jesus; An Essay in Johannine Christology* (B.T. Viviano, trans.; Leuven: Peeters; Minneapolis: Fortress).

Bond, Helen K.

1998   *Pontius Pilate in History and Interpretation* (Cambridge: Cambridge University Press).

Borg, Marcus

2002   'The Jesus Seminar from the inside', *QRT* 98: 21–7.

1994   *Jesus in Contemporary Scholarship* (Valley Forge: Trinity Press International).

Borgen, Peder

1993   'John 6: tradition, interpretation and composition', in Alan Culpepper (ed.), *Critical Readings of John 6* (BIS, 22; Leiden: E.J. Brill): 95–114.

1990   'John and the Synoptics', in David L. Dungan (ed.), *The Interrelations of the Gospels* (Macon, GA: Mercer University Press, 1990): 408–58.

1983   *Logos Was the True Light; And Other Essays on the Gospel of John* (Trondheim: Tapir Publishers).

1979   'The use of tradition in John 12:44-50', *NTS* 26: 18–35.

1965   *Bread from Heaven* (NovTSup, 11, Leiden: E.J. Brill).

1959   'John and the Synoptics in the passion narrative', *NTS* 5: 246–59.

Boring, M. Eugene, Klaus Berger and Carsten Colpe (eds)
    1995   *The Hellenistic Commentary to the New Testament* (Nashville: Abingdon).
Bornkamm, Gunther
    1960   *Jesus of Nazareth* (1956 in German; New York: Harper & Row).
Bretschneider, Karl Gottlieb
    1820   *Probabilia de Evangelii et Epistolarum Joannis Apostoli indole et origine erudi-
             torium iudiciis modeste subiecit* (Leipzig: J.A. Barth).
Bridges, Linda McKinnish
    1987   'The aphorisms in the Gospel of John: a transmissional, literary, and sociological
             analysis of selected sayings' (Ph.D. Dissertation, The Southern Baptist
             Theological Seminary).
Broadhead, Edwin K.
    1995   'Echoes of an exorcism in the Fourth Gospel', *ZNW* 86: 111–19.
Brodie, Thomas L.
    1993   *The Quest for the Origin of John's Gospel; A Source-Oriented Approach*
             (Oxford: Oxford University Press).
Brown, Colin
    1984   *Miracles and the Critical Mind* (Exeter: Paternoster; Grand Rapids: Eerdmans).
Brown, Raymond E.
    2003   *An Introduction to the Gospel of John*, Francis Moloney (ed.) (New York:
             Doubleday).
    1994   *The Death of the Messiah* (2 vols; New York: Doubleday).
    1979   *The Community of the Beloved Disciple* (New York: Paulist Press).
1966, 1970   *The Gospel according to John* (2 vols; Garden City: Doubleday).
    1965   *New Testament Essays* (Garden City: Image Books).
    1962   'The problem of historicity in John', *CBQ* 24: 1–14; also published in *New
             Testament Essays* (Garden City: Image Books, 1965): 187–217.
    1961   'Incidents that are units in the Synoptic Gospels but dispersed in St John', *CBQ*
             23: 143–61; also published in *New Testament Essays* as 'John and the Synoptic
             Gospels: a comparison' (Garden City: Image Books, 1965): 246–71.
Bruce, F.F.
    1980   'The trial of Jesus in the Fourth Gospel', in R.T. France and David Wenham
             (eds), *Gospel Perspectives; Studies of History and Tradition in the Four Gospels*
             (vol. 1, Sheffield: JSOT Press): 7–20.
Bruns, J. Edgar
1966–67   'The use of time in the Fourth Gospel', *NTS* 13: 285–90.
Bryan, Christopher
    1993   *A Preface to Mark: Notes on the Gospel in Its Literary and Cultural Settings*
             (Oxford: Oxford University Press).
Bühner, Jan-A.
    1977   *Der Gesandte und sein Weg im vierten Evangelium* (WUNT II, 2; J.C.B. Mohr
             (Paul Siebeck)).
Bull, Robert J.
1976–77   'An archaeological footnote to "Our fathers worshipped on this mountain",
             John IV. 20', *NTS* 23: 460–62.
    1975   'An archaeological context for understanding John 4:20', *BA* 38: 54–9.
Bultmann, Rudolf
    1971   *The Gospel of John: A Commentary* (G.R. Beasley-Murray, R.W.N. Hoare, and
             J.K. Riches, trans.; Oxford: Blackwell, 1971).
    1963a   *History of the Synoptic Tradition* (J. Marsh, trans.; 3rd edn; London/New York:
             Blackwell/Harper & Row).
    1963b   'Rudolf Bultmann's Review of C.H. Dodd: in *The Interpretation of the Fourth
             Gospel*', W.G. Robinson, trans.; *HDB* 27:2:9–22.

Burge, Gary
    1987   *The Anointed Community* (Grand Rapids: Eerdmans).
Burridge, Richard A.
    2004   *What Are the Gospels? A Comparison with Graeco-Roman Biography* (2nd
             edn; Cambridge: Cambridge University Press).
Burridge, Richard A. and Graham Gould
    2004   *Jesus Now and Then* (Grand Rapids: Eerdmans).
Byrskog, Samuel
    2000   *Story as History – History as Story: The Gospel Tradition in the Context of
             Ancient Oral History* (WUNT, 123; Tübingen: J.C.B. Mohr (Paul Siebeck)).
Caird, George B.
    1968–9   'The Glory of God in the Fourth Gospel: An exercise in biblical semantics', *NTS*
             15: 265–77.
Capper, Brian J.
    1998   '"With the oldest monks…": Light from Essene history on the career of the
             Beloved Disciple?', *JTS* 49: 1–55.
Carson, Donald A.
    1991   *The Gospel According to John* (Leicester: Inter-Varsity Press; Grand Rapids:
             Eerdmans).
    1981   'Historical tradition in the Fourth Gospel: After Dodd, what?', in R.T. France
             and David Wenham (eds), *Gospel Perspectives* (vol. 2; Sheffield: JSOT Press):
             83–145.
Casey, Maurice
    1996   *Is John's Gospel True?* (London: Routledge).
    1991   *From Jewish Prophet to Gentile God; The Origins and Development of New
             Testament Christology* (Cambridge: James Clarke & Co.).
Casey, Robert P.
    1945   'Professor Goodenough and the Fourth Gospel', *JBL* 64: 535–42.
Cassidy, Richard J.
    1992   *John's Gospel in New Perspective* (Maryknoll: Orbis Books).
Chamberlin, Theodore J. and Christopher A. Hall (eds)
    2000   *Realized Religion; Research on the Relationship between Religion and Health*
             (Philadelphia & London: Templeton Foundation Press).
Charlesworth, James
    1995   *The Beloved Disciple; Whose Witness Validates the Gospel of John?* (Valley
             Forge, PA: Trinity Press International).
    1992   (ed.) *Jesus and the Dead Sea Scrolls* (New York: Doubleday).
    1988   *Jesus Within Judaism: New Light from Exciting Archaeological Discoveries*
             (New York: Doubleday).
Ciholas, Paul
    1982   'The Socratic and Johannine *Sēmeion* as divine manifestation', *Perspectives in
             Religious Studies* 9: 251–65.
Coakley, James F.
    1988   'The anointing at Bethany and the priority of John', *JBL* 107: 241–56.
Collins, Raymond F.
    1991   *John and His Witness* (Collegeville: The Liturgical Press).
Cribbs, F. Lamar
    1979   'The agreements that exist between St Luke and St John', *SBL 1979 Seminar
             Papers*: 215–61.
    1973   'A study of the contacts that exist between St Luke and St John', *SBL 1973
             Seminar Papers*: 1–93.

1970 'A reassessment of the date of origin and the destination of the Gospel of John', *JBL* 89: 38–55.

Culpepper, R. Alan.
2000 *John, the Son of Zebedee* (Minneapolis: Fortress).
1998 *The Gospel of John and Letters of John* (Nashville: Abingdon).
1983 *Anatomy of the Fourth Gospel: A Study in Literary Design* (Philadelphia: Fortress Press).

Culpepper, R. Alan, and Clifton Black (eds)
1996 *Exploring the Gospel of John* (Louisville, Kentucky: Westminster / John Knox Press).

Denaux, Adelbert
1992 'The Q-Logion: Mt. 11:27/Lk. 10:22 and the Gospel of John', in Adelbert Denaux (ed.), *John and the Synoptics* (Leuven: Louvain University Press and Peeters):163–99.

Dewey, Kim E.
1980 '*Paroimiai* in the Gospel of John', *Semeia* 17: 81–99.

Dodd, C.H.
1963 *Historical Tradition in the Fourth Gospel* (Cambridge: Cambridge University Press).
1953 *The Interpretation of the Fourth Gospel* (Cambridge: Cambridge University Press).

Donahue, John R. (ed.)
2005 *Life in Abundance; Studies of John's Gospel in Tribute to Raymond E. Brown* (Collegeville: Liturgical Press).

Drummond, James
1904 *An Inquiry into the Character and Authorship of the Fourth Gospel* (New York: Charles Scribner's Sons).

Dunn, James D.G.
2003 *Jesus Remembered* (Grand Rapids: Eerdmans).
1991 'John and the oral tradition', in Henry Wansbrough (ed.), *Jesus and the Oral Gospel Tradition* (Sheffield: JSOT): 287–326.
1983 'Let John be John', in Peter Stuhlmacher (ed.), *Das Evangelium und die Evangelien* (WUNT, 28; Tübingen: J.C.B. Mohr): 309–39.

Du Rand, J.A.
1986 'Plot and point of view in the Gospel of Jesus', in J.H. Petzer and P.J. Hartin (eds), *A South African Perspective on the New Testament* (Leiden: E.J. Brill): 149–69.

Ehrman, Bart D.
1999 *Jesus: Apocalyptic Prophet of the New Millennium* (Oxford / New York: Oxford University Press).

Evans, C.F.
1977 'The Passion of John', in *Explorations in Theology 2* (London: SCM Press Ltd): 50–66.

Evans, Craig A.
1996a *Life of Jesus Research; An Annotated Bibliography* (rev. edn; NTTS, 24; Leiden: E.J. Brill).
1996b 'The passion of Jesus: History remembered or prophecy historicized?', *BBR* 6: 159–65.
1989 'Jesus' action in the Temple: Cleansing or portent of destruction?', *CBQ* 51: 237–70.
1982 'The function of Isaiah 6:9-10 in Mark and John', *NovT* 24:2: 124–38.

Fagal, Harold E.
    1978   'John and the Synoptic tradition', *Scripture, Tradition, and Interpretation* (Grand Rapids: Eerdmans): 127–45.
Farrer, Austin
    1952   *A Study in St Mark* (New York: Oxford University Press).
Forestell, James T.
    1974   *The Word of the Cross* (AnBib, 57; Rome: Biblical Institute Press).
Fortna, Robert T.
    1988   *The Fourth Gospel and its Predecessor: From Narrative Source to Present Gospel* (Philadelphia: Fortress).
    1970   *The Gospel of Signs: A Reconstruction of the Narrative Source Underlying the Fourth Gospel* (SNTSMS, 11; Cambridge: Cambridge University Press).
Fowler, James
    2004   'A response to the use of psychological theory in Paul Anderson's *The Christology of the Fourth Gospel; Its Unity and Disunity in the Light of John 6*', in J. Harold Ellens and Wayne Rollins (eds), *Psychology and the Bible; A New Way to Read the Scriptures* (vol. 4; Westport, CT: Praegers/Greenwood Publishers): 246–76.
    1984   *Becoming Adult, Becoming Christian* (San Francisco: Harper & Row).
    1981   *Stages of Faith* (San Francisco: Harper & Row).
France, R.T.
    1983   'Jewish historiography, Midrash, and the Gospels', in R.T. France and D. Wenham (eds), *Gospel Perspectives* (vol. 3; Sheffield: JSOT Press): 99–127.
Fredriksen, Paula
    1999   *Jesus of Nazareth, King of the Jews* (New York: Knopf).
Freyne, Sean
    1992   'Locality and doctrine – Mark and John revisited', in F. Van Segbroek, C.M. Tuckett, J. Van Belle and J. Verheyden (eds), *The Four Gospels* (vol. 3; Leuven: Leuven University Press): 1889–1900.
Funk, Robert W.
    1996   *Honest to Jesus; Jesus for a New Millennium* (San Francisco: Harper SanFrancisco).
Funk, Robert W. and the Jesus Seminar
    1998   *The Acts of Jesus: The Search for the Authentic Deeds of Jesus* (San Francisco: Harper SanFrancisco).
Funk, Robert W., Roy W. Hoover, and the Jesus Seminar
    1993   *The Five Gospels: The Search for the Authentic Words of Jesus* (New York: Macmillan).
Gadamer, Hans Georg
    1989   *Truth and Method* (2nd rev. edn; New York: Crossroad).
Gardner-Smith, Perceival
    1938   *Saint John and the Synoptic Gospels* (Cambridge: Cambridge University Press).
Glasson, T.F.
    1963   *Moses in the Fourth Gospel* (SBT, 40; Naperville: Allenson).
Goodenough, Erwin R.
    1945   'John: A primitive Gospel', *JBL* 64: 145–82.
Goodspeed, J. Edgar
    1937   *An Introduction to the New Testament* (Chicago: University of Chicago Press).
Grigsby, Bruce
    1985   'Washing in the Pool of Siloam – a thematic anticipation of the Johannine Cross', *NovT* 27: 227–35.
Gunther, John J.
    1979   'The Alexandrian Gospel and Letters of John', *CBQ* 41: 581–603.

Haenchen, Ernst
    1984   *A Commentary on the Gospel of John* (Hermeneia Critical and Historical Commentary on the Bible, 2 vols; Robert W. Funk and Ulrich Busse, eds; Robert W. Funk, trans.; Philadelphia: Fortress, from the 1980 edn).

Hägerland, Tobias
    2003   'John's Gospel: a two-level drama?', *JSNT* 25.3: 309–22.

Harner, Philip B.
    1970   *The 'I Am' of the Fourth Gospel* (Philadelphia: Fortress).

Headlam, Arthur C.
    1948   *The Fourth Gospel as History* (Oxford: Blackwell).

Hengel, Martin
    2000   *The Four Gospels and the One Gospel of Jesus Christ* (John Bowden, trans.; London: SCM).
    1989   *The Johannine Question* (John Bowden, trans.; London: SCM; Philadelphia: Trinity Press International).
    1985   *Studies in the Gospel of Mark* (John Bowman, trans.; Philadelphia: Fortress).
    1981   *The Charismatic Leader and His Followers* (James C.G. Reid, trans.; Edinburgh: T&T Clark).

Higgins, Angus J.B.
    1960   *The Historicity of the Fourth Gospel* (London: Lutterworth).

Hill, Charles E.
    2004   *The Johannine Corpus in the Early Church* (Oxford: Oxford University Press).
    1998   'What Papias said about John (and Luke): a "new" Papian fragment', *JTS* 49: 582–629.

Hofrichter, Peter L.
    2002   (ed.) *Für und wider die Priorität des Johannesevangeliums* (TTS, 9; Hildesheim, Zürich, New York: Georg Olms Verlag).
    1997   *Modell und Vorlage der Synoptiker; Das vorredaktionelle 'Johannesevangelium'* (TTS, 6; Hildesheim, Zürich, New York: Georg Olms Verlag).

Holquist, Michael
    1990   *Dialogism – Bakhtin and his World* (New York: Routledge).

Horsley, Richard A.
    1985   '"Like one of the prophets of old": two types of popular prophets at the time of Jesus', *CBQ* 47: 435–63.

Hoskyns, Edwyn C.
    1947   *The Fourth Gospel* (Francis N. Davey, ed.; London: Faber & Faber).

Howard, Wilbert Francis
    1931   *The Fourth Gospel in Recent Criticism and Interpretation* (London: The Epworth Press).

Jackson, H. Latimer
    1918   *The Problem of the Fourth Gospel* (Cambridge: Cambridge University Press).
    1906   *The Fourth Gospel and Some Recent German Criticism* (Cambridge: Cambridge University Press).

James, William
    1902   *The Varieties of Religious Experience; A Study in Human Nature* (Mineola: Dover).

Käsemann, Ernst
    1968   *The Testament of Jesus According to John 17* (trans. Gerhard Krodel; Philadelphia: Fortress Press).

Kealy, Sean P.
    2002   *John's Gospel and the History of Biblical Interpretation* (2 vols; Lewiston: Mellen Press).
    1978   *That You May Believe (The Gospel of John)* (Northampton: Slough).

Keener, Craig S.
>   2003   *The Gospel of John; A Commentary* (2 vols; Peabody: Hendrickson).
Kieffer, Rene
>   1985   'L'Espace et le temps dans L'Évangile de Jean', *NTS* 31: 393–409.
King, J.S.
>   1983   'There and back again', *The Evangelical Quarterly* 55: 145–57.
Koester, Craig R.
>   2003   *Symbolism in the Fourth Gospel: Meaning, Mystery, Community* (2nd edn; Minneapolis: Fortress Press).
>   1995   'Topography and theology in the Gospel of John', in Astrid Beck, Andrew Bartelt, Paul Raabe, and Chris Franke (eds), *Fortunate the Eyes That See* (Grand Rapids: Eerdmans): 436–48.
Köstenberger, Andreas J.
>   1999   *Encountering John: The Gospel in Historical, Literary and Theological Perspective* (Grand Rapids: Baker).
Kuhn, Thomas S.
>   1996   *The Structure of Scientific Revolutions* (3rd edn; Chicago and London: University of Chicago Press).
Kümmel, Werner Georg
>   1984   *Introduction to the New Testament* (Howard Clark Lee, trans.; rev. edn; London: SCM).
Kundsin, Karl
>   1925   *Topologische Überlieferungsstoffe im Johannesevangelium* (Göttingen: Vandenhoeck).
Küng, Hans
>   1966   *On Being a Christian* (New York: Pocket Books).
Kuschel, Karl-Josef
>   1992   *Born Before All Time? The Dispute over Christ's Origin* (John Bowden, trans.; New York: Crossroad).
Kysar, Robert
>   2002   'The de-historicizing of the Gospel of John', (unpublished paper presented at the John, Jesus, and History Group of the national SBL meetings).
>   1999   Review of *The Christology of the Fourth Gospel* by Paul N. Anderson, *RBL* 1: 38–42.
>   1993   *John, the Maverick Gospel* (revised edn; Atlanta: Westminster / John Knox).
>   1985   'The Fourth Gospel: A report on recent research' (*ANRW* II; Berlin: 2389–2480).
>   1975   *The Fourth Evangelist and His Gospel; An Examination of Contemporary Scholarship* (Minneapolis: Augsburg).
Lea, Thomas D.
>   1995   'The reliability of history in John's Gospel', *JETS* 38.3: 387–402.
Lee, Edwin Kenneth
>   1966   'The historicity of the Fourth Gospel', *CQR* 167: 292–301.
>   1956-7   'St. Mark and the Fourth Gospel', *NTS* 3: 50–8.
Lightfoot, Joseph Barber
>   1893   *Biblical Essays* (intro. Philip E. Highes; 2nd edn; Grand Rapids: Baker Book House, 1979).
Lightfoot, Robert H.
>   1956   *St. John's Gospel; A Commentary* (C.F. Evans, ed.; Oxford: Clarendon Press).
Lincoln, Andrew T.
>   2000   *Truth on Trial: The Lawsuit Motif in the Fourth Gospel* (Peabody: Hendrickson).

Lindars, Barnabas
    1972   *The Gospel of John* (London: Marshall, Morgan & Scott, 1972; Grand Rapids: Eerdmans, 1981).
    1971   *Behind the Fourth Gospel* (London: SPCK).
Loader, William R.G.
    1989   *The Christology of the Fourth Gospel; Structure and Issues* (BET, 23; Frankfurt / Bern / New York / Paris: Peter Lang).
    1984   'The central structure of Johannine Christology', *NTS* 30: 188–216.
Loder, James E.
    1998   *The Logic of the Spirit; Human Development in Theological Perspective* (San Francisco: Jossey-Bass Publishers)
    1981   *The Transforming Moment; Understanding Convictional Experiences* (San Francisco: Harpers).
MacGregor, G.H.C.
    1928   *The Gospel of John* (New York: Harper and Brothers).
MacKay, Ian Donald
    2004   *John's Relationship with Mark* (WUNT II, 182; Tübingen: J.C.B. Mohr (Paul Siebeck)).
Martyn, J. Louis
    2003   *History and Theology in the Fourth Gospel* (3rd edn; Louisville: Westminster / John Knox Press).
Matera, Frank J.
    1990   'Jesus before Annas: John 18:13-14, 19-24', *ETL* 66: 38–55.
Matson, Mark
    2001   *In Dialogue with another Gospel? The Influence of the Fourth Gospel on the Passion Narrative of the Gospel of Luke* (SBLDS, 178; Atlanta: Society of Biblical Literature).
Meeks, Wayne
    1966   'Galilee and Judea in the Fourth Gospel', *JBL* 85: 159–69.
Meier, John P.
    2001   *A Marginal Jew; Rethinking the Historical Jesus; vol. III: Companions and Competitors* (New York: Doubleday).
    1994   *A Marginal Jew; Rethinking the Historical Jesus; vol. II: Mentor, Message, and Miracles* (New York: Doubleday).
    1991   *A Marginal Jew; Rethinking the Historical Jesus; vol. I: The Roots of the Problem and the Person* (New York: Doubleday).
Minear, Paul S.
    1983   'The original functions of John 21', *JBL* 102: 85–98.
Moloney, Francis J.
    2000   'The Fourth Gospel and the Jesus of history', *NTS* 46: 42–58.
Montefiore, Hugh
    1962   'Revolt in the desert?', *NTS* 8: 135–41.
Morris, Leon
    1995   *The Gospel according to John: The English Text with Introduction, Exposition and Notes* (rev. edn; NICNT; Grand Rapids: Eerdmans).
    1969   *Studies in the Fourth Gospel* (Exeter: Paternoster; Grand Rapids: Eerdmans).
Mulder, H.
    1978   'John 18:28 and the date of the crucifixion', in T. Baarda, A.F.J. Klijnn, and W.C. Van Unnik, eds (*Miscellanea Neotestamentica* 48; Leiden: E.J. Brill, 1978): 87–105.
Mussner, Franz
    1966   *Historical Jesus in the Gospel of John* (W.J. O'Harah, trans.; New York: Herder & Herder).

Neirynck, Frans
    1977   'John and the Synoptics', in Marinus de Jonge (ed.), *L'Évangile de Jean* (BETL, 44; Leuven: University Press): 73–106.
Nicol, W.
    1972   *The Sēmeia in the Fourth Gospel; Tradition and Redaction* (NovTSup, 32; Leiden: E.J. Brill).
Nolloth, C.F.
    1929   'The Fourth Gospel and its critics', *Hibbert Journal* 28 (1929): 124–36.
O'Day, Gail R.
    1986   *Revelation in the Fourth Gospel; Narrative Mode and Theological Claim* (Philadelphia: Fortress).
Orton, David E. (ed.)
    1999   *The Composition of John's Gospel; Selected Studies from Novum Testamentum* (Readers in Biblical Studies, 2. Leiden: Brill).
Painter, John
    1993   *The Quest for the Messiah: The History, Literature and Theology of the Johannine Community* (Edinburgh: T&T Clark, 2nd edn; Nashville: Abingdon).
Palmer, Michael F.
    1977   'Can the historian invalidate Gospel statements? Some notes on dialectical theology', *The Downside Review* 95: 11–18.
Pancaro, Severino
    1969   'A statistical approach to the concept of time and eschatology in the Fourth Gospel', *Biblica* 50: 511–24.
Parker, Pierson
    1962   'John the Son of Zebedee and the Fourth Gospel', *JBL* 81: 35–43.
    1956   'Two editions of John', *JBL* 75: 303–14.
    1955   'Bethany beyond Jordan', *JBL* 74: 257–61.
Peterson, Norman, R.
    1993   *The Gospel of John and the Sociology of Light* (Valley Forge: Trinity Press International).
Plummer, Eric
    1997   'The absence of exorcisms in the Fourth Gospel', *Bib* 78: 350–68.
Polanyi, Michael
    1962   *Personal Knowledge* (New York: Harper & Row).
    1946   *Science, Faith and Society* (Chicago: University of Chicago Press).
Porter, Stanley E.
    2000   *The Criteria for Authenticity in Historical-Jesus Research; Previous Discussion and New Proposals* (JSNTSS, 191; Sheffield: Sheffield Academic Press).
Potter, R.D.
    1959   'Topography and archaeology in the Fourth Gospel', *StEv.* I: 329–37.
Powell, Mark Allan
    1998   *Jesus As a Figure in History: How Modern Historians View the Man from Galilee* (Louisville: Westminster / John Knox Press).
Quast, Kevin
    1989   *Peter and the Beloved Disciple; Figures for a Community in Crisis* (JSNTSupS, 32 Sheffield: Sheffield Academic Press).
Reich, Ronny
    1995   '6 stone water jars', *Jerusalem Perspective* 48: 30–33.
Reimarus, Hermann Samuel
    1970   *Reimarus: Fragments* (C.H. Talbert, ed.; R.S. Fraser, trans.; Philadelphia: Fortress, original 1778).

Reinhartz, Adele
    1989   'Jesus as prophet: predictive prolepses in the Fourth Gospel', *JSNT* 36: 3–16
Rensberger, David
    1988   *Johannine Faith and Liberating Community* (Philadelphia: Westminster Press).
Riches, John
    1993   *A Century of New Testament Study* (Cambridge: Lutterworth Press).
    1980   *Jesus and the Transformation of Judaism* (London: Darton, Longman & Todd).
Riesner, Rainer
    1987   'Bethany beyond the Jordan (John 1:28): topography, theology and history in the Fourth Gospel', *TynB* 38: 29–63.
Ricoeur, Paul
    1965   *History and Truth* (Charles A. Kelbley, trans.; Evanston: Northwestern University Press).
Ringe, Sharon H.
    1999   *Wisdom's Friends; Community and Christology in the Fourth Gospel* (Louisville: Westminster / John Knox Press).
Roberts, Colin H.
    1935   *An Unpublished Fragment of the Fourth Gospel in the John Rylands Library* (Manchester: Manchester University Press).
Robinson, James M.
    1959   *The New Quest of the Historical Jesus* (London: SCM).
Robinson, J. Armitage
    1908   *The Historical Character of St. John's Gospel* (London: Longmans-Green).
Robinson, John A.T.
    1985   *The Priority of John* (J.F. Coakley, ed.; London: SCM).
    1984a   '"His witness is true": a test of the Johannine claim', in Ernst Bammel and C.F.D. Moule (eds), *Jesus and the Politics of His Day* (Cambridge: Cambridge University Press): 453–77 (also in *Twelve More New Testament Studies*: 112–37).
    1984b   *Twelve More New Testament Studies*. (London: SCM Press).
    1959   'The new look at the Fourth Gospel', *StEv* 73: 338–50 (reprinted in *Twelve More New Testament Studies*, London: SCM, 1962: 94–106).
Salmon, Victor
    1976   *The Fourth Gospel; A History of the Textual Tradition of the Original Greek Gospel* (Matthew J. O'Connell, trans.; Collegeville: The Liturgical Press).
Sanday, William
    1872   *The Authorship and Historical Character of the Fourth Gospel* (London: Macmillan).
Sanders, E.P.
    1993   *The Historical Figure of Jesus* (London: Penguin).
    1985   *Jesus and Judaism* (London: SCM; Philadelphia: Fortress).
Schleiermacher, Friedrich
    1975   *The Life of Jesus* (S. Maclean Gilmour, trans.; Mifflintown, PA: Sigler Press; from the 1864 edn, Philadelphia: Fortress).
Schnackenburg, Rudolf
1968, 1980, 1982 *The Gospel According to St. John* (3 vols; Kevin Smyth, trans.; London: Burns & Oates; New York: Herder & Herder/Seabury).
Schneiders, Sandra
    1999   *Written that You May Believe; Encountering Jesus in the Fourth Gospel* (New York: Crossroad).
Schnelle, Udo
    1992   *Antidocetic Christology in the Gospel of John* (Linda Maloney, trans.; Minneapolis: Fortress).

Schwartz, Eduard
    1907–08 'Aporien im vierten Evangelium' (four essays), *NGG* 1:342–72; 2: 115–48; 3:149–88; 4:497–560.
Schweitzer, Albert
    1964, 2001   *The Quest for the Historical Jesus* (trans. W. Montgomery from the 1906 edn; New York: Macmillan, 1964); also see *The Quest of the Historical Jesus* (first complete edition, John Bowden, trans.; Minneapolis: Fortress, 2001).
Schweizer, Eduard
    1996   'What about the Johannine "parables"?', in R. Alan Culpepper and C. Clifton Black (eds), *Exploring the Gospel of John* (Louisville: Westminster John Knox, 1996): 208–19.
Scobie, Charles H.H.
    1982   'Johannine geography', *SR* 11: 77–84.
Segovia, Fernando F. (ed.)
    1996, 1998   *What is John?'* (2 vols; Atlanta, Georgia: Scholars Press).
Shellard, Barbara
    1995   'The relationship of Luke and John: a fresh look at an old problem', *The Journal of Theological Studies* 46 (New Series): 71–98.
Siegman, E.F.
    1968   'St. John's use of the Synoptic material', *CBQ* 30: 182–98.
Smalley, Stephen
    1978   *John: Evangelist and Interpreter* (Exeter: Paternoster).
    1968–69   'The Johannine Son of Man sayings', *NTS* 15: 278–301.
Smart, W.A.
    1946   *The Spiritual Gospel* (New York and Nashville: Abingdon-Cokesbury Press).
Smith, Barry D.
    1991   'The chronology of the Last Supper', *WTJ* 53: 29–45.
Smith, C.W.F.
    1982   '*Res Bibliographicae* – John and the Synoptics', *Biblica* 63: 102–13.
    1963a   'Tabernacles in the Fourth Gospel and Mark', *NTS* 9: 130–46.
    1963b   'John 12 and the question of John's use of the Synoptics', *JBL* 82: 58–64.
Smith, D. Moody
    2001   *John Among the Gospels; Second Edition* (Columbia, SC: University of South Carolina Press) (first edn 1992).
    1999   *John* (Nashville: Abingdon).
    1993   'Historical issues and the problem of John and the Synoptics', in Martinus C. de Boer (ed.), *From Jesus to John* (JSNTSupS, 84; Sheffield: JSOT): 252–67.
    1965   *The Composition and Order of the Fourth Gospel: Bultmann's Literary Theory* (New Haven: Yale University Press).
Smith, P. Gardner-
    1938   *Saint John and the Synoptic Gospels* (Cambridge: Cambridge University Press).
Smith, Philip Vernon
    1926   *The Fourth Gospel: Its Historical Importance* (London: SPCK; New York / Toronto: Macmillan).
Smith, Robert Houston
    1902   'Exodus typology in the Fourth Gospel', *JBL* 81: 329–42.
Söding, Thomas
    2003   'Incarnation and Pasch: the historical Jesus in John's Gospel', *TD* 50:3: 203–10.
Spitta, Friedrich
    1910   *Das Johannes-Evangelium als Quelle der Geschichte Jesu* (Göttingen: Vandenhoeck & Ruprecht).

Staley, Jeffrey L.
1996   *Reading with a Passion: Rhetoric, Autobiography, and the American West in the Gospel of John* (New York: Continuum).
1988   *The Print's First Kiss: A Rhetorical Investigation of the Implied Reader in the Fourth Gospel* (SBLDS, 82; Atlanta: Scholars Press).

Stibbe, Mark W.G.
1994   *John's Gospel* (London and New York: Routledge).
1992   *John as Storyteller: Narrative Criticism and the Fourth Gospel* (Cambridge: Cambridge University Press).

Strachan, R.H.
1925   *The Fourth Evangelist: Dramatist or Historian?* (London: Hodder and Stoughton).

Strauss, David Friedrich
1977   *The Christ of Faith and the Jesus of History; A Critique of Schleiermacher's The Life of Jesus*, (Leander Keck, ed., trans., and intro.; Philadelphia: Fortress Press; 4th German edn, 1865).
1972   *The Life of Jesus Critically Examined*, in Peter C. Hodgson (ed. and intro.; George Eliot, trans.; Philadelphia: Fortress Press, 1972, originally 1835–6).

Streeter, B.H.
1936   *The Four Gospels; A Study of Origins* (London: Macmillan).
1929   *The Primitive Church; Studies with Special Reference to the Origins of the Christian Ministry* (London: Macmillan).

Sturch, R.L.
1978   'The alleged eyewitness material in the Fourth Gospel', *Studia Biblica* II: 313–27.

Sutcliffe, Edmund F.
1960   'Baptism and baptismal rites at Qumran?', *HJ* 1.3: 179–88.

Taylor, Joan E.
1997   *The Immerser: John the Baptist within Second Temple Judaism* (Grand Rapids: Eerdmans).

Temple, William
1939   *Readings in St. John's Gospel* (London: Macmillan).

Theissen, Gerd, and Annette Merz
1998   *The Historical Jesus: A Comprehensive Guide* (John Bowden, trans.; London: SCM; Minneapolis: Fortress).

Theissen, Gerd and Dagmar Winter
2002   *The Quest for the Plausible Jesus; The Question of Criteria* (M. Eugene Boring, trans.; Louisville: Westminster / John Knox Press).

Theobald, Michael
2002   *Herrenworte im Johannesevangelium* (HBS, 34. Freiburg: Herder).

Thompson, Marianne M.
1996   'The historical Jesus and the Johannine Christ', in R. Alan Culpepper and C. Clifton Black (eds), *Exploring the Gospel of John* (Louisville: Westminster John Knox): 21–42.
1988   *The Humanity of Jesus in the Fourth Gospel* (Philadelphia: Fortress).

Twelftree, Graham H.
1999   *Jesus the Miracle Worker: A Historical and Theological Study* (Downers Grove: InterVarsity).

Van Belle, Gilbert
1994   *The Signs Source in the Fourth Gospel: Historical Survey and Critical Evaluation of the Semeia Hypothesis* (Leuven: Louvain University Press and Peeters).

Van der Watt, Jan G.
    1995   'The composition of the Prologue of John's Gospel: the historical Jesus intro-
            ducing divine grace', *WTJ* 57: 311–32.
Waetjen, Herman C.
    2004   *The Gospel of the Beloved Disciple; A Work in Two Editions* (New York and
            London: T&T Clark).
Wahlde, Urban C. von
    1990   *The Johannine Commandments: 1 John and the Struggle for the Johannine
            Tradition* (New York: Paulist Press).
    1989   *The Earliest Version of John's Gospel: Recovering the Gospel of Signs*
            (Wilmington, Delaware: Michael Glazier).
    1979   'The terms for religious authorities in the Fourth Gospel: a key to literary-
            strata?', *JBL* 98: 231–53.
Walker, Norman
    1960   'The reckoning of hours in the Fourth Gospel', *NovT* 4: 69–73.
Wead, David W.
    1970   *The Literary Devices in John's Gospel* (Basel: Friedrich Reinhardt
            Kommissionsverlag).
Webb, Robert L.
    1991   *John the Baptizer and Prophet* (Sheffield: JSOT Press).
Wellhausen, Julius
    1907   *Erweiterung und Änderungen in vierten Evangelium* (Berlin: G. Reimer).
Wendt, Hans Hinrich
    1902   *The Gospel According to St. John; An Inquiry into its Genesis and Historical
            Value* (Edward Lummis, trans.; Edinburgh: T&T Clark; New York: Charles
            Scribner's Sons).
Wenham, David
    1998   'A historical view of John's Gospel', *Themelios* 23: 5–21.
Westcott, Brooke Foss
    1908   *The Gospel According to St. John* (vols I and II; London: John Murray).
Willett-Newhart, Michael
    1992   *The Wisdom Christology of the Fourth Gospel* (San Francisco: Edwin Mellen
            Press).
Williams, Catrin H.
    2000   *I Am He: The Interpretation of 'Anî Hû' in Jewish and Early Christian
            Literature* (Tübingen: J.C.B. Mohr (Paul Siebeck)).
Wills, Lawrence M.
    1997   *The Quest of the Historical Gospel: Mark, John, and the Origins of the Gospel
            Genre* (London: Routledge).
Wilson, John F.
    1989   'Archaeology and the origins of the Fourth Gospel: Gabbatha', in James E.
            Priest, W. Royce Clark, and Ronald L. Tyler (eds), *Johannine Studies; Essays
            in Honor of Frank Pack*, (Malibu, CA: Pepperdine University Press): 221–30.
Witherington, Ben, III
    1995   *John's Wisdom: A Commentary on the Fourth Gospel* (Cambridge: Cambridge
            University Press).
Yarmey, A.D.
    1984   'Age as a factor in eyewitness memory', in G.L. Wells and E.L. Loftus (eds),
            Eyewitness Testimony; Psychological Perspectives (Cambridge: Cambridge
            University Press): 142–54.

INDEX OF REFERENCES